TONG SING

TONG SING

THE 'KNOW EVERYTHING BOOK'

中國三位一体

CHINESE TRINITY

BASED ON THE ANCIENT CHINESE ALMANAC
Dr Charles Windridge
EDITORIAL CONSULTANT: CHENG KAM FONG

 THREE RIVERS PRESS · NEW YORK

To Samantha, Juli and John

Acknowledgment

Christina Morris for her invaluable assistance
in the secretarial field.

Published by Three Rivers Press, New York, New York.
Member of the Crown Publishing Group.

Random House, Inc. New York, Toronto, London, Sydney, Auckland
www.randomhouse.com

Originally published in Great Britain by Kyle Cathie Ltd in 1999.

THREE RIVERS PRESS is a registered trademark and the Three Rivers Press
colophon is a trademark of Random House, Inc.

Printed in Singapore

Design by Robert Updegraff

Library of Congress Cataloging-in-Publication Data is available upon request.

ISBN 0-609-807331

10 9 8 7 6 5 4 3 2 1

First American Edition

CONTENTS

公雞同小雞

INTRODUCTION

The Chinese Almanac is a remarkable work in that it represents an attempt at the codification of all knowledge. It could fairly be described as the oldest encyclopedia in the world, for it has been in continuous publication from about 2250 B.C. (or so some authorities would have us believe), when the original was compiled by the best of China's astrologers and sages, and on the command of the Emperor Yao, who perceived that everyone would benefit, particularly the farmers, if the seasons were fixed. It is revised and reissued each year, but the bulk of the ancient text remains unaltered and its archaic language is not readily understood. In Taiwan the book is called the Farmers' Almanac, but in Hong Kong it is known as the *Tong Sing*, which means "Know All Things Book." It is a compendium of information about astrology, divinatory procedures, traditional beliefs, festivals, and so forth.

Dates and other data in the *Tong Sing* are based on the lunar calendar. The Chinese use the Western-style calendar, which is based on solar movements, for official purposes, but they prefer the lunar calendar for astrology and agricultural advice, because the times for sowing and harvesting are better decided by the influences of the moon than those of the sun. The lunar year begins on a variable day which, in the Western calendar, is in late January or early February.

The *Tong Sing* is essentially folkloric in content, but beneath the myths and traditions there is a great deal of practical thinking, and the information about agricultural procedures, health measures and the like is quite reliable. Divinations in China are based on known facts, intelligent observation and logical inference. They are often more in the nature of those proverbs which are universal truths and bits of profound wisdom.

However, the almanac does not neglect the needs of the modern world and contains sections on currencies, postal information, official statistics, etc.

Although this book contains many sections which appear in the original *Tong Sing*, it is essentially my own work and is neither a faithful reproduction nor a plagiarized version. It has arisen from the interest in Chinese culture that is frequently expressed by customers of my wife's Chinese restaurant. My wife, who is Chinese, has no eloquent command of English and is, in any case, far too busy to enter into lengthy discourse. So the task of answering the constant barrage of questions has largely fallen to me.

Because the questions tended to cover the same subjects over and over again, I prepared a series of leaflets, illustrated with my own drawings, giving some of the answers, which I had researched in Chinese texts, notably the *Tong Sing* and *I Ching*, or "Book of Changes." It occurred to me that this information might be of interest to people other than those who frequented my wife's restaurant, and this book is the outcome.

THE CHINESE LANGUAGE

The following notes will help you to understand the Chinese words used in this book.

THE LANGUAGES OF CHINA

1. We may speak of the Chinese language, but there are over a hundred languages and dialects in China.
2. The main and official language is Mandarin, which is spoken more in the north than in the south of China.
3. Cantonese is the main language in the south.
4. The same written characters are used for all the Chinese languages, and so, though the Chinese may not understand each other when speaking, they can always understand each other when expressing themselves in writing.
5. Some of the less common languages are as follows: Wu in the Zhejiang and Jiangsu provinces; Fujianese in the Fujian province and Taiwan; Hakka in the Guangxi and Guangdong provinces; Hunanese in the Hunan province.
6. Wenyen is a literary language which is only understood by the educated.
7. Putonghua, devised by the Chinese government, and based upon Mandarin, is the "national tongue," or lingua franca, for the whole of China.
8. There are more people speaking Chinese than any other language.

CHINESE CHARACTERS

1. The written language of China is visual not phonetic.
2. In its early development, its characters represented real things – plants, people, animals and objects.
3. In its later stages, the characters were simplified for ease in writing them, and so became more symbolic than pictorial.
4. These characters were adapted to represent abstractions. Examples: a fire to represent *anger* or *passion*, a ship to represent *travel*, and a snake to represent *poison*.
5. These characters, or ideograms, as they are properly called, may be combined to make other words. Thus, the character for mountain is combined with the character for *sheep* to make "mountain-sheep," which is the Chinese name for a goat.
6. In recent years, the Chinese government has adopted Paihua, which is a simplified way of writing Chinese characters.

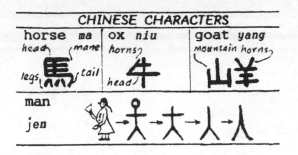

CHINESE CHARACTERS		
horse ma	ox niu	goat yang

ANGLICIZING CHINESE WORDS

1. Chinese words can be written in Anglicized forms, that is, by using the letters of the English alphabet.

2. There are several systems of transcription, which causes inconsistency and confusion. Thus, Confucius may be written as K'ung Fu-tzu or Kong Fuzi, Lao Zi as Lao-tze or Lao-tzu, Chou dynasty as Zhou dynasty, Peking as Beijing, Fukien as Fujian, and Mao Tse-tung as Mao Zedong.

3. The policy with this book is to use the Hanyu-Pinyin system of transcription, which was introduced by the Chinese government in 1979, and is now the official system of China.

4. Exceptionally, transcriptions are given in the Wade-Giles system, which is older, where they have become accepted into the English language, and so are more likely to be familiar to readers. Thus, "The Book of Changes," which is written as *Yijing* in Pinyin, is better known to the people of the West as the *I Ching*, and Guangzhou, a port in the south of China, is better known in the West as Canton.

5. It is helpful if one knows the correct pronunciation of letters used in transcriptions.

Pinyin	Wade	as in		Pinyin	Wade	as in
b	p	<u>b</u>at		x	hs	it<u>ch</u>
c	ts	be<u>ts</u>		z	ts	en<u>ds</u>
ch	ch'	e<u>tch</u>		zh	ch	<u>j</u>ump
d	t	<u>d</u>irt		t	t'	<u>t</u>op
g	k	ber<u>g</u>		r	j	u<u>r</u>ge
k	k'	<u>k</u>in		y	y	l<u>i</u>en
q	ch	<u>ch</u>in		j	ch	<u>g</u>in

The world created by Pangu

CHINA IN BRIEF

With an area of 3,661,500 square miles (448,328,500 hectares) and a population of over 1.2 billion people, the People's Republic of China – Chung Hua Jen-Min Kung-Ho Kuo – is the third largest country in the world. It is richly endowed with minerals, forests and other natural resources. Its main features are as follows:

BOUNDARIES
North: Mongolia, Siberia
South: Bangladesh, Burma, Laos, Vietnam, South China Sea
East: Korea, Yellow Sea, East China Sea
West: India, Nepal, Turkestan

REGIONS
Greater China contains China proper, which has 21 provinces and five autonomous regions: Manchuria, Inner Mongolia, Tibet, Xinjiang, Yunnan and the "special region" of Hong Kong. The most populous regions are Sichuan and Guangdong. Sichuan is the largest province.

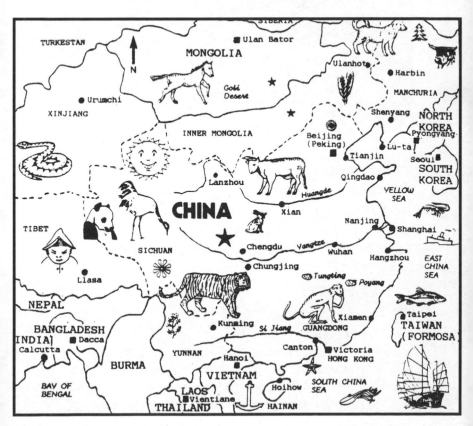

Temple of the Five Genii

CAPITAL
Beijing

CHIEF CITIES
Shanghai, Canton (Guangzhou), Chungjing, Nanjing, Tianjin, Wuhan, Harbin, Kunming, Xian, Shenyang (Mukden), Lu-ta (Talien), Chengdu, Lanzhou

CHIEF PORTS
Shanghai, Canton, Tianjin, Lu-ta, Hangzhou, Qingdao, Xiamen

MOUNTAINS
Himalayas, Khinghan, Shantung, Kun Lun, Chin Ling, Tien Shan. The Chin Ling range separates the basins of the Huangde and Yangtze rivers, so dividing China into north and south, two regions which are distinct and different in climate and agricultural produce.

RIVERS
Huangde, Yangtze, Si Jiang

LAKES

Tungting, Poyang, Tai

CLIMATE

Temperatures range from near-arctic in the north to subtropical in the south. Two seasons: wet and dry. The south-west monsoon blowing from the Indian Ocean brings heavy rain in June and September.

maize

FAUNA

Monkeys, tigers, bears, wolves, river dolphins, Yangtze alligators, etc. In the west, there are rare creatures such as the giant panda and lesser panda, which are found nowhere else in the world. Some of them are in danger of extinction.

FLORA

Bamboo, maple, ebony, mulberry (for silkworms), camphor, laurel and a wide range of medicinal herbs.

sugar cane

AGRICULTURE

Mainly confined to the fertile river valleys. Irrigation and crop rotation are practiced. Products include rice, wheat, maize, sorghum, millet, barley, tea, soya beans, sugar cane, fruit, vegetables, cotton, pork and poultry.

INDUSTRIES

Mining, textiles, engineering, food processing, iron and steel working. Products include coal, oil, iron, zinc, steel, paper, porcelain, lacquerware, silk, antimony, tin, silver, timber.

Golden Temple, Kunming

EXPORTS
Tea, rice, beans, silk, cotton, tin, hides, spices.

RACES
The Chinese people comprise over 60 different races, including the Han (true Chinese), Mongols, Manchus and Tibetans. Some 90 per cent are Han.

RELIGIONS
Confucianism, Taoism, Buddhism

ART AND LITERATURE
Calligraphy, embroidery, carvings in wood, ivory, glass, lacquer and jade, enamelling, castings in bronze, porcelain, wood-block printing, water colors. Writing is done with a brush, for calligraphy is a highly esteemed art form. Chinese artists do not slavishly imitate nature; they try to produce something that is beautiful in itself.

TRANSPORT
Rickshaws and bicycles. Many roads and railways are under construction. The main cities have airports, for airplanes are certainly the best means of transport in a country as large as China.

CURRENCY
Yuan, jiao and fen. 1 yuan = 10 jiao = 100 fen.
1 jiao = 10 fen. Banknotes: yuan 10, 5, 2, 1;
jiao 5, 2, 1; fen 5, 2, 1. Coins: fen 5, 2, 1

WEIGHTS AND MEASURES
Length: 1 cun = 1.3 inches,
1 chi = 1.1 feet, 1 chang = 3.64 yards,
1 li = 546.8 yards, 1 gonli = .62 miles
Weights: 1 liang = 1.76 oz, 1 jin = 1.1 lb,
1 gongin = 2.2 lb
Area: 1 mu = 2.5 acres
Volume: 1 sheng = 2.1 pints

EMBLEMS
The national flag of China is red with five stars in the top left-hand corner. The central star is larger than the others, and represents the leading role of the Communist Party in the revolutionary struggle.

The national coat of arms depicts the Gate of Heavenly Peace in Tiananmen Square. It is surmounted by five stars and has a wreathlike surround of bunches of grain. There is a gearwheel below the surround.

哲学家 神曲虎氏

Lao Zi

巨人熊猫

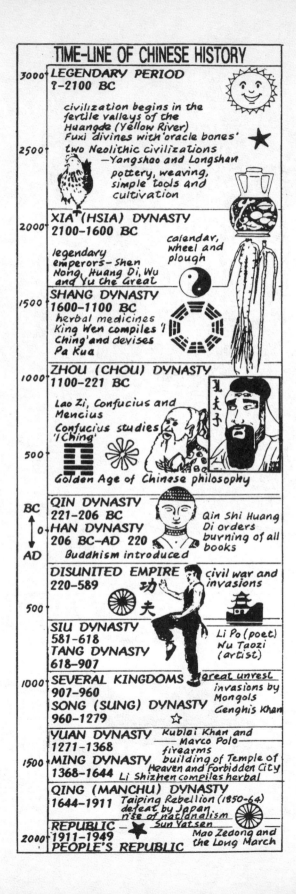

OLD CATHAY

THE LAND OF HAN

Better fifty years of Europe than a cycle of Cathay
Locksley Hall **Alfred, Lord Tennyson**

On the facing page, there is a timeline which shows, in the barest outline, the dynasties and other periods in Chinese history. Little is known about the early history of China because Qin Shi Huang Di (259–206 B.C.), the first emperor (see below), ordered the burning of all books, for he feared that freedom of thought and speech might create opposition to his rule.

Until recent times, China had little contact with the West, though a few merchants traveled to and from China via the Silk Road, which passes through the region to the north of the Kun Lun mountains in China, and reaches the West in Turkey and Iran, and which has been in existence since the time of ancient Rome. Marco Polo (1254–1324), a Venetian explorer, visited China, where he stayed for many years.

In 1514, a Portuguese ship sailed into the port of Canton (Guangzhou), and a trading center was established nearby at Macao. At the beginning of the nineteenth century, with the formation of the East India Company, the British began trading with China. By the end of that century, they controlled most of the foreign trade of China. In those days, China was called Cathay, or, quite often, "Old Cathay," no doubt because of its great antiquity.

The Han dynasty (206 B.C.–A.D. 220), which lasted for over 400 years, is the most significant in the history of China. It was a period of strong government, flourishing trade, literary activity and medical research. Buddhism was introduced and Confucianism re-established. The Chinese call themselves Han Jen (pronounced "Ren"), which means "People of Han," and their country the Land of Han.

Old Cathay

DYNASTIES

The Chinese dynasties in chronological order are as follows:

Xia 2100–1600 B.C.	Eastern Jin 317–420
Shang 1600–1100 B.C.	North and South Dynasties 420–589
Western Zhou 1100–770 B.C.	Sui 581–618
Eastern Zhou (Spring and Autumn Period) 770–476 B.C.	Tang 618–907
	Five Dynasties 907–960
Warring Kingdoms 476–221 B.C.	Song 960–1279
Qin 221–206 B.C.	Liao (Khitan) 916–1125
Western Han 206 B.C.–A.D. 24	Western Xia 1038–1227
Eastern Han 25–220	Jin 1115–1234
Three Kingdoms (Wei, Shu and Wu) 220–265	Yuan (Mongol) 1271–1368
	Ming 1368–1644
Western Jin 265–316	Qing (Manchu) 1644–1911

EARLY HISTORY

Little is known about the period before the Xia dynasty because, on the orders of the first emperor, all written records were destroyed. There are many legends about the early emperors, but archaeological evidence has revealed that they did exist, and that there were neolithic civilizations in the regions near Xian, in the Shaanxi province, and Jinan, in the Shandong province.

The Zhou Dynasty

The period of the Zhou (or Chou) dynasty was one of warfare and political and social unrest, but it was also one of great intellectual development. It was the Golden Age of Chinese philosophy, when Taoism evolved and medical practice became more sophisticated.

The First Emperor

Qin Shi Huang Di (259–206 B.C.), or "First Sovereign Ruler of the Qin," is regarded as the first emperor of China because his reign (221–206 B.C.), which lasted for only 15 years, introduced a system of language, culture and centralized bureaucracy which became the basis of the system of government in the later dynasties.

The Tang Dynasty

The Tang dynasty was another period of great advances, which included the completion of the Grand Canal between Beijing (Peking) and Hangzhou.

The Ming Dynasty

The Ming period also was one of great political and cultural development, reaching the height of its power under Emperor Yong Le, at which time a large Chinese fleet, commanded by the eunuch Zheng He, explored the west coast of Africa. Agriculture was improved, irrigation was introduced, and weaving, spinning, porcelain manufacture and other handicrafts were developed, and maritime trade with the West was established. In 1815, the first Portuguese ships arrived at Guangzhou (Canton), and were soon followed by the French, Dutch and English.

The Qing Dynasty

The most recent of the Chinese dynasties is the Qing (Manchu). Its main features may be summarized as follows: its first emperor, Fu Lin, was a prince of the Manchu tribe; the whole of China was conquered; Confucianism was adopted as the state religion; Western medicine, science and technology entered China; European powers forced China to open up to free trade; there were several wars with European nations in which China lost territories by unfair treaties.

The Last Emperor

The last emperor of China, and of the Qing (Manchu) dynasty, was Pu Yi (1906–67), or Henry Pu Yi, as he was known to his Western friends. He reigned for only a few years (1908–12) before his abdication and the establishment of the Republic of China under the presidency of Dr Sun Yatsen. As a three-year-old boy, he had been installed as emperor by Ci Xi, the empress dowager. She died shortly afterwards. Later, Pu Yi served as emperor (1934–45) of the Japanese puppet state of Manchukuo. His story has recently become well-known in the West thanks to the film *The Last Emperor*, directed by Bernardo Bertolucci.

EMPRESS
DOWAGER
CI XI

THE RECENT HISTORY OF CHINA

1839–52   **Opium War** arose from China's refusal to allow the British to import opium from India. Hong Kong ceded to Britain.

1850–64   **Taiping Rebellion** Revolt against Manchu rule. Twenty million lives lost. Rebels defeated by Western troops under General Gordon (1835–85).

1856–8   **Arrow War** British-French victory led to free trade in Chinese ports.

1894–5   **War with Japan** China defeated.

1900   **Boxer Rebellion** The Boxers, a secret society, rebelled against foreign intervention in Chinese affairs. Revolt crushed by joint Western forces.

1912   **Republic established by Sun Yatsen** (1866–1925) after abdication of Emperor Pu Yi.

1919–28   **Civil War** with fighting between warlords.

1928   **United China** under control of Kuomintang (Nationalist Party). Capital set up in Nanjing.

1930   **Communists split** with Kuomintang.

1931   **War with Japan** Manchuria seized by Japan.

1937–45   **War with Japan** Allies defeat Japan.

1945–49   **Civil War** between Kuomintang, led by Chiang Kaishek (1887–1975), and Communists, led by Chou Enlai (1868–76). Kuomintang defeated, and took refuge in Taiwan (Formosa).

1949   **People's Republic of China** established by Mao Zedong (1893–1976).

1951   **Annexation of Tibet**

1950–53   **Korean War** China supports North Korea. United Nations support South Korea.

THE PEOPLE'S REPUBLIC OF CHINA

In its constitution, the People's Republic of China is defined as a socialist state under the democratic dictatorship of the people, of whom the peasants and laborers are the leading class. The highest body of state authority is the National People's Congress, which is elected every five years through a complicated voting system involving the congresses at lower levels. The NPC is responsible for the nomination of the prime minister and government.

Some of the main features and events of the People's Republic are as follows:

• **National tribunals** expropriated land and distributed it among the peasants.

• **Mao Zedong** introduced New Democracy, which was a class-alliance between peasants, laborers and enlightened capitalists, who were those who had not collaborated with foreign powers.

• **In 1954**, the first five-year plan and Soviet-Stalinist economic policy came into operation; People's Communes came into being in 1958.

• **In the Great Leap Forward** of 1957, many people were engaged in labor projects; in 1959, Mao Zedong, the first president, relinquished his position to Liu Shaoqi.

• **Tibet, Xinjiang and Inner Mongolia** became autonomous regions; Manchuria and Yunnan were returned to China.

• **China broke with the Soviet Union**.

• **The Great Proletarian Cultural Revolution**, which began in the mid-sixties, was an attempt by Mao to counter the liberal policies of Liu Shaoqi and Deng Xiaoping.

• **In 1976, mass demonstrations** expressed the people's dissatisfaction with the political leadership.

• **Agricultural and political reforms** were introduced and the People's Communes were abolished; open markets were allowed.

• **Private property** was limited but not entirely prohibited; private enterprise was allowed in commercial and service industries.

After the death in 1976 of Mao Zedong, China began a long period of liberalization, technological expansion and friendlier relations with Western powers, under the leadership of Deng Xiaoping.

MEN OF DESTINY

*Some are born great, some achieve greatness,
and some have greatness thrust upon them.*

Twelfth Night **William Shakespeare**

History indicates that there have always been a few special people who, by their heroism, morality, intellect or administrative skill, are destined to achieve greatness, and who, in the process, may make a forcible impact on the destiny of mankind. But many heroes and other achievers go unsung, and so one may suspect that the mantle of greatness tends to fall on the shoulders of those who attract the most publicity, even if undeserved.

However, there can be little doubt that two of China's great men of destiny are Qin Shi Huang Di (259–206 B.C.), the first emperor of China, and Mao Zedong (1893–1976), popularly known as "Chairman Mao."

Qin Shi Huang Di

Qin Shi Huang Di (which means "First Sovereign Emperor of the Qin") ruled autocratically, often ruthlessly, but was very successful in attempting to unify the Chinese empire and improve its economy and system of administration. He introduced currency and a calendar, standardized weights and measures and the gauges of carriages, and unified the various systems of writing. He ordered that the walls from former kingdoms be joined together to make the Great Wall.

Mao Zedong

Courageous leader and inspired revolutionary, Mao Zedong entered the political arena during the turbulent days of the civil war in China. He dismantled the lingering remains of a corrupt and sinister imperialism, and established China as a leading world power and a people's democracy based on justice, social equality and economic stability. He was an intellectual, and wrote some fine poetry.

The enemy advances, we retreat.
The enemy halts, we harass,
The enemy tires, we attack.
The enemy retreats, we pursue.

Li Shizhen

Another of China's men of destiny is the eminent physician Li Shizhen (1517–1593), who lived at the time of the Ming dynasty (1368–1644). He devoted 37 years to the compilation of the *Ben Gao Gang Mu*, or "Outlines and Branches of Herbal Medicine," a comprehensive pharmacopoeia listing 2,000

Li Shizhen 1517–1593

herbal medicines, of which only about 300 are in common use today. In China, his work is still regarded as the main source of reference in medical science, and it has had considerable influence on medical studies in the West.

THE LEGENDARY EMPERORS

Some of China's great men are the legendary emperors – Wu, Huang Di and Shen Nong – who lived more than 5,000 years ago, and who studied the arts of agriculture and medicine. But little is known about them, for the first emperor ordered the burning of all written records.

It is, however, believed that these early emperors were great scholars. Yu the Great founded the Xia dynasty (c. 2100–1600 B.C.), which is regarded as the first imperial dynasty. He is credited with harnessing the power of water.

Huang Di, or "Yellow Emperor," who should not be confused with Qin Shi Huang Di, made a study of herbal medicines, and his wife, Lei Zu, discovered how to cultivate silkworms. It was Huang Di who instituted yellow as a symbol of the imperial family.

Shen Nong introduced agriculture and studied medicinal herbs. At a much later time, the medical discoveries of Huang Di and Shen Nong were described in a book compiled by some of the most eminent scholars of the Han dynasty (206 B.C.–220 A.D.).

It is interesting to note that items found by archaeologists in recent excavations have indicated that the so-called legendary emperors were real people.

GREAT MEDICAL MEN

The Chinese value health above all else and so it is hardly surprising that their most eminent physicians have been much esteemed and even revered. Of these physicians, the three most renowned are Hua Tuo (141–208), Zhang Zhong Jing (150–219) and Sun Simiao (581–682) .

Hua Tuo pioneered the use of "narcotic soups" as anaesthetics in treating abscesses and skin tumors. By the end of the Song dynasty

**Zhang Zhong Jing
150–219**

(960–1279), anaesthetics were well established as a technique in minor surgery.

About 200 B.C., Zhang Zhong Jing wrote *Shang Han Lun,* or "Discussions on Febrile Conditions." He also devised a chart of the human body to indicate the positions used in acupuncture.

Sun Simiao perceived that ill health was often due to dietary deficiencies. In his "Precious Prescriptions," published at the time of the Tang dynasty (618–907), he indicated that longevity could be attained by a wholesome diet, adequate exercise and regulated sexual habits. He died at the age of

Sun Simiao 581–682

101, so it is to be assumed that he practiced what he preached.

MEN OF LETTERS

The Chinese also value wisdom and so they highly esteem their philosophers, writers and other scholars, who include the poet Li Po, the artist Wu Taozi and the philosopher Mencius, who was second only to Confucius in influence.

Mencius (c. 372–289 B.C.) helped to establish Confucianism as the state religion, and his ideas became a component of the syllabus for civil service examinations.

COMMANDER OF THE FLEET

Although China has been invaded many times, the Chinese have never wanted to invade other countries, though they have always traded widely. During the time of the Ming dynasty (1368–1644), in the reign of the emperor Yong Le. a Chinese fleet commanded by the eunuch Zheng He sailed to the South Seas and established trading settlements. The first fleet even reached the eastern coast of Africa. Zheng He could therefore be regarded as China's one and only great navigator.

Great Wall

THE GREAT WALL OF CHINA

The Great Wall of China, which is about 3,950 miles in length, is a massive and magnificent monument to the perseverance, ingenuity and industry of the Chinese. It is said to be the only man-made structure which can be seen from outer space.

The best place to view the wall is at Juyongguan Pass, on Badaling Peak, about 53 miles from Beijing, where the wall is in a good state of repair. At the pass, one can make a close inspection of the bridge, watch-towers, parapets, battlements with their peep-holes and arrow-slits and arched gateways. The average height of the wall is 25 1/2 feet, the base width 21 feet, and the top width 22 feet.

The wall begins at the Jiayuguan Pass in the west, and then winds across deserts, grasslands and mountains until it reaches the Bohai Sea near the mouth of the Yalu River, which is on the South Korean border in the east. Because of its immense length, the Chinese call it Wan Li Chang Cheng, which means "Ten-thousand Li Wall." The li is a Chinese unit of distance, approximately equivalent to 1,640 feet.

The wall was repaired and reconstructed in the fourteenth century, during the period of the Ming dynasty (1368–1644), a project which took over 200 years. Watch-towers, at intervals of 1,312 feet, were erected for observing enemy movements, storing supplies and providing quarters for the garrison. Beacon towers for the communication of military information were erected alongside the wall. Communications were effected by means of fires, smoke signals and cannon shots.

Chinese writers have often likened the wall to an old giant dragon. Its tail did afford some protection for the Old Silk Road in the west. The eastern end, on the shores of the Bohai Sea, is called Lao Long Tou, which means "Old Dragon's Head." In Chinese mythology, mountains are likened to sleeping dragons. Earthquakes are their movements.

The Great Wall

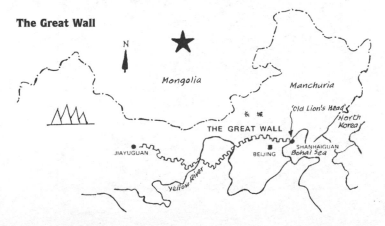

THE EMPEROR'S WARRIORS

About 25 miles to the east of the city of Xian, the capital of Shaanxi Province, lies the Mausoleum of Qin Shi Huang Di, the first emperor of the Qin (259–206 B.C.), and the site-museum of the Terracotta Army, which has received world-wide acclaim in recent years.

This mausoleum is reputed to be the largest tomb in the world. When it was constructed, it contained all those items necessary to create a subterranean universe in miniature: palaces, halls and towers,

Emperor's warrior, Xian

Tiger tally

rivers and lakes, rare art treasures, crossbows set to shoot automatically at grave robbers, a sun and moon of pearls, ducks and geese of gold and silver, pine trees and cypresses of precious stones, and lamps and fish-fat candles designed to provide permanent illumination. Of the surface structures, nothing has survived except the mound of the tumulus, which is overgrown with shrubs and weeds.

The vaults containing the warriors were discovered by accident in 1974 when some peasants of Yanzhai Commune were digging a well. The warriors they unearthed are life-size, and include foot soldiers, crossbowmen, charioteers and officers, some standing and some kneeling, armed with bronze swords and spears, and all in battle array, producing an awe-inspiring spectacle. There are three vaults, and it is possible that more will be found.

There is no shortage of *objets d'art* in China. Of particular interest are the items of pottery and the tallies which were used by the kings and emperors of ancient China as a proof of identity and an accreditation for an envoy or a general. They were the first "passports."

CHINESE ART

In Chinese art in the traditional modes, there is an absence of perspective and proportion, and the components – people, animals and objects – are generally stylized and more symbolic than real. Quite often, there are no more than one or two colors, but there are several shades of the same color, which are used to good effect. Perhaps this is a legacy from the time when a full range of colors was simply not available. However, there is no limit to the use of black; Chinese ink is renowned for its lasting and powerful quality.

In the picture below, the lily and the fish, which look unnatural, are almost as large as the girl; and the bird is as large as the mountains,

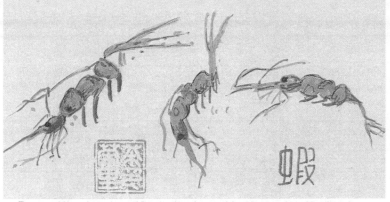

Done with a brush and in two colors, this picture is effective in its contrived simplicity.

which are unreal. What is portrayed is more of a product of the artist's mind than a faithful copy of nature. But this is an effective and well-established art-form in China, and one which we in the West would do well to copy occasionally.

But it is in the field of fine-quality pottery, called porcelain, that the Chinese excel artistically. Chinese potters have always been very skilful in the art of glazing, and have always produced designs of great elegance which are superior to anything similar in any other part of the world.

A paper-cut design of ancient origin

The well-known willow pattern first appeared on some of the porcelain ware that was made at the time of the Ming dynasty (1368–1644), during which period it was one of China's few exports to Europe. Surprisingly, the story associated with the willow pattern, in which a willow weeps for two tragic young lovers who are transformed into swallows, is English, not Chinese. This information often brings disappointment to those who have held a long-cherished but mistaken belief about the origin of this oft-told and charming story.

The designs on Chinese porcelain often include tortoises, peacocks and dragons, creatures which feature prominently in Chinese mythology. The imperial house of China was called the Dragon Throne, but this ceased when Sun Yatsen founded a republic in 1911.

A simulation of a woodcut

CHOPSTICKS

Chopsticks are eating utensils, and since the Chinese attach much importance to diet, it is not surprising that, over the centuries, the making of chopsticks has developed into an art form. Most chopsticks are mass-produced from wood, bamboo or plastic, but a few, generally of exquisite design, are hand-crafted from wood, bone or ivory, and their tops may be mounted with silver, gold or jade.

Chopsticks are mentioned in a book of the Western Han dynasty (206 B.C.–A.D. 24), so the Chinese have been using chopsticks for at least 2,000 years, and probably much longer. They are also used by the Koreans, Vietnamese, Japanese and some other peoples of the Far East; but they were invented by the Chinese.

Westerners are usually amazed at the skill and rapidity with which Chinese people manipulate their chopsticks when taking a meal. They can deftly pick up anything from large pieces of meat or fish to single peanuts or grains of rice, and they can easily cope with long and slippery items, such as noodles and oily slivers of vegetables.

Chopsticks are to the fingers what stilts are to the legs: they are useful extensions. They have four main advantages: being long, they provide much leverage; they prevent the fingers from being soiled by grease and food particles; they have no sharp points or cutting edges, and so are much safer than knives and forks; they are not made of metal, so they do not contaminate food. With Chinese meals, knives are not needed for cutting meat, fish, etc., for all the food items have been shredded, sliced or diced, and so are small enough to be picked up with chopsticks.

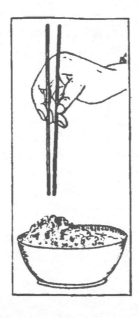

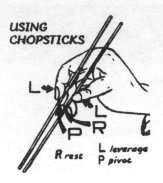

USING CHOPSTICKS

When chopsticks are being used, their lower ends appear to behave with a scissor-like motion, but this is an optical illusion. It is only the upper chopstick that moves.

Place one of the chopsticks, at about two-thirds of the distance from its tip, between your thumb and first finger and rest it on the edge of your third finger. Then place the other chopstick above the first, between your thumb and first finger, and pivot it on the end of the second finger, making sure that the tips of the chopsticks are together. Move the upper chopstick, keeping the lower one steady, in order to pick up food.

It is socially acceptable among the Chinese for you to hold your bowl under your chin and "shovel" rice into your mouth with the tips of your chopsticks held together.

Chopsticks are not the only sticks to be found in Chinese kitchens and dining-rooms. There are also some useful devices called joss-sticks – long, thin splinters of wood thinly coated with a mixture of clay, fragrant gum and a suitable oxidizing agent, such as saltpeter (niter), and which, when ignited, burn very slowly, emitting sweet-smelling fumes. The oxidizing agent provides oxygen, in which the gum burns, and the clay prevents too rapid burning of the gum.

Originally designed to be used as incense in temples, they are now used in any place where a soothing fragrance or an air-freshener is required. The Chinese use them for the same purpose that we, in the West, would use an air-freshener aerosol. But joss-sticks have the important advantage that they do no damage to the ozone layer.

The word *joss* means "idol" or "god." Thus, a joss-house is a temple. Seemingly, *joss* is a corruption of the Portuguese word *deos*, which means "god" and derives from the Latin word *deus*. Pronounce *deos* quickly and it has a sound similar to *joss*. Portugal was one of the first European nations to make contact with China, which explains how a Chinese idol has acquired a Latin name.

CHINESE LITERATURE

The chief glory of every people arises from its authors.

Samuel Johnson

The Chinese have also excelled in the field of literature, having produced some fine works in both prose and poetry. Unfortunately, these are not well known to the people of the West. The Chinese value wisdom, and so their excellent literary works indicate that they would be in full agreement with Dr Johnson's comment in this respect: "You can never be wise unless you love reading."

In earlier ages, Chinese authors and poets were also calligraphers and illustrators, and their works were often an impressive combination of various art forms, whose elegance has rarely been surpassed by modern publishers and printers with their inexpert reliance on mechanical, electronic and photographic aids. Their works were generally without blemish.

THE CONFUCIAN CLASSICS

The Confucian Classics are four canonical works – the *Shijing*, *Yijing*, *Shujing* and *Liji* – together with the *Chungiu*, which are so called because of their association with Confucius, though he did not write them.

Shijing is a collection of songs from the time of the Zhou dynasty (c.1100–221 B.C.), *Yijing* (known in the West as *I Ching*), is a book of divinations with sections which date from the time of the Shang dynasty (c.1600–1100 B.C.), *Shujing* contains documents and speeches from the Zhou period, *Liji* describes the classical rites, and *Chungiu*, or "Springs and Autumns," describes the history of the state of Lu, where Confucius was born, at the time of the Zhou dynasty.

Analects

The *Analects*, or "Lunyu," as this work is called in Chinese, is a collection of the sayings of Confucius. Some of these sayings are well known in the West, where they have assumed the status of proverbs.

> *Learning without thought is labor lost;*
> *thought without learning is dangerous.*
>
> *Have no friends not equal to yourself.*

Qu Yuan

Qu Yuan (330–295 B.C.) is one of China's great poets. He used verse as an outlet for his sorrow and disillusionment with the declining condition of China. He committed suicide, and is commemorated at the Dragon Boat Festival, which is held in the fifth lunar month every year.

Li Bai
Li Bai (also written as Li Taibo) was another eminent poet, who lived at the time of the Tang dynasty (618–907), and whose works were mainly in praise of nature.

Su Dongpo
Su Dongpo was one of the great poets of the period of the Song dynasty (960–1279), which was a time of cultural development. He also wrote in praise of nature, making many references to health and medicine.

Water Margin
Water Margin, or "All Men are Brothers," is one of the great classics of Chinese literature; and, though its setting is that of the Song period, it was written during the time of the Ming dynasty (1368–1644), when writers were beginning to make use of the vernacular, so that literature became available to all classes. In its essentials, this story is about a band of robbers who become engaged in charitable works.

Journey to the West
Journey to the West also appeared during the Ming period. It contains the legends of Sun Wukong, the quixotic monkey king, and describes the great journey of the monk Xuangzong.

Jin Ping Mei
Jin Ping Mei appeared during the seventeenth century, and is one of the first of the erotic novels. It gives explicit descriptions of the sexual activities of the nobility and the wealthy at that time.

Dream of the Red Chamber
Dream of the Red Chamber made its appearance during the eighteenth century. It is a sentimental love story which has always been popular with the younger generation, and is still widely read in China.

MEDICAL TEXTS
China has the finest system of preventive medicine in the world and there is no shortage of medical texts. Many of these have become established as classics which are of as much interest to the general reader as they are to the medical specialist. The best known of these are *Precious Prescriptions* by Sun Simiao, *Outlines and Branches of Herbal Medicine* by Li Shizhen, *Discussions on Febrile Conditions* by Zhang Zhong Jing, *Principles of Longevity* by Liu Ching, *The Internal Book of Huang Di*, compiled by the Han scholars, and *The Pharmacopoeia of Shen Nong*, also compiled by the Han scholars.

Tao Te Ching
Tao Te Ching, or "Classic of the Way and Power of Virtue and Nature," written by Lao Zi, has provided the Chinese with philosophical guidance and knowledge of Taoist principles since 666 B.C. It still has a strong influence on Chinese thought and behavior, and on their system of medicine.

Sima Qian

Sima Qian (145–86 B.C.) was China's first major historian and he succeeded in compiling a complete history of China.

Du Fu

Du Fu was a close friend of Li Bai. He wrote poetry about the lives of the common people and was highly critical of society.

THE LITERARY REVOLUTION

Modern Chinese literature is deemed to have begun with the so-called Literary Revolution of 1919.

Mao Dun and **Ba Jin** have both written influential novels about the decline of feudal China and the emergence of modern ideas. In *Midnight*, Mao Dun describes the fall of a wealthy family and thereby draws attention to social decadence.

Lu Xun is one of the most renowned of modern writers. He was very critical of the corruption in society. Initially he supported the policies of Mao Zedong, but later became openly critical of the Communists.

Lao She is another modern novelist. In *Rickshaw Boy* he writes about the sad condition of outcasts and draws attention to their misguided faith in the justice system.

Lin Yutang is probably the most accomplished of modern Chinese writers. In his epic novel *Moment in Peking*, published in 1939, he chronicles the collapse of traditional culture under Western influence. The novel tells the story of the tragic death of a mandarin's son just after the Boxer rebellion in 1900, when a British expeditionary force was entering Peking, thereby putting pressure on the weakened Manchu rulers and paving the way for Western science, technology and medicine. With these advances came the end of much of Old China, which is something that many Chinese have come to regret.

Reginald Johnson

Those who wish to view the demise of Old China through Western eyes, particularly as it affected the imperial court, could do no better than to read *Twilight in the Forbidden City*, a vivid and accurate account by Reginald Johnson, the English tutor of Pu Yi, the last emperor, who was compelled to abdicate when China became a republic.

Li Yu

Those with a weakness for pornography posing as literature could try an English translation of Li Yu's *The Carnal Prayer Mat*. It is a classic example of the Chinese erotic novel. Li Yu also wrote erotic plays, such as *Women in Love*, which are loaded with promiscuity, deviation and bawdiness. Such works were very popular in seventeenth-century China.

BEIJING

Beijing (Peking), situated in the Hopei province, is the capital city of the People's Republic of China, and is now a thriving metropolis and the political, financial and cultural center of China. With a population of more than eight million people, it is a large industrial and transport center, and has an international airport.

Beijing is really two cities: in the north, the Qing (Manchu) city, which includes the old imperial city and the Forbidden City; in the south, the Chinese city, which includes the Temple of Heaven.

AN ANCIENT CITY

Recent archaeological discoveries have shown that Peking Man, a primitive caveman, lived in the Zhoukoudian area on the south-western outskirts of Beijing about 500,000 years ago. During the time of the Zhou dynasty (c.1100–221 B.C.), a small market town called Ji arose at the place where Beijing now stands. It became larger and eventually it was adopted, in turn, as the capital of the Jin (1115–1234), Yuan (1271–1368), Ming (1368–1644) and Qing (1644–1911) dynasties.

The Hall of Prayer for Good Harvest in the Temple of Heaven, Beijing

OTHER CAPITALS

China has had other capitals. In ancient times, Xian, the main city of the Shaanxi province, was the capital of the Qin (221–206 B.C.) and Han (206 B.C.–A.D. 220) dynasties, though it was then called Changan, which means "Eternal Peace." In fact, eleven dynasties founded their capital in Xian. Between 1853 and 1864, the Taiping rebels made Nanjing their capital, as did the Guomindang (Nationalist) government between 1927 and 1949. Chongqing became the capital during the 1937 Sino-Japanese War. With the establishment of the People's Republic in 1949, Beijing again became the capital.

TOURISM

Beijing has much to offer tourists both culturally and in entertainments – modern hotels, parks, gardens, the famous Peking Opera and places of historical interest, including the Forbidden City, the Temple of Heaven, the Summer Palace and Tiananmen Square.

The international airport makes Beijing a good starting point for tours of China. Because of the immense distances involved, one should always travel by air. A typical tour of China is shown on the map below.

THE FORBIDDEN CITY

The imperial palace and Forbidden City, from which all foreigners and most Chinese were once excluded, is now a national museum, housing some of the relics of the pomp and splendor of the Dragon Throne. It was built during the fifteenth century, and it is where the Ming and Qing emperors lived in seclusion.

TIANANMEN SQUARE

Tiananmen Square, or Square of Heavenly Peace, contains the Monument to the People's Heroes and the sarcophagus of Mao Zedong.

CHINESE WISDOM

FESTIVALS

In the Chinese year, there are fourteen major festivals, though there are also a large number of minor festivals for local deities and suchlike.

The festivals briefly described below are given in order of importance, not in chronological order, for the dates of Chinese festivals are fixed by the lunar calendar, and so are variable.

NEW YEAR

This is by far the most popular of the Chinese festivals, though the celebrations now last for only three days, and not fifteen days, as they did formerly. It is an occasion for a family get-together, though there is still a great deal of ritual. The entertainments include eating, drinking, fireworks and masquerading as dragons. Gifts are exchanged, and peach trees and kumquat trees are bought for good luck. Before the New Year begins, all debts are settled and the house is swept clean. Workers get a special bonus of at least one month's extra wages.

CHINESE DOCTORS' DAY

Chinese doctors became very concerned about the influence of Western medicine, and so, on 17 March 1929, they petitioned the Nationalist government in Nanjing to support traditional Chinese medicine (TCM). Their petition was successful, and so, ever since, 17 March has been celebrated as Chinese Doctors' Day. This day has much significance for a people which values health as much as do the Chinese.

HUNGRY GHOSTS

This festival lasts for a whole month, though the main rituals are performed on the fifteenth day of the seventh month. It is an occult festival which creates an atmosphere of mystery and menace. According to tradition, it is an occasion when the spirits of the dead are allowed out of hell to visit the earth. The hungry ghosts are those who are not given ritual honors by their family. Perhaps they have died at sea and so have no known resting place, or the family line may have died out, or their descendants have neglected their filial duties. They may be people who have died violently, and so still feel attached to the earth. To placate these ghosts, people make offerings of food, joss sticks and other small gifts.

CHING MING

The springtime festival of Ching Ming is an occasion which involves visits to the family graves where offerings are made, joss sticks are burnt and respects are paid. However, this is not a sad occasion, for the Chinese regard their ancestors as being a part of the earth and still members of the family. It is not unusual for a Chinese family to have a picnic on the site of the graves of their ancestors.

CHUNG YEUNG

This is the autumn version of the spring festival. The Chinese visit the family graves twice a year.

DRAGON BOAT

This festival occurs on the fifth day of the fifth month, which is in late May or early June. It owes its origin to the death of Chu Yuen, an incorruptible court official who committed suicide by drowning in 288 B.C. The long and narrow dragon boats, which compete in races, may represent the boats which went out to try to save the unfortunate Chu Yuen.

TIN HAU

This festival is the birthday of Tin Hau, the Goddess of the Sea, and is held during the third lunar month. All the fishing boats in South China and Hong Kong participate in this event.

MOON DAY

This is a mid-autumn festival when people admire the autumn moon. This festival is a legacy from the days of moon worship.

TRADITIONS

Chinese folklore contains many quaint beliefs. Some belong to the realm of myths and fantasy; others are immensely practical. A few of these beliefs are set out below.

❊ Some lucky numbers are as follows: 2 running smoothly, 3 birth, 6 longevity, 9 immortality.

❊ If a couple wish to have a son, they must consume plenty of tofu (bean curd), bananas, mushrooms, carrots, lettuce, onions, cucumber, figs and noodles, and no meat and pickles, during the seven days before conception. If they wish to have a daughter, they must consume plenty of meat, fish and pickles.

❊ The body possesses two souls: *hun* or *shen*, which is of a higher and spiritual nature; and *po*, which is of a low and animal nature. When a person dies, his soul escapes from his body through a hole in the top of his head. When he dreams, his soul escapes and wanders

freely around the world. If his soul does not return, his body may be occupied by an evil spirit and continue to wander the world – as a hungry ghost, perhaps.

❀ If a person dreams about snow or losing his teeth, one of his parents will die.

❀ If a person hears the cry of a crow from the south between 3 a.m. and 7 a.m., it means that he will receive gifts. But, if he hears the cry between 7 a.m. and 11 a.m., there will be wind and rain, and between 11 a.m. and 1 p.m., there will be mistrust and quarrels.

❀ The Chinese tend to marry not only on a day which is favorable in some way, but also within an auspicious two-hour period.

❀ The first and fifteenth days of a lunar month are generally regarded as being the most propitious for occult rituals.

❀ If a man's ears burn between 11 p.m. and 1 a.m., there will be a harmonious relationship between him and his wife; but if they burn between 1 a.m. and 3 a.m., a guest is likely to arrive.

❀ 1, 4 and 7 are considered to be unlucky numbers. 1 signifies loneliness, and 4 and 7 signify death.

❀ Tortoiseshells and yarrow (milfoil) stalks are associated with good fortune. This explains why tortoiseshells were used in making the *I Ching*.

❀ At the beginning of the world, there was one abstract principle. This was the First Cause. When it first moved, its spirit produced the great male principle, or yang; when it rested, it produced the great female principle, or yin. These influences affected the whole universe, and in accordance with fixed laws, which are called *li*. See page 57.

❀ The operation of the universe is based upon three factors: *qi*, which is energy, *li*, which is the fixed laws, and *so*, which is mathematical principles. They express themselves as the outward form of nature, which is called *ying*.

❀ The Chinese use a Pa Kua mirror to reflect evil influences, and so changing their direction in order that they can do no harm. A Pa Kua mirror is a small mirror surrounded by the eight trigrams known as the Pa Kua.

❀ The three main religions of China – Taoism, Confucianism and Buddhism – are generally regarded as being components of one single religion. Many Chinese support all three religions, on the principle that the more religions one has, the better one's chances.

ANCIENT WISDOM

CHINESE COINS

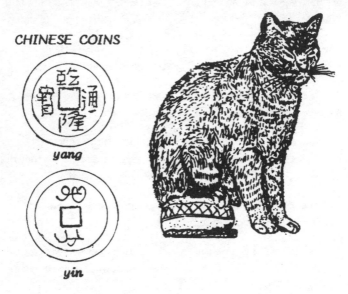

yang

yin

In a study of Chinese folklore, it is sometimes difficult for the Westerner to distinguish between what is myth and superstition and what is useful information of the kind that derives from many centuries of experience, observation and profound wisdom. But it is certainly the case that this ancient wisdom has served the Chinese well in their management of their everyday affairs, especially in the realms of health, diet and divination. Some examples of this folkloric sagacity are given below.

CHOOSING A CAT

In choosing a cat, it is important to by guided by the purpose it is to serve. Does one want a good mouser and ratter, or no more than a lovable bundle of fur? Would one prefer a male or a female? A female might mate with an undesirable tom-cat, which could lead to the production of undesirable kittens. On the other hand, a male might wander widely and deprive one of its company.

The *Tong Sing* says that a good cat has a short body – so that it can be agile – attractive eyes, a long tail and a tiger-like face. It will also have a strong and menacing voice, which will make rats and mice so afraid that they will die of fright. In this direction, it is helpful if its claws are sharp and long.

Apparently, a cat with a long body will be unfaithful and likely to go to another family. If it has a wide tail, it will be lazy. If it has a long face, it will kill chickens.

STARS FOR MARRIAGE

Certain stars are good omens for a happy marriage. Here, the term star is used loosely to include the planets, which in ancient times were described as "wandering stars."

For the woman: Venus, Saturn and Moon
For the man: Mars, Mercury and Jupiter

CURING HAIR LOSS AND GREYING

The Chinese have strong hair, so this remedy is probably less needed than it might be in the West.

Finely chop an apple, a carrot and a quarter of a lemon, add $1^3/_4$ pints boiling water and let stand until cool. Consume this liquid once daily for several weeks.

A GOOD COMPLEXION

To nourish the skin, and so improve the complexion, consume a simple meal prepared as follows once daily for several weeks:

Chop 3oz mushrooms and stir-fry them with 8oz soya bean sprouts and 1oz sesame seeds or $^1/_2$ teaspoon sesame oil.

SPOTS AND PIMPLES

Skin blemishes of various kinds can be reduced by drinking flower teas, such as chrysanthemum and dandelion, avoiding sugary and fatty foods and keeping free of constipation. It is also helpful to rub pimples and other spots with the cut end of a cucumber or a garlic clove.

CHINESE ACHIEVEMENTS

The Chinese certainly value achievement. The Tao of Achievement – one of the Eight Pillars of Taoism, which are the eight branches of Taoist philosophy and practice – indicates how success in living may be achieved by an analysis of the forces and patterns in nature, and developing strategies to deal with them.

It seems that the Taoist sages of ancient China anticipated modern scientific theories by over 3,000 years, for this analysis involves a study of the phenomena and laws of nature which, in this modern age, are defined by chemistry, physics, biology, astronomy, mathematics and other branches of science. It also involves a study of social philosophy, psychology and the arts of divination, or the forecasting of events. The Taoists believe that accurate divination is possible because the universe is cyclical in its operation, and events that have occurred will occur again. They believe that time is illusory, as did the physicist Albert Einstein (1879–1955).

The Chinese have achieved a great deal in the intellectual field. For example, their sages had a profound knowledge of mathematics. They were using mensuration in surveying and astrology; they were aware of

*Heaven and earth do not
communicate with each other,
and so the superior man does
not boast of his virtues and
makes light of his problems.*

I Ching

the optical law of lateral inversion and Newton's Third Law of Motion –
"action and reaction are equal and opposite" – and they understood
binary numbers, which constitute the essential principle of the electronic
computer. They regarded time as being "distance between events," for
they understood that, if there were no events, such as the rotation of
the earth, the swing of a pendulum and the heartbeat, we would have
no perception of time.

Many of the devices and ideas for which the people of the West claim
credit were invented or discovered by the Chinese many centuries before
they were known in Europe. Spectacle lenses, gunpowder, coinage,
banknotes, gearwheels, movable type and the calculus, odometer,
astrolabe and magnetic compass are but a few of their achievements.

But it is in the realm of medicine that the Chinese have especially
excelled. Some of the medicines recently "discovered" by the medical
scientists of the West were being administered by Chinese physicians
nearly one thousand years ago. Two examples are ephedrine for the
treatment of asthma, and the iodine-rich black ash from burnt seaweed
for the treatment of goiter. By the end of the Han dynasty (206 B.C.–
A.D. 220), anaesthetics were in common use, and the circulation of the
blood had been discovered.

But the greatest achievement of the Chinese is their mastery of the art
of living, which they owe largely to Qin Shi Huang Di, the first emperor,
who laid the foundations of an efficient system of administration; to
Lao Zi, who advocated harmony with nature and within the body; and
to Confucius, who advocated harmony in society and within the family.

THE ART OF LIVING

The art of living is surely to be as healthy as one can, for as long as one can, and as contentedly as one can.

**The gold in one's heart is far more precious
than the gold in one's purse.**
Analects Confucius

**Our main purpose in life should not be to hanker
after a heaven in the sky, which probably does not
exist, but to create a heaven on earth for each
other by effecting complete harmony between the
yin and yang forces within us and around us.**
I Ching

**What you do not want done to yourself,
do not do to others.**
Analects Confucius

**To administer medicines for illnesses which have
already developed is akin to the conduct of a man
who begins to dig a well after he has become thirsty.**
The Internal Book of Huang Di

**Treat hot illnesses with cooling medicines,
and cold illnesses with warming medicines.**
The Pharmacopoeia of Shen Nong

Delicious dishes banish potions and pills;
Nourishing food is the cure for most ills.
Chinese Traditional

When going to an eating-house,
make sure it is one that is full of people.
Chinese Proverb

A man may have a long and healthy life if he
regularly takes wholesome food and proper
exercise and effects an emission twice monthly or
twenty-four times annually.
Precious Remedies Sun Simiao

Wine is a beautiful gift from heaven which,
if not taken immoderately,
brings great joy and disposes of melancholy.
Li Shizhen

Those who say they can explain Tao do not
understand it,
and those who understand it do not say.
Tao Te Ching Lao Zi

Men and women are meant to
love and complement each other.
I Ching

Do not be afraid of paper tigers.
Chinese Proverb

Do not tread on the tiger's tail.
Chinese Proverb

By the accident of good fortune a man may rule the world for a time.
But by the virtue of love he may rule the world for ever.
Tao Te Ching Lao Zi

Do not consider any vice trivial, and so practice it;
do not consider any virtue trivial, and so neglect it.
Chinese Proverb

Shall I tell you what true knowledge is?
When you know, to know that you know,
and when you do not know, to know that you do
not know – that is true knowledge.
Analects Confucius

Sadness, disquiet, ambition without talent, greed,
jealousy, excessive joy, idleness, drunkenness, over-
sleeping, decrepitude and over-strenuous activity are
wounds, and when they have amassed to the highest
level, exhaustion and death will soon follow.
Therefore, to keep alive, one must not look, listen,
sit, drink, eat, work, rest, sleep, walk, exercise, talk
or dress too much.
Nei Pien Ko Hung

However great the ills a man may have to bear,
he but adds to them when he allows himself
to give way to despair.
Analects Confucius

If you love men and they are unfriendly,
look into your love;
if you rule men and they are unruly,
look into your wisdom.
Mencius

Wooden printing block

The Chinese have great respect for the written word, and so, by tradition, their books are made with much expertise. Years ago, their printing was done with wooden blocks, each with a character exquisitely carved in relief. These blocks were the forerunner of metal type. The Chinese also used clay and metal blocks, but they were not very effective.

These are examples of images that were frequently used to illustrate the written text.

**To the ruler, people are heaven;
to the people, food is heaven.**
Traditional

**As there is ornament in nature, so shall there be in society;
but its place is secondary to what is substantial.**
I Ching

Government is something to be endured with much patience – and much forgiveness.
Traditional

The answer you seek is within you, but it may be hard to find.
Confucius

It would be a mistake to say that there is no ruler of the universe; but, on the other hand, there is not a Gentleman in Heaven judging our moral transgressions.
Chu Hsi

**When one, seeing the peril,
can arrest his steps,
is he not wise?**
I Ching

**Know your enemies; know yourself; in a hundred
battles, a hundred victories.**
Sun Tzu

**Let a hundred flowers bloom,
let a hundred schools contend.**
Mao Zedong

The sun is in the east.
That beauty is a lady.
She is in my house,
In my house.
She approaches me ritually,
And I accept her.
Shi Ching

The moon is in the east.
That beauty is a lady.
She is in my bedroom,
In my bedroom.
She approaches me ritually,
And I make off with her.
Shi Ching

FOUR SEASONS

Earth and sky meet,
four seasons merge,
wind and rain are gathered in,
and yin and yang are in harmony.

According to Taoist philosophy, the orderly operation of the universe, of which man is a component and to some extent a miniature version, is dependent upon the harmony created by the all-pervading complementary opposites of yin forces, which are seen as feminine or negative, and yang forces, which are masculine or positive.

This principle is well exemplified by the four seasons: summer, which is hot, is the complementary opposite of winter, which is cold, and spring, which is the season of growth, is the complementary opposite of autumn, which is the season of decline. Hotness and growth are regarded as yang, whereas coldness and decline are seen as yin.

THE TAI CHI

The symbol shown above represents the Tai Chi (also written as Tai Ji) – the "Supreme Ultimate" or " Supreme Absolute" – which embodies the yin (–) forces or poles and the yang (+) forces or poles. It is the Taoist concept of a deity – and an inanimate one! – and the First Cause of the universe and the origin of life.

Order and harmony throughout the universe and within the human body are maintained by the perpetual state of balance between these opposing forces. Without this balance, there would be chaos. Yin signifies negativity, as with passivity, weakness, night, decline and death, whereas yang signifies positivity, as with activity, strength, day, birth and growth. A yin force and a yang force attract each other, but two yin forces or two yang forces repel each other. It is a basic principle of physics: "Unlike poles attract; like poles repel."

POSITIVITY AND NEGATIVITY

On the Tai Chi symbol, the black yin segment contains a small white yang circle, and the white yang segment contains a small black yin circle, which is a symbolic way of saying that yin contains a little yang, and yang contains a little yin, and neither yin nor yang can ever be entirely predominant. In fact, there are degrees of positivity and negativity.

This notion of positivity and negativity is one which is well known to physicists and chemists. A temperature of, say, 120°F is negative when compared with a temperature of 195°F, but positive when compared with 68°F. Likewise, a temperature rise from 32°F to 120°F is much larger than a rise from 200°F to 212°F. This is one of the many instances where the sages of ancient China anticipated the methods of modern science. This notion also explains the Chinese love of compromise and their avoidance of extremes of conduct. They often take the view that what is desirable may not be much better or more significant than what is apparently undesirable.

SCIENTIFIC HARMONY

The yin-yang principle should not be dismissed lightly as superstition, for it is consistent with modern scientific ideas about the structure of matter and the nature of energy. An atomic bomb is a spectacular example of what may happen when there is a shift in the fine balance between yin and yang. Furthermore, this principle is in accord with the scientific tenet of predestination or "cause and effect." As Albert Einstein put it, "God does not play dice."

Science provides many examples of complementary opposites in nature: light and shadow, acceleration and deceleration, positive and negative charges of electricity, evaporation and condensation, freezing and melting, synthesis and decay in the metabolism of plants and animals, etc. The atom contains positive and negative charges (protons and electrons). The yin-yang principle is also in accord with the numbering system used by computers, in which 1 is positive and 0 is negative.

TAOISM

Lao Zi, 6th century B.C.

*Man can only achieve personal harmony
in accepting nature and the inevitable.*

Tao Te Ching Lao Zi

Taoism is possibly the oldest and most profound religion in the world,
though it is more of a way of life and a philosophical system than a
religion in the Western sense of the term. In its purest form, it contains
much that is commendable, for it encourages a style of thought which is
similar to that of modern Western science, and it has made an
enormous contribution to the development of the medical arts. With its
emphasis on harmony with nature, it makes a perfect complement to
Confucianism, which places emphasis on harmony in society.

Unfortunately, Taoism has debased forms which often contain
elements of superstition and polytheistic religion; in the past, it has
been associated with animism, alchemy, witchcraft and elixirs of
immortality, practices which are very different from the scholarly
approach of Lao Zi, who is regarded as its founder. Perhaps the greatest
debasement was due to the influences of Mahayana Buddhism during
the sixth century, whereby it acquired the character of a religious
system.

Lao Zi (also written as Lao-tse or Lao-tzu), who is generally depicted
holding the Peach of Immortality in his hand, lived during the sixth
century B.C. and was a contemporary of Confucius. Although he is
regarded as the founder of Taoism, it is likely that some of its precepts
were formulated by Huang Di, or "Yellow Emperor," one of the legendary

emperors. Lao Zi's name, which means "Old One" or "Old Boy," derives from an ancient legend which informs us that he was born in strange circumstances.

One night in 666 B.C., a woman was so shocked by the sight of a falling star that she became pregnant. Sixty-two years later, she gave birth to a silver-haired son who was fully capable of articulate speech. This was Lao Zi. This theme of a portentous star and a human conception without male involvement is similar to that of legends from other parts of the world, and is some indication of the influence of astrology in those ancient times. It also indicates that there is no limit to credibility.

At the age of 160, just before his death, Lao Zi wrote a book containing 5,000 characters which became the inspiration for the *Tao Te Ching*, or "The Classic of the Way and Power of Virtue and Nature." This is regarded as the primary Taoist text, though there are others, which are known collectively as the Taoist Patrology. About 300 B.C., two hundred years after the compilation of *Tao Te Ching*, the Taoist scholar Chuang Chou wrote the *Chuang Tzu*, which is an exposition of the teachings of Taoism. This work is also regarded as part of the core of Taoist thought.

But there is a certain enigma about Taoist teachings, for people are persuaded to seek Tao or "the Way," but there is no clear indication of how this might be achieved. As Lao Zi said, "Those who say they can explain Tao do not understand it, and those who understand it do not say." One may wonder if Taoism once functioned as a *tong*, or brotherhood, similar to one of those secret societies in the West whose members do their good work by stealth. But whatever the mysteries of Taoism, it is certainly the main source of the desire for harmony which is the chief motivation and *raison d'être* of so many of the Chinese.

In the Book of Genesis, the Bible provides an account of the creation of the world. Similar stories are to be found elsewhere, for men have always sought for knowledge of the origin of life and the universe. This traditional Chinese story explains how the world was created by Pangu.

Before the world began, there was nothing except an egg-shaped primeval mass and the universal principle of yin and yang, which is the origin and the spirit of all matter and life. Pangu, the creator of the world, was fashioned from yin and yang. Every day, during a period of 18,000 years, he underwent nine changes. He also labored, with the help of four creatures – a dragon, a tortoise, a unicorn and a phoenix – to mold the mass into the shape which is now the earth. In this process, the clear and pure elements condensed to form the stars, sun and moon, and the dark and impure elements condensed to form the earth. The earth, the heavens and Pangu himself grew larger until, one thousand years later, he died. Then his body was amazingly transformed. His flesh became the soil, his blood the lakes and rivers, his breath the wind, his sweat the rain, his hair the plants, his left eye the sun, his right eye the moon, and his voice thunder. The parasites feeding on his body became the various members of the human race.

Chinese intellectuals, particularly the Taoist philosophers, accept that the cosmic principle of yin and yang has always existed. It is not only the basis of all Chinese philosophy, science and medicine but also an ever-present and all-pervading influence in the social affairs and everyday life of the Chinese.

However, though the rest of the story may once have had its attractions for the Chinese peasantry, it would never have been taken seriously by the Taoist sages. They have never conceived of humans in godlike form or, worse still, gods in human form, and would have regarded such beliefs as naïve or grossly pretentious. A universe under the governance of a deity with human qualities would not have been their notion of the way to cosmic harmony.

Taoists tend toward healthy agnosticism, "neither denying nor slighting Heaven," as Confucius said. They regard nature as self-creating, self-adjusting and possessed of its own spirituality. Every force and movement is an aspect of that spirituality. Acceptance of nature and its inevitable workings is more rewarding than the pursuit of knowledge which will always be limited. Even the most intelligent of us has little chance of discovering the origin of the universe. It could be that the universe has no origin. If it is cyclical, as Einstein suggested, it will have no beginning and no end. But we do not know, for we have no access to the Omnipotent or the Unknowable. Taoism may be the only religion that does not have a basis in blind faith, which is the enemy of reason. For thinking people, it has much to offer.

THE EIGHT PILLARS

The emperors of ancient China were keen to find elixirs and other devices by which they could achieve immortality. They did not realize their objective, nor was that possible, but the researches in that direction had not been entirely unfruitful, for they had yielded a wide range of health foods, herbal medicines and exercises which inhibit the ageing process, so extending the life span – and longevity is surely the next best thing to immortality. The peach is used in Chinese medicine as a treatment for ailments of the heart and circulation and other conditions associated with ageing. This explains why the peach is regarded as a symbol of longevity and immortality.

It is doubtful if Lao Zi had any serious beliefs in regard to immortality, for the *Tao Te Ching* indicates that he was a person who sought an understanding of the cosmos in terms which were more materialistic than mystical. The factual thinking of the Taoists is contained within the Eight Pillars, which are the branches of Taoist philosophy and practice. Most of the emphasis is on health, longevity, remedial treatments and harmonious relationships, which shows that their thinking was essentially practical.

The Taoist Pillars are described in outline below. Each *tao* is symbolized by one of the trigrams of the Pa Kua (or Ba Gua), as is indicated by the numbers in the illustration opposite. The Pa Kua is a symbol which, according to long tradition, was invented by Wen, father of Wu (c. 1100 B.C.), the first Zhou king. It was once widely used for divinatory purposes, and is a component of the *I Ching*, a classical work of great antiquity.

1
TAO OF PHILOSOPHY
the meaning and purpose of life, human destiny,
the laws of nature, social development and health.

2
TAO OF REVITALIZATION
the promotion of health and longevity by
exercise and meditation.

3
TAO OF BALANCED DIET
foods and dishes which are varied,
harmoniously blended and essentially vegetarian.

4
TAO OF FORGOTTEN FOOD
health foods, dietary remedies and
herbal medicines to supplement the diet.

5
TAO OF HEALING
the regulation and improvement of vital energy
and the repositioning of prolapsed organs by massage,
acupressure and other forms of manipulation.

6
TAO OF SEX WISDOM
eugenics, birth control and sex
as a therapy and to strengthen the ties of love.

7
TAO OF SUPREMACY
the achievement of mastery of one's situation,
oneself and others by divinatory devices, including astrology,
fingerprinting, numerology, personology and directionology.

8
TAO OF ACHIEVEMENT
stratagems by which the individual may adjust to the laws of
nature and society, and which include a practical and analytical
study of the sciences, philosophy and psychology.

Perhaps the most significant of the Eight Pillars is that of revitalization, or rejuvenation, for it is the basis of the many exercise techniques which are employed in traditional Chinese medicine. The internal exercises, which are those used to treat the internal organs, fall into three categories: those to promote correct posture and movement, those to increase stamina by elevating the energy levels, and those to induce healing by breathing techniques.

Some of these practices, such as birth control and eugenics, which are recent developments in the West, have been known to Chinese philosophers and physicians for thousands of years.

Fingerprints as a means of identifying criminals were first used in the United Kingdom in 1901. But the Taoists have long been aware that a person's fingerprints are an indicator of his personal character and career potential.

QI

One of the fundamental concepts of Taoist philosophy and medicine is *qi* (also written as *chi*), which means "vital energy" or "life-force," though it is sometimes translated as "breath," "air" or "spirit." This is what the *Nei Jing*, or "The Classic of Internal Medicine," one of the ancient Taoist texts, says about *qi*:

> The origin and regulation of life, birth, growth and change is *qi*, which is the law obeyed by all the myriad things of both earth and the heavens. *Qi*, on the exterior, envelopes both earth and the heavens; and, in the interior, it activates them. It is the source from which the sun, moon and stars derive their light, and the wind, rain and thunder derive their existence, and the four seasons and all animals and plants derive their birth, growth, gathering and storage. These things are brought about by *qi*, on which all life depends, as does mankind.

In the Western World, *qi* has been likened to *élan vital*, or "life-force," a concept postulated by the French philosopher Henri Bergson (1859–1941). This notion has since been repudiated by other French philosophers – but they could be wrong. It is ironic that some of the intellectuals in the West, particularly in the field of religion, lay claim to knowledge of a kind which no one is likely to possess, and which is in the nature of speculation and fantasy, yet will adamantly reject the Taoist concept of *qi*, for whose existence there is an abundance of evidence.

Modern Western science probably provides the best explanation of *qi*, though it is not one that Taoist philosophers would necessarily accept in its entirety. The heat and light in the sun and other stars are forms of nuclear energy. The moon is illuminated by light from the sun. Wind and rain and other weather phenomena are due to solar radiation and the position of the earth in relation to the sun. Thunder is the noise of atmospheric electrical discharges, which are a form of energy. Clearly, the compilers of the *Nei Jing*, which was produced about 2,000 years ago, had a remarkable perspicacity.

The energy required by plants and animals derives from solar radiation, which means that it is atomic in origin. During photosynthesis, green plants trap the energy of sunlight in combining carbon dioxide from the atmosphere with water from the soil to form sugar, which in turn is changed into starch. This energy is released when plants are consumed by animals. Oxidation occurs within the body tissues when oxygen from the air which is introduced by the breathing organs – lungs, gills, etc. – combines with carbon in the nutrients from the food consumed to form carbon dioxide, and energy is released. The carbon dioxide is expelled by the breathing organs. These processes can be briefly summarized as what chemists describe as an endothermic reaction, in which energy is acquired, and an exothermic reaction, in which energy is released.

It would seem that the Taoists were being quite reasonable in assuming that *qi* is contained in all things, including sunlight, water, air, plants and animals.

Taoist physicians take the view that *qi* in the human body can only be effective if it is in the right amount, of the right kind and in the right position. Thus, *qi* associated with the kidneys is kidney-*qi*, that of the liver is liver-*qi*, that in the wrong position or of the wrong amount is evil-*qi*, rebellious-*qi* or stagnant-*qi*, that which is particularly good, for one reason or another, is protective-*qi* or nourishing-*qi*, and that from air, which is obtained by breathing exercises, is pure-*qi*. *Qi* may be yin or yang. Yin-*qi* is associated with coldness or depression, and yang-*qi* with warmth or excitement. This is figurative language, but it is remarkably accurate by the standards of 1000 B.C. A useful analogy is the powered steering of a vehicle. All the energy is supplied by the engine, but it is not effective unless the driver ensures that the vehicle is steered in the right direction.

Yuan-qi, or "primordial vital energy," is the original and perfect energy with which a person is born, and which slowly deteriorates until the last day of life. The rate of deterioration determines the span of life. *Yuan-qi* is the energy in the egg from which the person has developed, and which is initially inert but, like a coiled spring, has the capacity to create movement and exert a force, and so initiate the period of life.

THE ELEMENTS

Another fundamental concept of Taoism, closely linked with the concept of *qi* and the yin-yang principle, is that of the five elements. In order of importance these are water, fire, wood, earth and metal. They have much significance in traditional Chinese philosophy, science, astrology and medicine; they are frequently mentioned in Chinese stories and poems; they strongly permeate Chinese folklore; and to some extent they exert an influence on the everyday affairs of the Chinese.

STUDYING THE FIVE ELEMENTS

In attempting to make a serious study of the five elements, one finds oneself confronted with an odd mixture of mystery, superstition and commonsense facts, and it is small consolation to know that this mixture has baffled some of the best minds in the Western world – and, one suspects, some of the best minds in China, too. The modern Chinese attitude toward the five elements seems to be much the same as Western people's attitude toward the contents of the Old Testament of the Bible: many are "true believers"; others keep an open mind. For, although the Chinese are great traditionalists, they are also a pragmatic people, and it is unlikely that many accept without some degree of scepticism all the components of their traditional lore.

WHAT ARE THE FIVE ELEMENTS?

In trying to define the five elements, it is less difficult to say what they are not than what they are. Certainly they have no equivalence to the four elements of the ancient Greeks – air, earth, fire and water – which were thought to be the basic constituents of all matter. Nor are they connected to the hundred or so natural elements of modern chemistry – oxygen, hydrogen, carbon, sulphur, iron, etc. – which are able, in their various combinations, to produce a wide variety of compounds. The five elements are not material and bear only a slight resemblance to reality. Generally, in this context, fire is not real fire, water is not real water, and so on.

The elements can be briefly, if somewhat inadequately, defined as qualities and influences. Thus, those things which have the quality of heat, such as a fever or sunshine, are thought to be associated with or influenced by the element fire. For obvious reasons, ancient Chinese philosophy describes the sun as the "fire force." For less obvious reasons, the heart is called the "fire organ" – because the body is kept warm by the blood circulated by the pumping action of the heart. Similarly, the kidneys and the sense of taste are associated with the element water, because urine (produced by the kidneys) and sea water both have a salty taste. Metals are often shiny, so anything shiny, such as glass or a polished surface, might be associated with metal, or the shininess might be ascribed to the influence of this element.

Ancient Chinese philosophy also used the elements as symbols to denote influences which, though not fully understood, were known to be real, such as the alternation of the seasons, the motions of the planets, some of the functions of the body and those concepts which in modern Western science are denoted by letters from the Greek alphabet (such as π) or explained in terms of the laws of nature as postulated by astronomy, chemistry, physics, biology, and so on.

A MATTER OF LANGUAGE

Although the origins of the five elements are shrouded in mystery, it is reasonable to conjecture that their development coincided with that of language, which was an unsophisticated concept thousands of years ago. There is some evidence to show that yin-yang symbols were being scratched on tortoiseshells at a time when most people were barely literate. The single word "fire," whose meaning was clear to everyone, would have had to suffice in a situation where such subtleties as heat, warmth, temperature, dryness, excitement, passion, energy, and so on, were simply not available. Similarly, "water" would have encompassed coldness, wetness, moisture, dew, flow, and so forth.

A MATTER OF PHILOSOPHY

The *Huai nan Tzu* or "The Book of Huai Nan," which was written for one of the ancient princes and contained 21 volumes, explained how heaven and earth became yin and yang, how yin and yang became the four seasons, and how yang produced fire, its essence becoming the sun.

The Confucian sage Zhou Tunyi (1017–73) wrote these words about yin and yang:

> Yin arises from tranquillity, whereas yang arises from activity. When tranquillity reaches its maximum, activity begins, and then, when the activity reaches its maximum, there is a return to tranquillity. This alternation of yin and yang yields the five agents water, fire, wood, metal and earth; and, when they are in harmony, the four seasons proceed smoothly.

In a work called the *Shu Ching*, it is said that the purpose of water is to soak and fall; that of fire to heat and rise; that of wood to be crooked or straight; that of metal to obey or alter; and that of earth to influence sowing and harvest. So the five elements give rise, respectively, to the five tastes recognized by the Chinese – saltiness, bitterness, sourness, dryness and sweetness.

These philosophical explanations may seem a bit far-fetched to the modern reader, but they do contain a certain logic, and it must be remembered that the ancient sages were operating without much of the concrete evidence that might be available today.

RELATIONSHIPS

The table below shows some of the relationships of the five elements. It is obvious why fire is related to Mars, red and bitterness, but some of the other connections cannot be so easily discerned.

Water	Fire	Wood	Metal	Earth
❀	❀	❀	❀	❀
Mercury	Mars	Jupiter	Venus	Saturn
❀	❀	❀	❀	❀
black	red	green	white	yellow
❀	❀	❀	❀	❀
salt	bitter	sour	dry	sweet
❀	❀	❀	❀	❀
fear	joy	anger	fretfulness	desire
❀	❀	❀	❀	❀
six	seven	eight	nine	five
❀	❀	❀	❀	❀
pig	horse	rooster	dog	ox

A MATTER OF MEDICINE

In traditional Chinese medicine, the five elements, together with five colors, are used to symbolize the relationships between treatments and organs, for the vital organs are associated with the emotions, some herbal medicines have distinctive tastes, and some bodily conditions are characterized by odors. This symbolism would have been useful at a time when physicians possessed only limited scientific data.

Water	Fire	Wood	Metal	Earth
❀	❀	❀	❀	❀
kidneys	heart	liver	lungs	spleen
❀	❀	❀	❀	❀
black	red	green	white	yellow
❀	❀	❀	❀	❀
salt	bitter	sour	pungent	sweet
❀	❀	❀	❀	❀
putrid	acrid	rancid	rank	fragrant
❀	❀	❀	❀	❀
fear	joy	anger	worry	desire
❀	❀	❀	❀	❀
cool	hot	windy	dry	wet

It should be understood that the first medical practitioners in China were shamans, or witch-doctors, whose treatments were combinations of sound remedies and magical practices; and one can be sure that the patients, if not the shamans, were prepared to believe that the elements had beneficial influences.

A MATTER OF ASTROLOGY

The five elements have much significance in Chinese astrology, which is based on a 60-year cycle comprised of two lesser cycles, the Ten Heavenly Stems and the Twelve Earthly Branches. The Ten Heavenly Stems are denoted by the five elements, each in its yin and yang aspects, and the Twelve Earthly Branches are denoted by the names of 12 animals – the so-called Chinese years. Each year has the name of one of the animals, is associated with one of the elements and is either yin or yang. For example, 1966 was a horse, fire and yang year, indicating the strong influence of a fiery-tempered horse; 1959 was a pig, earth and yin year, indicating the influence of a fairly reliable pig. Throughout the 60-year cycle, there are 60 different combinations, with the same combination occurring only once every 60 years. Thus 1930 was a horse, metal and yang year, as was 1990.

In the West it is a popular misconception that the Chinese attach much importance to the year-animals. In fact, Chinese astrologers prefer to denote the years by the names of the Earthly Branches, which are:

1	TZU
2	ZHOU
3	YIN
4	NAO
5	CHEN
6	SZU
7	WU
8	WEI
9	SHEN
10	YU
11	XU
12	HAI

The characteristics of the year-animals are described more fully on pages 116–121.

CONFUCIANISM

Confucius (Kung Fu-tze)
551–479 B.C.

In its role as a moral force, Confucianism is no less important than Taoism, but it is much more easily understood – and followed – for it is essentially a social philosophy. There is no rivalry between Confucianism and Taoism, for they tend to operate in such widely different areas, with Confucianism placing all the emphasis on social order and justice, and Taoism placing all emphasis on health and co-operation with nature. But they are certainly complementary, for an orderly and just society is the product of healthy-minded individuals, and vice versa. But, in any case, the Chinese are pragmatic in these matters, and are prepared, as determined by their needs, to accept – or reject – components of any religion.

Confucianism has been defined as a code of social ethics in the scholarly tradition, and an all-embracing political ideology and way of life, but with all the emphasis on the rights and wrongs of human conduct and the need for self-discipline. It was the state religion at the time of the Han dynasty (206 B.C.–A.D. 220), and it still is the greatest moral force in China, and has been instrumental in producing a stable society based on stable family life, which in turn has produced stable individuals. Its moral values are unassailable, and have no basis in superstition, giving the Chinese a strong lead socio-politically over the rest of the world.

Little is known about the personal life of Confucius (551–479 B.C.). His name, as we know it, is a Latinized version of Kon Fuzi (or Kung Fu-tze), his Chinese name, which was devised by the Jesuit missionaries. He was born at Qufu, in the state of Lu. His sayings, many of which have become globally-distributed proverbs, indicate that he was a person of profound wisdom, great benevolence and trenchant logic. These sayings were written down by his students, and form a collection called the *Lunyu*, or "Analects."

Confucianism is world-oriented. Confucius made only vague references to heaven; he contended that virtue brings its own rewards – as does vice – and that a heaven on earth could be attained if everyone behaved with wisdom, justice, sincerity, charity and propriety. The main aim of Confucianism is to produce the *zhunzi* (*chun-tzu*), which means "true gentleman" or, more literally, "superior man," who will behave correctly in all situations. Who could deny that much human misery – a living hell – is due to human selfishness and folly?

CONFUCIUS SAYS...

When you have faults,
do not be afraid to abandon them.

Study the past if you would divine the future.

In this life, bad news is always
followed by good news.

From a man's mouth may come forth sharp arrows
to wound, and fiery brands to burn. Take good heed,
then, that neither issue from your mouth.

By keeping silence when we ought to speak, much
may be lost. By speaking when we ought to keep
silent, we are wasting words. The wise man is
careful to do neither.

Do not consider any vice trivial,
and so practice it;
nor any virtue trivial,
and so neglect it.

Learning without thought is labor lost;
thought without learning is perilous.

BUDDHISM

Buddha 563–483 B.C.

Buddhism is an offshoot of Hinduism, and was founded by Siddhartha Gautama, an Indian ascetic, about 500 B.C. He was given the title Buddha, which means "Enlightened One." Its adherents strive to achieve nirvana, which is release from suffering by meditation and righteous conduct involving the "noble eightfold path" of correctness in belief, conduct, speech, resolve, occupation, effort, contemplation and meditation. They believe that there are "four noble truths": life is sorrow; desire brings sorrow; when desire ceases, sorrow ends; desire is ended by following the "noble eightfold path." They also believe that, as their souls transmigrate from one animal body to another in a lengthy series of reincarnations, their past misdeeds and misery, called *karma*, will be gradually forgotten. The sacred writings of the Buddhists are known as the *Lotus Scriptures*.

Buddhism is the third largest religion in China, and it has a large following; but, for many Chinese, particularly the Confucians, it is very much an alien religion, and they regard its mysticism and priestly caste with a suspicion that is not wholly ill-founded. They consider the doctrine of reincarnation to be nonsensical, and the celibacy of the priesthood to be unnatural. Moreover, a Buddhist temple contains altars, burning candles, grotesque statues and other paraphernalia which put it on a par with the churches in the West, but do not impress the Confucians, who are averse to superstition.

The Mahayana Buddhism practiced in China is a debased form with a heaven and a trinity, which consists of Buddha Sakyamuni, Buddha of the Past and Buddha of the Future, together with Bodhisattvas and other beings in various modes of salvation. It is very much a religion of personal convenience, for it readily accepts deities from other religions, and belief in a monotheistic deity is a matter of choice for the individual.

On the other hand, Buddhists are a peace-loving people, which makes them a good influence; and, since they are opposed to the slaughter of animals, they have evolved a wide range of delectable and health-giving vegetarian dishes which have done much to improve the health of the Chinese. It was the Buddhist monks who popularized the tea-drinking habit, and tea is beneficial to the health in a variety of ways. They also devised some of the hard styles of kung fu, or martial arts, as a means of self-defence, but which now provide opportunities for keep-fit exercises, and which have meditative overtones that help to promote a sound state of mental health by reducing stress.

lotus

ALMANACS

WHAT IS AN ALMANAC?

In its simplest form, an almanac is a calendar with some astronomical data and other useful information – festivals, weather signs, times of sowing and harvesting, etc. – which would have been a great boon in bygone ages, when such data was not readily available. The *Tong Sing*, or "Chinese Calendar," was an almanac of this kind when it was first published, many centuries before the birth of Christ.

THE FIRST ALMANACS

The Romans had almanacs which indicated the dates of their religious festivals. In ancient Egypt, the almanacs were stone tablets on which the movements of the planets were recorded. The almanacs used in ancient times in Denmark and Norway were blocks of wood or brass on which notches were cut to indicate important dates.

The first printed almanac in Europe was published in 1457 at Vienna, in Austria. It indicated the dates of the full moon and the motions of the planets. It also contained forecasts of fires, droughts and famines, and there were symbols to aid those who could not read.

MODERN ALMANACS

In recent times, almanacs have become much more elaborate, and are now crammed with useful information, most of which is of current interest. Such almanacs, which are of encyclopaedic quality, are sometimes called yearbooks because a new edition is published at the beginning of each year, with the calendar-type information being updated. The *British Almanac* was published in 1828, but the one which is best known is *Whitaker's Almanack* (with an archaic spelling).

Many almanacs, such as *Wisden Cricketer's Almanack*, are of a specialist nature. Nautical almanacs provide for the needs of mariners, for they contain the astronomical data which is required for navigational purposes.

Some almanacs provide information on astrology and horoscopes. Probably the most famous and enduring of these is *Old Moore's Almanac*, founded in 1700 by Francis Moore. His title for it was *Vox Stellarum*, which means "voice of the stars."

TONG SING

The *Tong Sing* is an almanac which is particularly worthy of study, for it is not only remarkable in being the oldest book of its kind in the world but it has been considerably increased in size since it was first published about 2250 B.C. (as its archaic language leads us to believe). In past centuries, the most talented of China's astrologers and soothsayers made their contributions, and it is now an encyclopaedia of essential knowledge, especially in regard to divination, agriculture, diet and health. Its only disadvantage is that most of its language is archaic because its content is much as it was in ancient times, though the calendar-type information is updated each year.

ASTRONOMY OR ASTROLOGY?

Astronomy and astrology are two terms which are commonly confused. According to the dictionaries, astronomy is the scientific study of the celestial bodies, whereas astrology is the study of the influence of the celestial bodies on human affairs. However, in ancient times there was no such distinction. The astrologers were also astronomers, and it would be a mistake to think that astrologers were solely engaged in the making of horoscopes, that is, using the stars as a means to forecast human destiny. It would also be a mistake to dismiss astrology lightly as being so much superstition, for divination by the stars does have certain merits.

THE WORK OF THE ASTROLOGERS

Astrologers were primarily engaged in the pursuit of astral knowledge of a useful kind, including that required for navigation and the making of an accurate calendar. An increase in knowledge of geometry, algebra, trigonometry and the earth were by-products of their researches. During the thirteenth century, Chinese astrologers built an observatory at Kaifeng. They found a value for π (*pi*) of 3.142, and constructed such instruments as the magnetic compass, seismograph, astrolabe and planetarium. It is interesting to note that they did not use the compass for navigation. Could they have discovered that a magnetic compass does not indicate true north?

CALENDARS

And that inverted Bowl we call The Sky,
Whereunder crawling coop't we live and die,
Lift not thy hands to It for help – for It
Rolls impotently on as Thou or I.

Rubáiyát of Omar Khayyám

A calendar is a chart or other device indicating the various divisions of the year – months, weeks and days. These are natural divisions, but they cannot be exactly equated. A lunar month, which is the time taken by the moon to revolve around the earth, is about $29\frac{1}{2}$ days, which is more than four weeks. A solar year, which is the time taken by the earth to revolve around the sun, is 365 days, 5 hours, 48 minutes and 46 seconds, so more than the 365 days of a calendar year, but less than the 366 days of a leap year.

This explains why calendars are slightly inaccurate and occasionally need to be corrected. The calendar used in the West during the medieval period became so inaccurate over the centuries that, in 1752, September was officially shortened by 11 days. This led to great alarm and even rioting, as many people thought that they had been cheated of 11 days of their lives!

Early men measured time by observing the seasonal changes or watching the stars and constellations which regularly appear and disappear. The people of ancient Egypt used the yearly overflowing of the Nile as a measure of the length of a year.

The Egyptians, Babylonians, Assyrians and Romans devised calendars, but all had imperfections. The Roman calendar, called the Julian calendar because it was instituted by Julius Caesar (c. 102–44 B.C.), is the origin of the calendar that is now used throughout the world.

Time measurement requires a convenient starting-point. With Christians, it is the birth of Christ, and so dates are B.C., meaning "before Christ," or A.D., meaning *Anno Domini* ("in the year of our Lord"). With Muslims, it is the Hegira, or Muhammad's flight from Mecca (A.D. 622). With the ancient Romans, it was the year of the founding of Rome (c. 753 B.C.), and dates were given as AUC, meaning *ab urbe condita* ("from the founding of the city"), or *anno urbis conditae* ("from the year of the founding of the city"). For Jews, it is the date of the creation of the world that is given in their scriptures (3761 B.C.).

The ancient Assyrians and Persians began their year at the autumn equinox (21 September), and the ancient Egyptians at the winter solstice (21 December). At one period, the Christian Church chose 25 December as New Year's Day; and, in the fourteenth century, it became 25 March, Annunciation Day.

When the Julian calendar was found to be inaccurate by ten days, Pope Gregory XIII (1502–85) ordered a revision. An extra day was inserted every fourth year – the leap year – but it is omitted when the leap year is the last year of the century. The Gregorian calendar is now in official use in all countries.

With the calendar, as with so many intellectual endeavors, we owe much to Islamic culture. In the twelfth century, Omar Khayyám, meaning "Omar the Tentmaker," was commissioned by Malik Sháh, the Seljuq sultan, to make a correction to the solar calendar, and this he did with remarkable accuracy. His correction, called the Jalalaean era, was a closer approximation to the true length of the year than that in the Gregorian calendar. Omar was a mathematician, astronomer, philosopher and poet. He wrote the *Rubáiyát*, a poetical work of 1,300 quatrains. His *Al Jebr*, from which the English word "algebra" derives, was regarded as an authoritative work.

THE MOON

*Eerie, silent and spectral, an orb or crescent of pale silver
mirroring the Sun, shedding a cold and austere light and casting
formless and gloomy shadows among the indefinable recesses on
a darkened earth, remote but friendly and familiar, majestic
though mysterious, gliding gently across the star-spangled
firmament, the Moon, Queen of the Night, does have a quality of
potent magic . . .*

For official purposes, the Chinese use the Western-style calendar; but, in
the rural areas and for making horoscopes and fixing festivals, they use the
lunar calendar, for the moon occupies a central position in Chinese folklore.
The term lunar derives from the Latin word *luna*, meaning "moon."

THE LUNAR YEAR

The lunar year contains 13 months of 28 days. In China, New Year's Day
falls on a varying date at the end of January or the beginning of February.

THE CALENDAR YEAR

The year of the Western calendar contains 12 months which are not
based on the movement of the moon, and are of various lengths. They
can be remembered by this doggerel.

Thirty days hath September,
April, June and November.
All the rest have thirty-one,
Excepting February alone,
Which has twenty-eight days clear,
And twenty-nine each leap year.

TIDES

The water in the oceans is attracted by the moon's gravity, and it builds up on the side of the earth nearest to the moon, for it is here that the moon's gravitational force is greatest. To compensate, the water also builds up on the other side of the earth, and so, at any time of the day, there are two high tides, and two corresponding low tides, one on each of the opposite sides of the earth.

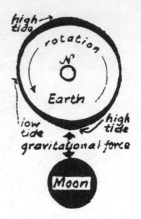

THE MOON'S MOVEMENTS

The moon revolves in an elliptical orbit around the earth. A single revolution takes about 28 days. It also rotates on its axis, which takes 28 days.

AN ECLIPSE OF THE MOON

One cannot always see the moon even on a clear night because it is sometimes in the earth's shadow. This is called an eclipse of the moon.

THE PHASES OF THE MOON

A lunar month is defined as the time between one full moon and the next. At the beginning of a lunar month, the moon is a thin crescent. This is a new moon. After about seven days, it is a half moon. In the middle of the month, it is a disc, white and shining. This is a full moon. These shapes are called the phases of the moon.

The apparent shape of the moon is the part of it in sunlight that you can see as it revolves about the earth. At the end of its first week of revolution, it is said to be in its first quarter; at the end of the third week, it is in its last quarter. This is what you see:

A Its illuminated surface is facing away from the earth, so it cannot be seen. B New moon (crescent). C Half moon (first quarter). E Full moon. G Half moon (last quarter). H Old moon.

THE FAR SIDE OF THE MOON

The moon always presents the same side to us because its period of rotation equals its period of revolution – about 28 days. But, in 1959, the Russians launched Lunik 3 on a journey around the moon. Photographs were taken, and so the far side of the moon was seen for the first time.

LUNIK 3

OTHER MOONS

The moon is the earth's satellite. Some of the other planets have satellites, or moons. Saturn has nine, Jupiter has twelve, Uranus has five, Neptune has two, and Mars has two – Phobos and Deimos. Without a doubt, there are many other moons in the solar systems in the Via Lactea, or "Milky Way," which is the galaxy to which the earth belongs.

URANUS and two of its moons

Phobos   Deimos

MARS

THE MAN IN THE MOON

Those dark patches on a full moon, which one can see on a clear night, have the appearance of a face, which children call the Man in the Moon. Of course, there is no Man in the Moon. The dark patches are valleys and volcanic craters, which were once thought to be seas and oceans.

MOON DAY

Every year, on 15 August, which is the time of a full moon, the Chinese hold a great festival that they call Moon Day. It has its origin in an old legend about a beautiful and virtuous queen who is so dismayed by the misconduct of her husband, the king, that she consumes a magic tablet which enables her to ascend to the moon, where she resides for ever. It is a charming story. And so it seems that the Chinese have a Lady in the Moon!

月
球
公
主

THE MOON AND MONEY

The Western calendar was introduced into China in 1912, when it became a republic under the presidency of Sun Yatsen. This greatly alarmed the workers because they feared that, instead of receiving 13 lunar monthly payments of wages each year, to which they were accustomed, they would receive only 12 calendar-month payments. But they did not lose out, for arrangements were officially made for them to receive an extra month's payment as a bonus at the end of the year.

MOON MAGIC

In ancient times, the moon was worshipped as a goddess who greatly influenced human affairs, and it often played an important part in the magical and religious rites of early peoples, as it still does among some of the primitive races in certain parts of the world. It could well be that Stonehenge, in southern England, which may have been used for astrological purposes by the Druids and other priesthoods, was the scene of human sacrifices, probably young maidens, at the time of a full moon.

As recently as 1900, there were a few people who believed that witches held their covens, or assemblies, and rode through the sky, seated on broomsticks, when the moon was at its fullest. It was also believed that people who are mentally unstable behave with more than their usual eccentricity at the time of a full moon. This was a common belief in China.

STONEHENGE   c.1450 BC

TIME

With his theory of relativity and notion of a space-time continuum, Einstein would have us believe that time is an illusion. Perhaps we are living in the eternal present, and the passage of time is like a toy train travelling on a circular track – coming from nowhere and going nowhere, but effectively deceiving our sensory organs.

Some physicists and engineers are of the opinion that it is acceleration rather than time which should be a fundamental quantity in our system of measurement, presumably on the principle that the intensity of an action is more significant than its speed.

TIME AND THE SENSES

We would be unwise to regard these philosophical concepts about time as being far-fetched nonsense, for we could be as wrong in so doing as were the "flat-earthers" of the Middle Ages who adamantly refused to believe that the earth is a sphere. But, then, they were merely accepting the evidence of their own senses. Alas, man is very prone to illusions. The wide variety in the many forms of religious belief should be sufficient indication of this.

However, in our everyday affairs, we must assume that time is both real and measurable, for it seems to govern our whole existence.

THE WORLD IN THE MIDDLE AGES

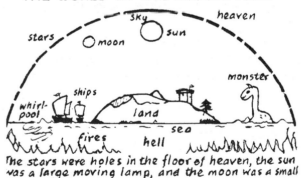

The stars were holes in the floor of heaven, the sun was a large moving lamp, and the moon was a small moving lamp.

TIME AND THE CHINESE

The Chinese have related time to their system of five directions – north, south, east, west and center; and five elements – earth, fire, wood, water and metal. It is involved in the making of horoscopes, and it plays no little part in medical treatments for jet lag and insomnia; and it is a fact that blood sugar is at its lowest level in the early morning.

MEASURING TIME

Generally, when we are busy or happy, time seems to pass quickly, but when we are unoccupied or unhappy, it seems to drag. We cannot rely on our senses for the accurate measurement of time.

The motions of the moon and stars, the apparent motion of the sun and seasonal changes are adequate for measuring long periods of time, but they are not suitable for measuring small time intervals. For this, special instruments must be used.

TIME MEASURERS

For measuring small periods of time, the Chinese have used shadow clocks, candle clocks, sand-glasses and clepsydras, or water clocks. The sundial is a type of shadow clock. The position and length of the shadow indicates the time. The shortest shadow is at midday, when the sun is overhead. Strangely enough, it seems that the Chinese did not use mechanical clocks until they were introduced into China by the Jesuit missionaries during the fourteenth century.

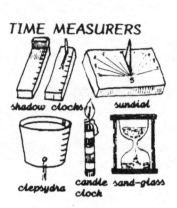

TIME MEASURERS

shadow clocks / sundial

clepsydra / candle clock / sand-glass

ZODIAC EXERCISES

For astrological work, the Chinese divide the day into 12 two-hour periods, which roughly correspond with the signs of the zodiac used in the West.

The Taoists devised a set of 12 healing exercises by which each of the 12 vital organs can be treated with the appropriate exercise during the two-hour period when its activity is at its maximum.

Zodiac Exercises

1–3 a.m. liver	1–3 p.m. ileum
3–5 a.m. lungs	3–5 p.m. bladder
5–7 a.m. colon	5–7 p.m. kidneys
7–9 a.m. stomach	7–9 p.m. pericardium
9–11 a.m. spleen	9–11 p.m. triple-warmers
11–1 p.m. heart	11–1 a.m. gall-bladder

ASTROLOGY

Although they had no telescopes, the astrologers of ancient times made accurate observations which laid the foundations of modern astronomy.

The Gao Cheng Observatory near Kaifeng was built by the astronomer Gao Shoufing in the thirteenth century. He calculated that one complete revolution of the earth around the sun takes 365.2425 days.

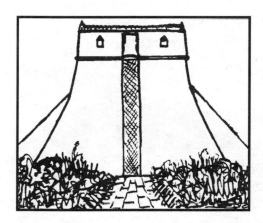

THE UNIVERSE

The universe as it appeared to the people of ancient China.
Earth is square; heaven is round.

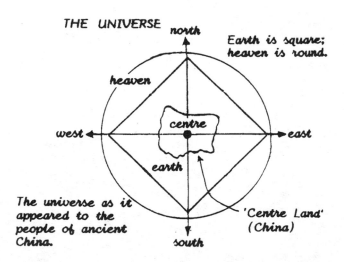

THE UNIVERSE

north

Earth is square; heaven is round.

heaven

west

centre

east

earth

The universe as it appeared to the people of ancient China.

'Centre Land' (China)

south

THE SOLAR SYSTEM

In ancient times, the astrologers were not aware of the existence of the very distant planets; nor did they know the difference between a star and a planet. A star shines because it is incandescent; a planet shines because it reflects light from the sun, which is a small star and the center of the solar system. Planet means "wanderer."

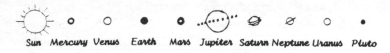

Sun Mercury Venus Earth Mars Jupiter Saturn Neptune Uranus Pluto

NORTHERN SKY AT NIGHT

Polaris (Pole Star) is indicated by an arrrow.

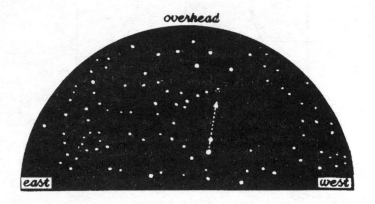

overhead

east   west

CONSTELLATIONS

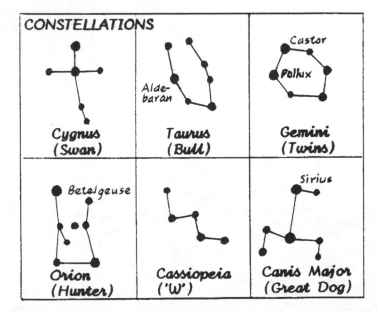

CONSTELLATIONS		
Cygnus (Swan)	Taurus (Bull) Aldebaran	Gemini (Twins) Castor Pollux
Orion (Hunter) Betelgeuse	Cassiopeia ('W')	Canis Major (Great Dog) Sirius

ECLIPSE OF THE SUN

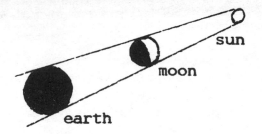

METEOR

A meteor is a tiny piece of material moving through space at high speed which becomes incandescent when it meets the earth's atmosphere. If it does not burn out completely and falls to the earth, it is called a meteorite.

A comet is a larger body appearing at regular intervals and travelling in an elliptical orbit around the sun. A good example is Halley's comet, which returns every 75 years.

Meteors and comets are the falling stars and stars of good omen in the old legends, but they are not true stars.

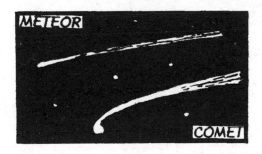

HOROSCOPES

Astrology, whether it be Chinese or in the Western style, is mainly used nowadays for making horoscopes, and it does contain some elements of superstition; but, even so, it should not be lightly dismissed as being so much nonsense, for the knowledge gleaned by earlier astrologers laid the foundations for modern astronomy.

The professional astrologer, as distinct from the itinerant fortune-teller, is honest and skilful, in the manner of a physician making a diagnosis, or a meteorologist making a weather forecast, and so will provide accurate predictions, coupled with some sound advice, based upon astral charts, logical thinking, shrewd observations and known facts about a person's character and past history.

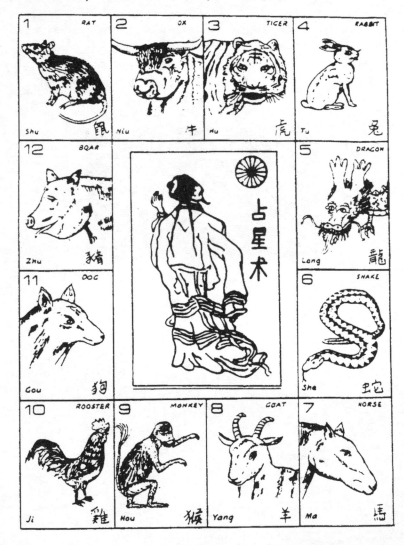

Chinese astrology is based on a cycle of 12 years, each being named after an animal. According to an old legend, Buddha summoned all the animals to appear before him at the time of the full moon just before his departure from the earth. But only 12 obeyed his call. As a reward, he named each of the years after one of the animals in the order in which they had arrived: Rat, Ox (Buffalo), Tiger, Rabbit (Hare), Dragon, Snake, Horse, Goat (Sheep), Monkey, Rooster, Dog and Pig (Boar). The Ox, Rabbit, Snake, Goat, Rooster and Pig are yin, and the Rat, Tiger, Dragon, Horse, Monkey and Dog are yang.

According to Chinese astrology, a person's destiny and character are determined by the animal which governs the year in which they were born. Thus, a person who is born in the Year of the Rooster will have a tendency to be vain, moody and talkative; and a person born in the Year of the Ox will be strong, reliable and calm. Herein, perhaps, lies the true value of a Chinese horoscope, for the person who emulates the good qualities of the animal of their birth-year is likely to have a more successful future and be a worthier person than he might be otherwise.

The characters of the year-animals are briefly:

Rat	survival	**Horse**	tolerance
Ox	endurance	**Goat**	art
Tiger	courage	**Monkey**	fantasy
Rabbit	virtue	**Rooster**	candor
Dragon	wisdom	**Dog**	idealism
Snake	luck	**Pig**	honesty

In this connection, it is interesting to note that, in China, the two most respected year-animals are the Rat and the Dragon. This is because the former is a good survivor, and the latter has great wisdom, and the Chinese greatly value these qualities.

The Chinese years used in astrology are lunar years, and begin on a variable date at the end of January or the start of February. This can be misleading. For example, a person born in the early part of January 1953, would be regarded as being born in 1952, which is a Dragon year in the lunar calendar, and not 1953, which is a Snake year. A list of the dates of the Chinese years for the whole of the twentieth century, together with other relevant information, is given below.

Chinese astrology is based on two cycles, which are the 12-year cycle of animals and the ten components comprising the five elements – metal, water, wood, fire and earth – each in both the yin, or negative (–), and the yang, or positive (+), aspects. Every 60 years, the two cycles combine to give a complex 60-fold cycle. Thus, 1906 was a fire + Horse year, as was 1966, which came 60 years later. Similarly, 1921 was a metal – Rooster year, as was 1981. The table overleaf indicates many other combinations.

CHINESE HOROSCOPES

There are three main components in the construction of a Chinese horoscope. They are the animals which govern the year, month and two-hour period when a person was born. But some influences are exerted by the element of the year-animal, the yin/yang nature of the year-animal, and the yin/yang nature of the element of the year-animal. These influences determine personality, career prospects and compatibility in friendship and marriage.

1900	Jan	31	Rat metal +	1928	Jan	23	Dragon earth +
1901	Feb	19	Ox water –	1929	Feb	10	Snake earth –
1902	Feb	8	Tiger water +	1930	Jan	30	Horse metal +
1903	Jan	29	Rabbit water –	1931	Feb	17	Goat metal –
1904	Feb	16	Dragon wood +	1932	Feb	6	Monkey water +
1905	Feb	4	Snake wood –	1933	Jan	26	Rooster water –
1906	Jan	25	Horse fire +	1934	Feb	14	Dog wood +
1907	Feb	13	Goat fire –	1935	Feb	4	Pig wood –
1908	Feb	2	Monkey earth +	1936	Jan	24	Rat fire –
1909	Jan	22	Rooster earth –	1937	Feb	11	Ox fire –
1910	Feb	10	Dog metal +	1938	Jan	31	Tiger earth +
1911	Jan	30	Pig metal –	1939	Feb	19	Rabbit earth –
1912	Feb	18	Rat water +	1940	Feb	8	Dragon metal +
1913	Feb	6	Ox water –	1941	Jan	27	Snake metal –
1914	Jan	26	Tiger wood +	1942	Feb	15	Horse water +
1915	Feb	14	Rabbit wood –	1943	Feb	5	Goat water –
1916	Feb	3	Dragon fire +	1944	Jan	25	Monkey wood +
1917	Jan	23	Snake fire –	1945	Feb	13	Rooster wood –
1918	Feb	11	Horse earth +	1946	Feb	2	Dog fire +
1919	Feb	1	Goat earth –	1947	Jan	22	Pig fire –
1920	Feb	20	Monkey metal +	1948	Feb	10	Rat earth +
1921	Feb	8	Rooster metal –	1949	Jan	29	Ox earth –
1922	Jan	28	Dog water +	1950	Feb	17	Tiger metal +
1923	Feb	16	Pig water –	1951	Feb	6	Rabbit metal –
1924	Feb	5	Rat wood +	1952	Jan	27	Dragon water –
1925	Jan	25	Ox wood –	1953	Feb 14		Snake water –
1926	Feb	13	Tiger fire +	1954	Feb	3	Horse wood +
1927	Feb	2	Rabbit fire –	1955	Jan	24	Goat wood –

Examples of usage:

A person born on 30 January 1938 falls into the Chinese year that began in February 1937 and so has an Ox personality. But 31 January 1938 is the first day of the New Year, so a person born on that day has a Tiger personality.

Year	Month	Day	Sign		Year	Month	Day	Sign
1956	Feb	12	Monkey fire +		1984	Feb	2	Rat wood +
1957	Jan	31	Rooster fire −		1985	Feb	20	Ox wood −
1958	Feb	18	Dog earth +		1986	Feb	9	Tiger fire +
1959	Feb	8	Pig earth −		1987	Jan	29	Rabbit fire −
1960	Jan	28	Rat metal +		1988	Feb	17	Dragon earth +
1961	Feb	15	Ox metal −		1989	Feb	6	Snake earth −
1962	Feb	5	Tiger water +		1990	Jan	27	Horse metal +
1963	Jan	25	Rabbit water −		1991	Feb	15	Goat metal −
1964	Feb	13	Dragon wood +		1992	Feb	4	Monkey water +
1965	Feb	2	Snake wood −		1993	Jan	23	Rooster water −
1966	Jan	21	Horse fire +		1994	Feb	10	Dog wood +
1967	Feb	9	Goat fire −		1995	Jan	31	Pig wood −
1968	Jan	30	Monkey earth +		1996	Feb	19	Rat fire +
1969	Feb	17	Rooster earth −		1997	Feb	8	Ox fire −
1970	Feb	6	Dog metal +		1998	Jan	28	Tiger earth +
1971	Jan	27	Pig metal −		1999	Feb	6	Rabbit earth −
1972	Jan	16	Rat water +		2000	Jan	27	Dragon metal +
1973	Feb	3	Ox water −		2001	Jan	24	Snake metal −
1974	Jan	23	Tiger wood +		2002	Feb	12	Horse water +
1975	Feb	11	Rabbit wood −		2003	Feb	1	Sheep water −
1976	Jan	31	Dragon fire +		2004	Jan	22	Monkey wood +
1977	Feb	18	Snake fire +		2005	Feb	9	Rooster wood −
1978	Feb	7	Horse earth +		2006	Jan	29	Dog fire +
1979	Jan	28	Goat earth −		2007	Feb	18	Pig fire −
1980	Feb	16	Monkey metal +		2008	Feb	7	Rat earth +
1981	Feb	5	Rooster metal −		2009	Jan	26	Ox earth −
1982	Jan	25	Dog water +		2010	Feb	14	Tiger metal +
1983	Feb	13	Pig water −		2011	Feb	3	Rabbit metal −

2000 YEAR OF THE DRAGON

The year 2000 is not only the first year of the third millennium since the birth of Christ, but also a Dragon Year in Chinese tradition. So it could be a propitious year for those born in a Year of the Dragon, for the Dragon is associated with wisdom, magic and generosity.

However, there can be some confusion with dates. In the Western calendar, the Chinese year 2000 begins on 5 January 2000, and ends on 23 January 2001. Moreover, there is some doubt about the date of the birth of Christ, with some experts even claiming that Christ was born about 5 B.C.!

THE DRAGON

The Dragon is a mythical monster with a scaly body, clawed feet, a long tail and massive fire-breathing jaws. It sometimes has batlike wings. Its English name drives from the Greek word *drakon*, meaning "serpent." It is the subject of many legends, and it is often associated with the heroes of folklore, such as St George and Beowulf.

This legendary creature commonly features in the literature and the social and ceremonial life of China. It was the emblem of the imperial family of China, and always appeared on its flags prior to 1912, when China became a republic, founded by Sun Yatsen, thus ending the power of the Qing (Manchu) dynasty and the Dragon Throne.

There are, in fact, many different kinds of dragons, each with its own functions, powers and rank, but all are quixotic, and sometimes friendly, sometimes not. The Chinese belief in dragons is understandable, for there are some creatures with a dragon-like appearance. An example is the Komodo dragon, *Varanus komodoensis*, a large monitor lizard found in Indonesia. The dinosaurs which once roamed the earth were also dragon-like creatures. Their fossilized bones are reputed to have medicinal properties, and they are commonly used in Chinese medicines.

The Dragon, or Long, as it is called in China, symbolizes heaven, energy and masculinity in Chinese cosmology.

THE CHINESE CALENDAR

Because the Chinese year is determined by the movement of the Moon, not the apparent movement of the Sun, it begins on a variable date in January or February. Thus, the Years of the Dragon for the twentieth century are as follows:

1904	16/2–4/2
1916	3/2–23/1
1928	23/1–10/2
1940	8/2–27/1
1952	27/1–14/2
1964	13/2–2/2
1976	31/1–18/2
1988	17/2–6/2

GENERAL HOROSCOPE FOR DRAGON YEARS

Order: 5th
Direction: ESE
Season: spring
Element: wood
Hours: 7–9 a.m.
Yin/yang: +
Month: April
Zodiac: Aries

Personality: quixotic, enigmatic, witty, artistic, original in thought, humorous, perfectionistic, generous.

Career: athletics, politics, medicine, law

Friendship marriage: affectionate, magical

Compatibility: Rat, Monkey

FINDING THE YEAR-ANIMALS

The year beginning in January 2000 is a Dragon Year, the following year (2001) is a Snake Year, then a Horse Year and so on. The other year-animals can be found by counting in twelves. For example, the next Dragon Year will be 2000 + 12 = 2012, the next Snake Year 2001 + 12 = 2013, and the next Horse Year 2002 + 12 = 2014.

2001
YEAR OF THE
SNAKE

The Year of the Snake begins on 24 January 2001 in the Western calendar. The Snake is associated with good fortune, talent and wisdom.

THE SNAKE

Snakes are legless reptiles with long cylindrical bodies and scaly skin; they have movable elastic-like bones in the head and jaws which enable them to swallow animals much larger than themselves. Some species of snakes are quite harmless, but many kill their prey by constriction, such as the python and anaconda, or by means of venom in their fangs, such as cobras and vipers. They move swiftly and silently in so doing, which explains why they have a reputation for being vicious and cunning. It also explains why, in Chinese astrology, people born in a Year of the Snake are considered to be shrewd and ruthless in their determination to achieve success.

As a snake grows, it casts off its old skin, which is replaced by a new skin developing beneath it, and so the skin of a snake is always smooth and unblemished. This, no doubt, explains why Chinese astrology associates the Snake with youthfulness.

The Snake, or She, as it is called in China, symbolizes earth, darkness and femininity in Chinese cosmology.

GENERAL HOROSCOPE FOR SNAKE YEARS

Order:	6th
Direction:	SSE
Season:	spring
Element:	fire
Hours:	7–11 a.m.
Yin/yang:	–
Month:	May
Zodiac:	Taurus

Personality:	instinctively wise, proud, determined, talented, courageous when necessary, lucky, always successful, youthful.
Career:	finance, politics, law, stage, business
Friendship marriage:	jealous, possessive
Compatibility:	Rooster, Ox

NEW YEAR RECIPES

At New Year in China, it is the custom to serve dishes that are in some way related to the year-animal. For example, a fiery-tasting soup would be appropriate for the year of the Dragon, as a pork dish would be for the Year of the Pig. The quantities given here serve four people.

DRAGON SOUP

3 spring onions
2 slices fresh ginger
2 pinches black pepper
2 teaspoons dark soy sauce
1 tablespoon curry powder
2¹/₂ pints chicken stock

Chop the onions and add them, together with the other ingredients, to the stock. Stir well, bring nearly to the boil, and then simmer gently for 5 minutes.

In the West, this dish is called mulligatawny soup. It originated in India.

DRAGON RICE

This dish is really prawn fried rice, but the prawns are provided with "wings" to give them a vaguely dragonlike appearance.

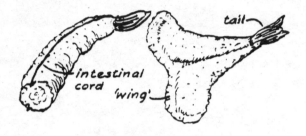

2 eggs
4oz large cooked
    whole prawns
cornstarch
cooking oil for
    deep-frying

Beat the eggs. Clean the prawns, removing the head, legs and shell, but leaving the tail intact. Split them lengthwise, remove the intestinal cord with the tip of a knife, flatten them, dip them first in beaten egg and then in cornstarch, and deep-fry until golden brown. Drain well and serve at once with egg fried rice.

Prawns prepared in this way are sometimes called prawn cutlets. It is important to use large prawns or even king prawns.

CHICKEN FUYUNG

A chicken dish is suitable for the Year of the Rooster.

1 sprig fresh parsley
7 eggs
¹/₄ teaspoon salt
pinch of black pepper
5oz cooked chicken
1 large mushroom
3 spring onions
1 tomato
2 tablespoons peanut oil

Chop the parsley finely. Beat the eggs well, add the salt, pepper and parsley, and stir. Shred the chicken, chop the mushroom, onions and tomato, mix them together and stir-fry in the oil over fairly high heat for about 2 minutes. Add the egg mixture and continue to stir-fry until the egg is set. Serve immediately.

PORK BALLS WITH CABBAGE

This recipe is for the Year of the Pig. Pork dishes are very popular in China.

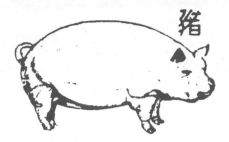

12oz lean pork
2oz mushrooms
1 tablespoon cornstarch
1 tablespoon meat/chicken stock
1 teaspoon salt
2 tablespoons soy sauce, light/dark
4 spring onions or 1 leek
1lb cabbage, preferably Chinese
3 tablespoons cooking oil

Finely chop the pork and mushrooms, add the cornstarch, stock, $\frac{1}{2}$ teaspoon salt and 1 tablespoon soy sauce, mix well and shape into 10–12 balls of equal size.

Chop the onions/leek and cabbage, stir-fry together in the oil over fierce heat for 2 minutes. Add $\frac{1}{2}$ pint water, 1 tablespoon soy sauce and $\frac{1}{2}$ teaspoon salt, bring to the boil. Place the pork balls on top of the cabbage, cover, simmer for 15–20 minutes and serve at once.

FRIED RABBIT

The rat and the rabbit are distantly related, and so this recipe would be suitable for either the Year of the Rat or the Year of the Rabbit.

1 fresh dressed rabbit
2 egg whites
1 teaspoon salt
4 teaspoons cornstarch
cooking oil for deep-frying
4 spring onions
4 tablespoons peanut oil
2 tablespoons light soy sauce
6 tablespoons chicken stock

Wash the rabbit, dry on kitchen paper and cut into 8 pieces of equal size. Beat the egg whites until frothy, add the salt and 2 teaspoons of cornstarch, and mix together. Dip the pieces of rabbit into the mixture, allow to stand for 15 minutes, and then deep-fry until tender.

Chop the onions and stir-fry in the peanut oil at high heat for about 15 seconds, add the pieces of rabbit, the soy sauce and the stock, and cook at medium heat for 4–5 minutes.

POACHED TROUT

Both snakes and fish are cold-blooded creatures, and so a fish dish would be suitable for the Year of the Snake.

1 trout
1 spring onion
2 tablespoons cornstarch
1 pint milk/chicken stock
1/4 teaspoon salt
2 teaspoons lemon juice

Gut and clean the trout, but do not remove the head, tail and fins. Immerse in gently simmering water in a wok, continue to simmer for 10 minutes, drain, place in a flat dish and keep warm.

Chop the onion very finely. Mix the cornstarch with just enough of the milk/stock to make a smooth paste.

Put the remaining milk/stock into a wok, add the salt, onion, cornstarch paste and lemon juice, bring to the boil, constantly stirring, simmer for 2 minutes and pour on to the trout. Serve at once.

FRIED LAMB

Lamb is similar to goat's meat and dog meat in flavor and texture, making fried lamb an appropriate dish for the Year of the Goat or the Year of the Dog.

1lb lamb
6 spring onions
2 tablespoons light soy sauce
1 teaspoon salt
2 tablespoons peanut oil
4 teaspoons dry sherry
3 teaspoons sesame oil

Slice the lamb thinly, chop the onions and mix together with the soy sauce and salt. Heat the peanut oil in a wok or pan. When very hot, add the meat mixture and stir-fry until cooked. Add the sherry and sesame oil, stir lightly and serve with vegetables.

CHICKEN WITH NUTS

For obvious reasons, a dish with nuts is appropriate for the Year of the Monkey.

3oz mixed nuts:
   walnuts, cashew nuts, almonds and peanuts
12oz cooked chicken
1 spring onion
2 teaspoons cornstarch
2 tablespoons peanut oil
2 pinches of salt
1 tablespoon light soy sauce

Blanch the nuts by immersing them in boiling water for 5 minutes. Remove the skins with a cocktail stick or a pin. Cut the chicken into 1/2-inch cubes, chop the spring onion, and mix the cornstarch with sufficient water to make a thick liquid.

Stir-fry the nuts in the oil at high heat for about 1 minute, and then add the rest of the ingredients and stir-fry over medium heat for a further 2 minutes. Serve at once.

FRUIT SALAD

This dish is suitable for all festive occasions.

1 apple
1 pear
6 strawberries
1 orange
1 small melon
12oz can of
   litchis

Wash the fresh fruits, peel, core and cut the apple and pear into wedges, trim the strawberries, peel and separate the orange into its segments, cut the melon into cubes, discarding the seeds and peel, and drain the litchis. Mix the pieces together and store in a refrigerator until required. Serve very cold.

OYSTER SAUCE BEEF

Lean beef is a solid red meat of firm texture, as is the flesh of the horse, so a beef dish would be suitable for both the Year of the Ox and the Year of the Horse.

1 teaspoon cornstarch
10oz beef steak
1 tablespoon light soy sauce
1 teaspoon sugar
1 teaspoon rice wine or
   sherry
3 tablespoons peanut oil
1 small carrot
2oz mangetout
2 mushrooms
1 stick celery
1 spring onion
3 thin slices ginger root
¼ teaspoon salt
2 tablespoons oyster sauce
3 tablespoons chicken
   stock

Mix the cornstarch with just enough water to make a smooth liquid. Thinly slice the beef, put into a shallow dish with the soy sauce, sugar, wine and cornstarch, and leave to marinate for 30 minutes.

Pre-heat a wok and add 2 tablespoons of peanut oil. Stir-fry the beef for about a minute, remove, drain and keep warm.

Slice the carrot, mangetout, mushrooms, celery and onion. Heat a further tablespoon of oil in the wok and stir-fry the vegetables, together with the ginger, for about 2 minutes. Add the beef, salt, oyster sauce and stock, blend and heat gently for about 2 minutes. Serve with a dip-in sauce.

FISH WITH GINGER

A fiercely hot dish such as this is suitable for the Year of the Tiger.

1lb cod or haddock in
   4 fillets
2 tablespoons peanut oil
3oz butter
1 tablespoon grated ginger
   root
4 sprigs parsley or coriander
4 lemon wedges

Wash and dry the fish. Heat the oil in a wok and fry gently for a few minutes until tender.

Melt the butter in a small pan, add the ginger, stir until well mixed and pour over the fish. Serve garnished with the parsley or coriander and the lemon wedges.

HOROSCOPES
AND
PROPHECIES

PROPHECIES

Myself when young did eagerly frequent
Doctor and Saint, and heard great Argument
About it and about; but evermore
Came out by the same Door as in I went.

Rubáiyát of Omar Khayyám

People have always had a great interest in human destiny, with the individual wanting to know what the future holds. They have generally been prompted by fear of death, illness or some other calamity, or by joyful anticipation of wealth, prestige or some other form of worldly success. It does seem that anticipation is more meaningful than realization.

But people have good cause to be anxious about the future, for they are constantly operating under a cloud which is due to their intelligence, of which they are so inordinately proud. We are the only animals on earth with prior knowledge of our own demise – and well in advance. It is this intelligence which has also rendered us capable of gross cruelty and refined deception, including self-deception. Lest the future be less favorable to our interests than we might wish, we have entertained dreams of immortality or an afterlife where all will be good and beautiful. "Hope springs eternal in the human breast…"

There have always been prophets who are ready to satisfy the market in soothsaying. Some of the minor prophets are charlatans, as in the case with those who will readily assure you of a delightful destiny if you cross their palm with sufficient silver. Predictions from this source will

surely be unreliable, but this cannot be said of a physician's prognosis, a meteorologist's forecast or an economist's appraisal of commercial trends, for they are based on known facts and logical thinking, though they could rarely achieve complete accuracy.

Religion has produced many prophets. The Bible, for example, contains much prophetic wisdom, including that of Elijah and Solomon. In other religions, too, visionaries such as Lao Zi, Confucius and Muhammad produced inspired teachings which have done much for the health and happiness of mankind.

But there have always been sceptics, such as the Persian philosopher Omar Khayyám, who perceived that most of the sages and saints are neither as clever nor as virtuous as they would have us believe. Considering the present state of the world, it seems that Omar had a clear perception, for it is apparent that those in authority, who are supposed to be of exceptional talent, have not always served mankind well.

For the people of the ancient world, the main sources of prophecies were astrology, books of fate and oracles. Some well-known books of fate are the Bible, *I Ching*, *Tao Te Ching* and Virgil's *Aeneid*.

Apollo

A dictionary defines an oracle as a person or thing that serves as an infallible but mysterious guide or indicator in making profoundly wise and authoritative judgments. Such an oracle was the Temple of Apollo, the god of the sun, in Delphi, at the foot of Mount Parnassus in central Greece. The soothsayers of ancient Rome used the entrails of an animal as a means of making predictions. The blood sacrifice, so beloved of religionists, was probably intended to produce a favorable augury. Bribing the gods!

Chinese prediction-making, whether astrological or otherwise, has always been based upon past experience, logical thought and three scientific principles: there can be no effect without a cause; nothing occurs in isolation; and what has occurred before will occur again. These principles are explained in more detail on page 111.

Temple of Apollo, Delphi

THE YELLOW EMPEROR'S POEM AND SEASONS

One of the simplest ways of making predictions is the so-called Yellow Emperor's Poem and Four Seasons, which is a chart consisting of a poem and four pictures of the Yellow Emperor. The predictions are contained within the poem and are located by reference to the pictures.

It is certain that the Yellow Emperor (c. 2600 B.C.) did not write this poem; but no doubt the compilers of the *Tong Sing* assumed that the mention of his name would be a good, and perhaps a magical, influence, for he was the first of the legendary emperors, had enormous powers and was closely associated with divine beings and the forces of nature.

To use this system, you need to know the two-hour period in which you were born. Each two-hour period is assigned a reference number, as follows:

1	11 P.M–1 A.M.
2	1–3 A.M.
3	3–5 A.M.
4	5–7 A.M.
5	7–9 A.M.
6	9–11 A.M.
7	11 A.M.–1 P.M.
8	1–3 P.M.
9	3–5 P.M.
10	5–7 P.M.
11	7–9 P.M.
12	9–11 P.M.

Now find the reference number of your period of birth in the picture which corresponds with the season of your birth. Then locate this number in the lists of predictions-cum-advice given overleaf:

SPRING

1 Sleep well

2 Eat more

3 Disaster

4 Romance ahead

5 No hope

6 Much hope

7 Act quickly

8 Dress well

9 Friends needed

10 Trust no one

11 Wealth ahead

12 Stormy

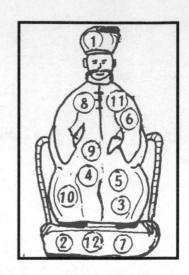

SUMMER

1 Eat less

2 Keep awake

3 Be alert

4 Deep friendship

5 Hopeful

6 Take care

7 Have trust

8 Certain joy

9 Sadness

10 Good luck

11 Black clouds

12 Sympathy coming

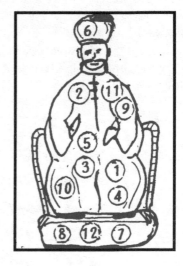

AUTUMN

1 Passion rules

2 Doubt

3 Satisfaction

4 Much pleasure

5 Be true

6 False dreams

7 Act soon

8 Worry not

9 Less hope

10 Success ahead

11 Good news

12 Danger

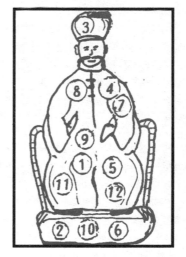

WINTER

1 Trust your family

2 Hope

3 Failure

4 News

5 Marriage

6 Be watchful

7 Icy

8 Good fortune

9 Be careful

10 Happiness

11 Bad news

12 Great surprise

You will notice that these predictions have a somewhat cryptic quality. This was no doubt intended. A little mystery is not out of place here, and in any case these predictions should not be taken too seriously.

You will also notice that you can select the appropriate prediction without referring to the pictures. Presumably a picture of the Yellow Emperor was meant to function as a charm.

CASTING YOUR OWN HOROSCOPE

A horoscope may be briefly defined as a personal prediction based upon data derived from the configuration of the heavenly bodies.

PREPARING HOROSCOPES

The preparation of Chinese horoscopes in the correct and traditional manner can be a complicated business requiring astrological data and reference books. It is essential that the person preparing the horoscopes should be observant, shrewd and knowledgeable about astrology and horoscopy, for there are a number of influences involved: year-animal, month and time of birth, year-animal element and fixed element. Anyone requiring an accurate Chinese horoscope is advised to consult a professional horoscope-maker.

But for the purpose of entertainment some of these influences can be partly ignored; and so by following the instructions on the next few pages, it is possible to prepare Chinese-style horoscopes quickly and easily without most of the complications associated with the procedures prescribed in the learned works on the subject. Inevitably, there will be some streamlining; but, for practical purposes, this will not make much difference.

A SCIENTIFIC APPROACH

Whether one considers the making of horoscopes, Chinese or Western, as a matter to be taken seriously or regarded as an innocent form of entertainment, one should be aware that the astrologers of the ancient world often adopted a scientific approach. The ancient Egyptians used a gnomon, or sundial, to measure time. The Greek philosopher Eratosthenes determined the earth's circumference by measuring the angle of the sun's rays, and this was done with great accuracy, which was no mean achievement. The Chinese astrologer Gao Shoufing accurately calculated the period of the earth's revolution around the sun as 365.2425 days.

ERATOSTHENES
276–192 BC

GAO SHOUFING
13th century

The Moving Finger writes; and, having writ,
Moves on; nor all thy Piety nor Wit
Shall lure it back to cancel half a Line,
Nor all thy Tears wash out a Word of it.

Rubáiyát of Omar Khayyám

It is known that the earth is influenced by the sun, moon, stars, planets and other celestial bodies. The gravitational forces of the moon and sun create the ocean tides and influence the weather, which, in turn, exerts an influence on agricultural activities and human conduct generally. Is it not said that some mentally unstable people behave more irrationally than usual when the moon is at the full?

Radioactive particles from outer space must have some effect on our health. It could well be that this cosmic radiation causes mutations, that is, alterations of the gene patterns in the reproductive cells of plants and animals, so creating new species. Although some of these astral influences are only barely discernible, and, therefore, generally immeasurable, there can be no doubt that they do exist. Moreover, it is more than likely that there are influences operating in the universe which are unknown to man.

THREE SCIENTIFIC PRINCIPLES

There are three scientific principles which have some bearing not only on horoscopes but on all forms of serious prediction-making.

1. There can be no effect without a cause. There are no accidents. What we describe as an accident is an event which is unforeseen or whose cause is not apparent, but which does nevertheless have a cause. An effect will give rise to another effect, and so every cause and effect is a component in many long series of causes and effects which have been in operation since the beginning of time. Free will is an illusion created by a person's inability to perceive all causes and effects. Our decisions are

decided by our emotional and intellectual make-up, which is the product of inheritance and environmental influences, both past and present. We may think we have a free choice, but whatever choice we make, there can only be one outcome, which has been preordained. The law of cause and effort is inexorable. A human being has no more free will than a computer has. This view is in accord with Taoist philosophy.

2. No event occurs in isolation. This is really an extension of the principle of cause and effect, but it is less concerned with history and more with immediate causes and effects, particularly those which tend to be imperceptible to the human senses. When a small pebble is thrown into a pond, the ripples reach all the sides of the pond, no matter how small the ripples or how large the pond. Radio waves reach all parts of the earth's surface, though they are so reduced in intensity that they need to be amplified if they are to be heard. Many human acts, such as small mannerisms and things said in passing, go largely unnoticed, but they will be noticed by, and be helpful to, any astute observer, and particularly to a maker of horoscopes.

3. What has occurred before will occur again. This principle stems from Einstein's concept of a cyclical universe. But it is difficult to conceive or accept that the whole of human history in all its detail could occur again at some future time. Yet, if time and space are cyclical or infinite, this is possible. Alas, we are unable to envisage infinity, and we can do no more than represent it by a mathematical symbol (∞). However, at an everyday level, it can be said that there is a certain sameness about human nature, and that the same or similar causes generally produce the same or similar effects. This often makes accurate predictions possible, for a person's behavior is sometimes an indication of his or her future.

CONSTRUCTING A HOROSCOPE

There are six components in the construction of a Chinese horoscope.

1. **The animal governing the year.**
2. **The animal governing the month.**
3. **The animal governing the two-hour period in which a person is born.**
4. **The element of the year-animal.**
5. **The yin/yang nature of the animal.**
6. **The yin/yang nature of the element of the year-animal.**

These components determine such items as personality, career prospects and compatibility in friendship and marriage, all of which are briefly stated in the year-animal charts on the pages that follow.

There are some lesser influences, but they can be disregarded for practical purposes.

As we have seen, six of the year-animals – Ox, Rabbit, Snake, Goat, Rooster and Pig – are yin, and six – Rat, Tiger, Dragon, Horse, Monkey and Dog – are yang.

THE ELEMENTS

By their alternation, yin and yang produce five elements – metal, water, wood, fire and earth – which, in turn, interact to produce all phenomena. But it must be understood that they are cosmic agents, not to be rigidly identified with the substances after which they are named. They have the same sort of significance as x, y, a, b and the other mathematical symbols.

The elements have yin and yang components. Examples:

METAL coin –, sword +

WATER lake –, cataract +

WOOD bamboo –, fir +

FIRE lamp –, furnace +

EARTH valley –, mountain +

The animal elements are interpreted as follows:

METAL resolute, powerful, individual, opulent

WATER creative, communicative, flexible, observant

WOOD moral, self-confident, co-operative, compassionate

FIRE inventive, decisive, dynamic

EARTH practical, reliable, prudent

Those which are yang (+) are powerful. Those which are yin (–) are less powerful.

THE MONTH AND TIME OF BIRTH

The animals governing the months are as follows:

OX January

TIGER February

RABBIT March

DRAGON April

SNAKE May

HORSE June

GOAT July

MONKEY August

ROOSTER September

DOG October

PIG November

RAT December

The two-hour periods and their governing animals are as follows:

RAT 11 p.m.–1 a.m.

OX 1 a.m.–3 a.m.

TIGER 3 a.m.–5 a.m.

RABBIT 5 a.m.–7 a.m.

DRAGON 7 a.m.–9 a.m.

SNAKE 9 a.m.–11 a.m.

HORSE 11 a.m.–1 p.m.

GOAT 1 p.m.–3 p.m.

MONKEY 3 p.m.–5 p.m.

ROOSTER 5 p.m.–7 p.m.

DOG 7 p.m.–9 p.m.

PIG 9 p.m.–11 p.m.

Thus, someone born at 4 a.m. in October 1988 will have most of the qualities of the Dragon, which will largely predetermine his or her destiny. To a lesser degree, they will have some of the qualities of the Dog (October); and, to an even lesser degree, some of the qualities of the Tiger (3 a.m.–5 a.m.).

COMPATIBILITY TRIANGLES

Each of the 12 animals in the Chinese cycle of years is allotted a direction, and their compatibility occurs where they are joined by the sides of an equilateral triangle.

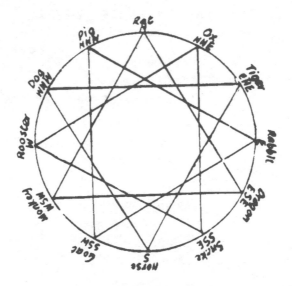

And so, for example, in friendship or marriage, the Rat is an ideal partner for the Monkey or the Dragon. On the other hand, the Rat would be sheer anathema to the Horse, Snake or Goat.

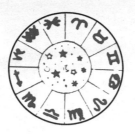

THE ZODIAC

Western-style horoscopes are based on the 12 signs of the zodiac –
Aquarius (Waterman), Pisces (Fishes), Aries (Ram), etc. – each of which
is assigned to a monthly period. But each of the 12 Chinese year-animals
is also assigned to one of the months, and so they may be approximately
equated with the zodiacal signs: RAT = Sagittarius, OX = Capricorn etc.

The zodiacal equivalents of the Chinese year-animals, together with
some other Western-style data – planetary ruler, flower, gem, lucky day,
lucky number, etc. – are shown in the year-animal charts on the next
three pages.

A SPECIMEN HOROSCOPE

Let us assume that a horoscope is being prepared for a person born at
10 a.m. on 9 February 1954. Most of the data needed will be found in the
Horse chart, that for February in the Tiger chart, and that for 10 a.m. in
the Snake chart. Combined, the data could take the following form:

10 a.m. 9 February 1954.

Year of the Horse (wood +)

Personality:
popular, carefree, optimistic, imaginative, practical,
lucky, courageous, handsome, charming, wise.

Career:
business, agriculture, art, stage, politics.

Romance:
amorous, faithful, sensitive.

Compatibility:
Dog, Tiger, Rooster.

**The personality traits are strong, for 1954 was a yang
year and the element wood indicates self-confidence.**

RAT

Order: 1st
Direction: N
Hours: 11 p.m. – 1 a.m.
Yin/Yang: +
Season: winter
Month: December

Personality: artistic, talented, charming, opportunist, lively, pleasure-seeking, sometimes unscrupulous, usually successful

Career: accountancy, law, business

Romance: sentimental, fickle

Compatibility: Dragon, Monkey

Examples: William Shakespeare (1564), Charlotte Brontë (1816)

Zodiac: Saggitarius
Ruler: Jupiter
Flower: carnation
Gem: turquoise
Colour: pale blue
Day: Thursday
Number: 3

OX

Order: 2nd
Direction: NNE
Hours: 1 – 3 a.m.
Yin/Yang: –
Season: winter
Month: January

Personality: very intelligent, calm but stubborn, industrious, deep and original in thought, reliable, a good leader

Career: finance, politics, law

Romance: faithful, sincere

Compatibility: Rooster, Snake

Examples: Adolf Hitler (1889), Charles Chaplin (1889)

Zodiac: Capricorn
Ruler: Saturn
Flower: cornflower
Gem: moonstone
Colour: green
Day: Saturday
Number: 4

TIGER

Order: 3rd
Direction: ENE
Hours: 3 – 5 a.m.
Yin/Yang: +
Season: winter
Month: February

3 TIGER

Hu 虎

Personality: lucky, powerful, proud, aggressive, courageous, a good leader, vivacious, impulsive, dignified, handsome

Career: stage, catering, army

Romance: sensitive, passionate

Compatibility: Horse, Dog

Examples: Sir Alec Guinness (1914), Dwight D. Eisenhower (1890)

Zodiac: Aquarius
Ruler: Uranus
Flower: daffodil
Gem: amethyst
Colour: blue
Day: Saturday
Number: 7

♅ Uranus

RABBIT

Order: 4th
Direction: E
Hours: 5 – 7 a.m.
Yin/Yang: –
Season: spring
Month: March

4 RABBIT

Tu 兔

Personality: shrewd, patient, cautious, diplomatic, sophisticated, cultured, old-fashioned, sympathetic, moody, affectionate, often artistic

Career: art, music, social work

Romance: affectionate, self-assured

Compatibility: Goat, Boar

Examples: Prince Edward (1964), Henry Wadsworth Longfellow (1807)

Zodiac: Pisces
Ruler: Neptune
Flower: lily
Gem: aquamarine
Colour: pale green
Day: Thursday
Number: 9

♆ Neptune

DRAGON

Order: 5th
Direction: ESE
Hours: 7-9 a.m.
Yin/Yang: +
Season: spring
Month: April

5   DRAGON

Long   龍

Personality: witty, quixotic, artistic, inventive and original in thought, enigmatic, perfectionist, humorous, generous, egotistical, aristocratic

Career: athletics, politics, medicine

Romance: affectionate, magical

Compatibility: Rat, Monkey

Examples: Harold Wilson (1916), Haile Selassie (1890)

Zodiac: Aries
Ruler: Mars
Flower: tulip
Gem: diamond
Colour: red
Day: Tuesday
Number: 8

♂ Mars

SNAKE

Order: 6th
Direction: SSE
Hours: 9-11 a.m.
Yin/Yang: −
Season: spring
Month: May

SNAKE

She   虫它

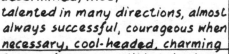

Personality: proud, determined, wise, talented in many directions, almost always successful, courageous when necessary, cool-headed, charming

Career: finance, politics, theology

Romance: possessive, jealous

Compatibility: Rooster, Ox

Examples: Abraham Lincoln (1809), Neil Kinnock (1942)

Zodiac: Taurus
Ruler: Venus
Flower: daisy
Gem: emerald
Colour: pink
Day: Friday
Number: 6

♀ Venus

HORSE

Order: 7th
Direction: S
Hours: 11 a.m. – 1 p.m.
Yin/Yang: +
Season: summer
Month: June

Ma

Personality: popular, friendly, carefree, optimistic, pleasure-seeking, imaginative, inquisitive, capable, practical, energetic, impulsive

Career: business, agriculture, art

Romance: amorous, faithful

Compatibility: Dog, Tiger

Examples: Franklin D. Roosevelt (1882), Earl of Snowdon (1930)

Zodiac: Gemini
Ruler: Mercury
Flower: marigold
Gem: agate
Colour: yellow
Day: Wednesday
Number: 5

Mercury

GOAT

Order: 8th
Direction: SSW
Hours: 1 – 3 p.m.
Yin/Yang: –
Season: summer
month: July

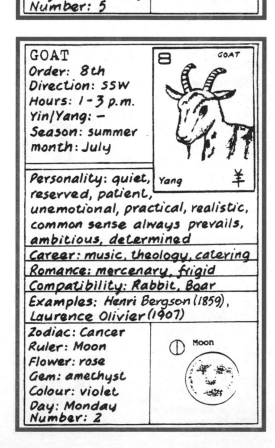

Yang

Personality: quiet, reserved, patient, unemotional, practical, realistic, common sense always prevails, ambitious, determined

Career: music, theology, catering

Romance: mercenary, frigid

Compatibility: Rabbit, Boar

Examples: Henri Bergson (1859), Laurence Olivier (1907)

Zodiac: Cancer
Ruler: Moon
Flower: rose
Gem: amethyst
Colour: violet
Day: Monday
Number: 2

Moon

MONKEY

9 MONKEY

Hou

Order: 9th
Direction: WSW
Hours: 3 – 5 p.m.
Yin/Yang: +
Season: summer
Month: August

Personality: lively, mercenary, oppor-tunist, self-centred, devious, amusing, companionable, extremely ambitious, always successful
Career: finance, politics, stage
Romance: fickle, insincere
Compatibility: Dragon, Rat
Examples: Charles Dickens (1812), Leonardo da Vinci (1452)
Zodiac: Leo
Ruler: Saturn
Flower: anemone
Gem: ruby
Colour: orange
Day: Sunday
Number: 1

♄ Saturn

ROOSTER

10 ROOSTER

Ji

Order: 10th
Direction: W
Hours: 5 – 7 p.m.
Yin/Yang: –
Season: autumn
Month: September

Personality: moody, dreamy, talkative, vain, outgoing, extravagant, over-confident, rarely successful unaided, dignified, handsome
Career: stage, music, advertising
Romance: optimistic, inconsiderate
Compatibility: Snake, Ox
Examples: Joyce Grenfell (1910), Katharine Hepburn (1909)
Zodiac: Virgo
Ruler: Mercury
Flower: azalea
Gem: sapphire
Colour: pale blue
Day: Wednesday
Number: 6

☿ Mercury

DOG

Order: 11th
Direction: WNW
Hours: 7–9 p.m.
Yin/Yang: +
Season: autumn
Month: October

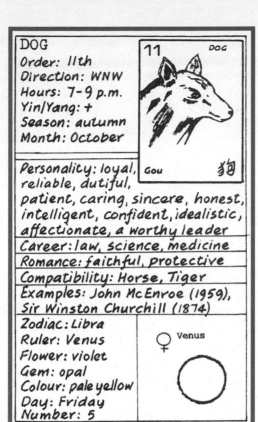

11 · DOG
Gou
狗

Personality: loyal, reliable, dutiful, patient, caring, sincere, honest, intelligent, confident, idealistic, affectionate, a worthy leader

Career: law, science, medicine

Romance: faithful, protective

Compatibility: Horse, Tiger

Examples: John McEnroe (1959), Sir Winston Churchill (1874)

Zodiac: Libra
Ruler: Venus
Flower: violet
Gem: opal
Colour: pale yellow
Day: Friday
Number: 5

♀ Venus

PIG

Order: 12th
Direction: NNW
Hours: 9–11 p.m.
Yin/Yang: −
Season: autumn
Month: November

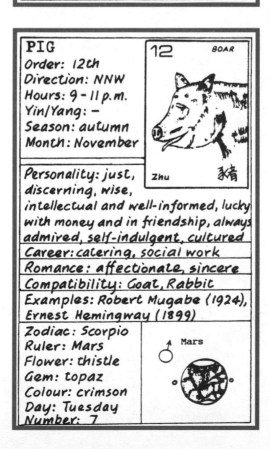

12 · BOAR
Zhu
豬

Personality: just, discerning, wise, intellectual and well-informed, lucky with money and in friendship, always admired, self-indulgent, cultured

Career: catering, social work

Romance: affectionate, sincere

Compatibility: Goat, Rabbit

Examples: Robert Mugabe (1924), Ernest Hemingway (1899)

Zodiac: Scorpio
Ruler: Mars
Flower: thistle
Gem: topaz
Colour: crimson
Day: Tuesday
Number: 7

♂ Mars

SECRETS OF FATE

Many people consult professional astrologers in the hope of discovering the secrets of their fate – those aspects of the future which seem to be completely hidden and quite unknowable.

Professional astrologers, as distinct from itinerant fortune-tellers, behave with honesty and skill, and in the manner of a detective conducting an investigation, though predictions are often based more on an interpretation of the subject's character and past history than on astrological devices. They take an objective view of those personal details about which the subject would be inclined to be subjective and thus unrealistic. The accuracy of these professionally made horoscopes sometimes comes as a great shock, pleasant or otherwise, to their recipients.

However, an unfavorable horoscope need not be too alarming, for horoscopes deal with tendencies rather than unchangeable facts, and people may alter their personality and predicted fate by a supreme effort of will. It is important here to distinguish between a person's fate, which is what will happen and has been preordained, and his or her predicted fate, which is what is likely to happen but may not. The outcome will not be known until a given event has occurred or not occurred. A person's decision to alter his or her predicted fate has also been preordained.

Horoscopes intended as entertainment need not be strictly accurate, but they should be made as palatable as possible. This can be effected by using skill and imagination in embroidering the bare astrological facts, making a sensible compromise between seemingly contradictory facts, telling the subjects those pleasant things about themselves that they want to hear and incorporating known facts about their habits and past history, which horoscopists can obtain easily enough if they keep their eyes and ears open.

Chinese astrologers are generally concerned only with predictions to do with health and safety, on the principle that to be forewarned is to be

A superior person can cope with an impasse. It is the inferior person who loses control at an impasse.

Lunyu

Good fortune is lighter than a feather,
yet no one knows how to carry it.
Misfortune is heavier than the earth,
yet no one knows how to avoid it.

Tao Te Ching

forearmed. Divination is an established medical technique and a component of a physician's consultation with a patient.

But those who prepare "What the Stars Foretell" predictions for the media often take refuge in vague and effectively meaningless generalizations: "Friday brings a sigh of relief," "Be positive in an affair of the heart," and "Your financial condition will improve." Such predictions are so unspecific that they could be interpreted to apply to almost anyone.

Certainly, we would like to have some predictions about world affairs for the next few years. If from a reliable source, these predictions could be accurate, but it would be interesting to see just how accurate they would prove to be. Perhaps they would answer pertinent questions.

Will there be dissension among the European states during the coming years? Will the uneasy peace in Northern Ireland come to an end? Will the peoples of Europe become more and more dissatisfied with the EU? What progress will be made in science and technology? And what of China and its rapidly advancing economic development?

In any of our predictions, which are our attempts to plot the course of fate, there are doubts. To some extent, fate will always be a closed book – a big secret. But there is no doubt about our ultimate fate. There is nothing so certain as death, although many people console themselves with the hope of an afterlife, and in past ages there have been those who have tried to achieve immortality by various means.

Some of the emperors of ancient China were regarded as demigods, and they expected their physicians and other learned men to search for herbs and other devices by which immortality could be achieved. But this search was abandoned when it became evident that this objective could not be realized. However, it had not been entirely unfruitful because, as by-products, its researches yielded a wide range of medicines and health foods that improved general health, inhibited the ageing process and so extended the life-span – which is surely the next best thing to everlasting life!

Some of these emperors relied on alchemists, who tried to create an elixir which would confer immortality on those who consumed it. Of course, they were not successful in this respect either, but they were successful in others, for they devised ageing-inhibitors and pills and potions to relieve pain and misery, so transmuting the leaden metal of human existence into the gold of a healthy, long and serene life.

These early emperors also employed diviners, for they had a great desire to know what the future held for them – no doubt on the wise principle that to be forewarned is to be forearmed. Some of these soothsayers were much favored and had influential positions in the imperial court, but not for long if their predictions came to nothing. Execution was the usual fate of those who failed the emperor in this regard, and many of them, in an attempt to please their master, tempted fate by making predictions and promises which could not always be fulfilled.

The most famous of these soothsayers was Liu Po Wen, also called Liu Chi, who was consultant adviser to Zhu Zhanzhang, the first emperor of the Ming dynasty (1368–1644). He has been described as the Chinese Nostradamus, for he made predictions that have since proved remarkably accurate. It is said that he was executed, despite the emperor's offer of protection and high rewards, not because he failed in his duties but because the emperor was envious – and perhaps even fearful – of his knowledge and influence.

Liu Po Wen's most prophetic and famous pronouncement to the emperor was written down in lyrical form and has the odd title "The Biscuit Poem of Liu Po Wen." Just how it came to be written and why it has this title is best explained by quoting a small part of a dialogue between the emperor and his adviser:

> *The emperor covered the bowl in which he had just placed a half-eaten biscuit, and then sent for Liu Chi (as he would have been called at court).*
>
> **Emperor** Tell me, sir, if you are good at making predictions and solving puzzles and so on, do you know what is contained in this bowl?
>
> **Liu Chi** (*counting his fingers*) It could be the sun, or it could be the moon, but I fancy that it is something that has been half-eaten by you.
>
> *The emperor removes the cover from the bowl and so reveals the biscuit.*

This poem is written in cryptic form and is difficult to understand, but it is generally assumed that it predicted the invasion of China by the Mongols (1449), the rise to power of the eunuch Zheng He (1568–1627), the foundation of the Manchu (Qing) dynasty (1644), the Opium War (1858), the war with Japan (1894–5), the reign of Pu Yi (1908–12), the beginning of the republic (1911) and many other events.

The poem was probably written about 1735 and all the prophecies in relation to the Ming and Qing dynasties are quite accurate, but since 1911 they have become vague and inaccurate. This had led some experts to believe that the work is a fraud of recent production, designed to reassure people that all would be well at a time when there was much unrest as a consequence of the Japanese invasion and the rise of Communism.

Emperor Zhu Zhanzhang

Hall of Supreme Harmony, Forbidden City, Beijing

YOUR FUTURE

Your future prospects for career and romance/marriage over the next ten years, based upon various Chinese methods of divination, are indicated by the stars in the table below: * poor, ** moderate, *** good, **** excellent. Thus, the career prospects in 2003 for a person born in a Rat-year are excellent. The accuracy – or inaccuracy! – of these predictions will become clear as the years go by.

CAREER

	RAT	OX	TIGER	RABBIT	DRAGON	SNAKE
2000	***	**	***	**	***	**
2001	**	***	***	*	***	**
2002	***	***	****	*	***	*
2003	****	***	****	**	**	***
2004	****	***	***	**	****	***
2005	*	****	***	***	****	***
2006	****	*	***	****	****	**
2007	****	**	***	***	***	***
2008	***	***	**	**	****	****
2009	***	***	***	*	****	***

	HORSE	GOAT	MONKEY	ROOSTER	DOG	PIG
2000	**	**	***	**	***	***
2001	*	**	***	**	**	****
2002	**	**	****	**	****	****
2003	***	***	**	*	***	***
2004	**	***	***	***	***	****
2005	**	**	**	*	***	****
2006	*	*	*	*	****	***
2007	***	*	***	**	****	***
2008	****	**	****	**	***	***
2009	**	***	**	***	****	****

*Sincerity reaches and affects
even pigs and fishes.*

I Ching

ROMANCE/MARRIAGE

	RAT	OX	TIGER	RABBIT	DRAGON	SNAKE
2000	***	***	**	***	***	**
2001	***	**	****	***	***	**
2002	***	**	***	**	****	**
2003	****	**	***	***	****	*
2004	***	****	**	***	****	*
2005	**	***	***	***	****	*
2006	**	***	****	****	****	**
2007	***	**	****	****	***	***
2008	*	*	***	***	***	**
2009	****	**	***	***	****	****

	HORSE	GOAT	MONKEY	ROOSTER	DOG	PIG
2000	***	**	***	**	***	***
2001	**	***	**	**	***	***
2002	***	**	**	**	****	****
2003	****	**	*	***	***	****
2004	****	**	***	***	***	****
2005	***	*	***	****	***	***
2006	**	**	****	***	***	***
2007	***	**	***	**	**	****
2008	***	**	****	***	**	**
2009	***	***	*	***	****	****

ELEMENTAL WOMEN

Many Chinese believe that a person's character and career are strongly influenced, on the *fung shui* principle, by the *qi*, or "energy," in the environment, of which there are five types: fire, earth, wood, water and metal. A woman can utilize this energy to create harmony in the environment, and enrich her life by using the inner energy of her body to produce outward beauty and charm.

Here are the character traits associated with the elements.

Fire: active, exuberant, impulsive, passionate, sensual, audacious, optimistic.

Earth: sensual, seductive, glamorous, artistic, self-aware, much admired.

Wood: sophisticated, elegant, popular, extrovert, alluring, aesthetic tastes, altruistic, independent.

Water: sensitive, gregarious, beguiling, popular, ethereal, romantic, imaginative, communicative.

Metal: fond of party-going, deeply erotic, intuitive, dramatic, astute, charismatic, volatile, extremist, single-minded, ambitious.

The wise woman will wear dresses, jewelry and make-up which will lend some enhancement to the good qualities in her temperament

I CHING
THE BOOK OF CHANGES

The best of the Chinese instruments for divination, and somewhat superior to astrology, is the *I Ching*, or "Book of Changes." This is a classical work of great antiquity, much older than the *Tong Sing*, and, in its origins, the oldest book in the world.

A BOOK OF PROFOUND WISDOM

But the *I Ching* is more than a book of fate and a divinatory oracle; it is a fount of profound wisdom, and provides much information about Chinese folklore and philosophy. Together with Taoism and Confucianism, it has strongly influenced the way of life of the Chinese for thousands of years, and has been instrumental in maintaining the essential fabric of their society. It is hardly surprising that it is the most influential and widely-read book in China, and the Chinese have as much respect, even reverence, for it as the people of the West have for the Bible, and some would regard it as being semi-sacred.

The *I Ching* is a source of wisdom for the talented and ambitious, consolation for the afflicted and desperate, and encouragement for all who value health, longevity and peace of mind, which is a clear indication that the sages of ancient China possessed immense practicality and perception. Their concern with the well-being and destiny of mankind outweighed all other considerations. For them, the art of living is to be contented and healthy and to live long. People who are successful in these aims are extremely wealthy in real terms, and other human aims are generally no more than vain illusions.

In using the *I Ching*, one may feel that one is making a close and personal contact with pre-eminently wise people – old friends, one might say – who lived many centuries ago. In this way, the sages of ancient China take command in a modern situation. But perhaps the passage of time has little effect on human nature.

Many people in the Far East, even the poorest, own a copy of the *I Ching*; they say it brings them good luck. This is not mere superstition, for those who have ready access to profound wisdom can count themselves fortunate.

The Path to Peace

THE ART OF LIVING

A study of the *I Ching* reveals the remarkable capacity of the Chinese for survival, and their fervent desire for harmony at all levels in all situations, which permeates and influences all aspects of their way of life. It is this desire for harmony, more than anything else, that has given the Chinese mastery of the art of living.

Most of the predictions and advice contained in the *I Ching* are to do with the establishment of harmony on the yin-yang principle. Good social and business relationships are largely a matter of compromise and a balanced view. This, one might think, has much to do with common sense and little to do with magic or superstition.

Repay kindness with kindness, and injury with justice.

***Analects* Confucius**

THE OLDEST BOOK IN THE WORLD

The *I Ching* is generally regarded as a product of Taoism, but it could be that, in its origins, it preceded Taoism by about 3,000 years. At a much later date, it was studied by Confucius, and a few of his followers, but not the eminent philosopher himself, contributed ten appendices.

The complete text, essentially as it is today, appeared at the time of the Han dynasty (206 B.C.–A.D. 220), probably in the reign of the emperor Jing Di. It was based on a much earlier work, produced by King Wen, one of the rulers of the Shang dynasty (c. 1600–1200 B.C.), though it is reasonable to assume that there were contributions from other sources.

The legendary sage Fuxi, who is supposed to have lived about 7,000 years ago, is said to have devised eight trigrams, called the Pa Kua, which are the mystic symbols that users of the *I Ching* employ in making divinations. In recent times, ox bones and tortoiseshells have been discovered bearing crude inscriptions of these symbols. These "oracle bones," as they are called, indicate that the *I Ching* is older than recorded history, and that, in its inspiration, it is undeniably the oldest book in the world.

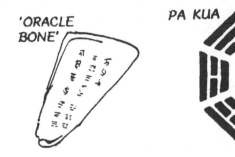

'ORACLE BONE'

PA KUA

The predictions produced by the *I Ching* are often uncannily accurate, which says much for the perspicacity of its compilers and makes one wonder if the sages of ancient China had knowledge not possessed by even the most learned men in the West.

WHAT ARE THE CHANGES?

The changes to which the *I Ching* refers are causes and effects, particularly those in the human condition, or what may be loosely described as human fate. The Chinese explain this in terms of the yin-yang principle that things tend to remain the same; although everything is in a constant state of flux, the changes are often more apparent than real, and what appears to be a change may be no more than a temporary displacement.

The faith that is born of knowledge finds its object in
an eternal order, bringing forth endless change,
through endless time, in endless space.

T. H. Huxley

Our senses often deceive us. Ice and steam, for example, are of a different appearance, but they are the same substance; a bald-headed man may look different when he is wearing a wig, but he is still the same person, or essentially so.

It is these ideas, together with an awareness of the sameness of human nature and human institutions, that enabled those sagacious compilers of the *I Ching* to make predictions which are as relevant to the needs of the people of today as they were to the needs of those living in ancient China.

THE VALIDITY OF THE I CHING

There could be no better testimony to the validity of the *I Ching* as a divinatory oracle than a list of some of the worthy persons who have used it in their work or extolled its virtues. Such a list would include some of the leading businessmen throughout the world, Chinese government officials and court judges. Japanese military and naval commanders in the Second World War (1939–45), Mao Zedong (1893–1975), General Chiang Kaishek (1887–1976), the German mathematician and philosopher Baron von Leibnitz (1646–1716), the Swiss psychologist and psychiatrist C. G. Jung (1875–1961) and the Swedish physicist Niels Bohr (1885–1962).

Among his many achievements, Leibnitz invented a mechanically operated calculator and a form of differential calculus, a branch of mathematics that is vital to the needs of modern engineering. In these particular endeavors, he was inspired by the *I Ching*. Jung regularly consulted the *I Ching* when treating patients, and Bohr perceived a concurrence between the yin-yang principle and the theories of atomic science.

An enthusiastic interest in the *I Ching* has in recent years been sweeping the United States, and a small computer which performs the selective functions of the *I Ching* is now available and is extensively used in stock-market transactions. Within the next few years, the *I Ching* may also become established in Britain as a superior alternative to astrology for making predictions.

THE I CHING ORACLE

There seems to be some mystery about the oracular powers of the *I Ching*, and the collective opinions of the experts who have studied the *I Ching* may be summarized as follows: "The exact nature of its functioning is beyond human comprehension, but it is a manifestation of an ultimate, yet unknown, reality, and it seems that its compilers were divinely inspired. However, it does give practical results, and it appears that, by clever suggestion, it prompts users to reveal some of the information, often containing great truths, which is deeply buried in their subconscious." But does the psychiatrist's couch not have a similar function? This may account for Jung's high regard for the *I Ching*.

However, the *I Ching* is certainly not "a book of magic spells," as it was once described by one of its translators, a clergyman. It is more of a retrieval system than an oracle or fortune-telling device based on guesswork. It obligingly returns the information put into it thousands of years ago, and does so with mathematical precision. One writer has made the comment: "To read and study the *I Ching* is to be in communication with the great intelligences of a long bygone age."

But the *I Ching* cannot be beyond human comprehension, at least not that of educated humans, for its makers were mere mortals, however inspired they may have been.

HOW THE I CHING FUNCTIONS

The *I Ching* selects predictions by means of combinations of complete and broken lines in 64 six-line figures, called hexagrams, of which no two are identical. A complete line is yang (positive), and represents 1 in the binary system of numbers; a broken line is yin (negative), and represents 0. In the decimal, or denary, system, the base number is 10, its multiples being 100, 1,000, 10,000, etc., and its submultiples $1/10$, $1/100$, $1/1000$, etc. In the binary system, the base number is 2, its multiples being 4, 8, 16, 32, 64, etc. and its submultiples $1/2$, $1/4$, $1/8$, etc. Thus, 3, 10, 16, 65 and $3/4$ on the binary system would be 11, 1010, 10000, 1000001 and 0.11.

The binary system is the basis of the modern electronic computer, in which a flow of current to the computer represents 1, and a non-flow or a weak flow represents 0. The *I Ching* is sometimes likened to a computer, but it is its user who should be likened to a computer. It is not the user who initiates responses in the *I Ching*, but the *I Ching* which initiates responses in the user.

THE HEXAGRAMS

The *I Ching* contains some appendices and other commentaries, mainly of a philosophical nature, but its main body consists of 64 hexagrams, which were formed by pairing the eight trigrams of the Pa Kua.

TRIGRAMS

yang

yin

The trigram containing three complete lines is regarded as yang, and those containing two complete lines are regarded as predominantly yang. The trigram containing three broken lines is regarded as yin, and those containing two broken lines are regarded as predominantly yin.

If each trigram is paired, in turn, with each of the remaining trigrams, 64 different hexagrams are formed, and these are also regarded as being yang or yin according to the number of complete (yang) and broken (yin) lines they contain. Each hexagram has a name, and is also numbered for ease of reference. Those which have odd numbers are yang, and those with even numbers are yin.

HEXAGRAMS

1 Qian
(Father)
yang

35 Jin
(Wealth)
yang

4 Meng
(Youth)
yin

48 Jing
(Hope)
yin

THE PREDICTIONS

Each of the hexagrams is attached to a prediction, which is in two parts – the judgment and the image.

The judgment is not so much a prediction as a piece of good advice of a general nature expressed as a proverb, a question or a statement of opinion.

The image, which is so called because it is often the converse of the judgment by being an answer to a question or an elucidation, generally indicates how the judgment may be achieved.

These predictions are usually very wordy, for the compilers of the *I Ching* allowed for all contingencies. Here is a brief example of a prediction:

12 PI (disharmony), yin. Judgement: Despite perseverance, the great departs and the small arrives. There is little benefit. Image: Disharmony reigns. The superior man hides his good qualities to avoid victimization.

SELECTING HEXAGRAMS

Traditionally, the Chinese use a bundle of yarrow sticks, which are stems of the yarrow (milfoil) plant, *Achillea millefolium*, to select hexagrams, and thereby cast predictions. This technique is mathematically accurate, but its processes are long-winded and complicated. They sometimes use a set of three Chinese coins.

However, a detailed study of these selection methods is beyond the scope of this book, and the reader who wishes to delve further into the intricacies of the *I Ching* is advised to obtain a reliable translation. Undoubtedly, the best of these is the German translation by Richard Wilhelm. It contains a commentary by C. G. Jung.

	1	34	5	26	11	9	14	43
	25	51	3	27	24	42	21	17
	6	40	29	4	7	59	64	47
	33	62	39	52	15	53	56	31
	12	16	8	23	2	20	35	45
	44	32	48	18	46	57	50	28
	13	55	63	22	36	37	30	49
	10	54	60	41	19	61	38	58

I CHING ENTERTAINMENT

The *I Ching* can be used for the fortune-telling type of entertainment, though some people would regard this as sacrilege, and a single coin can be used to select the hexagrams.

This is the procedure: assume that the head is yang, and the tail is yin. Toss the coin six times, and, starting at the top, draw the appropriate line for each throw – a complete line for a head (yang), and a broken line for a tail (yin). If, for example, the six throws yield *tail, tail, head, tail, head* and *tail*, the hexagram will be as shown below.

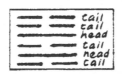

Now find the upper trigram among those shown at the top of the table above, and the lower trigram in the left-hand column. The number, which is 40, at the point of intersection of two imaginary lines from these trigrams, is the number of the prediction cast, and can be located in the list below. But it is important to understand that these predictions are purely for entertainment, and must not be taken seriously.

1.	Be bold to achieve success.
2.	Be persistent but cautious.
3.	Make friends. They may help you.
4.	Abide by the accepted conventions.
5.	Bold action will only provoke opposition.
6.	This is not a time for rash decisions.
7.	Be flexible in your thinking.
8.	Avoid scheming and unworthy motives.
9.	Know your limitations to avoid frustration.
10.	Be useful, industrious and tactful.
11.	Health, wealth and romance are yours.
12.	Abide by your moral principles.
13.	Do not favor unworthy people.
14.	Do not be niggardly with your wealth.
15.	Neither expect nor demand too much of life.
16.	Enjoy your good fortune humbly.
17.	Be true to yourself; be true to others.
18.	Make your own decisions.
19.	You are destined to succeed.
20.	Think carefully before taking action.
21.	Peace of mind will surely come.
22.	Right thoughts and right actions prevail.
23.	Avoid arrogance and insincerity.
24.	Your ambitions will be fulfilled.
25.	Listen to the promptings of your heart.
26.	Eschew shallow and unprofitable pursuits.
27.	Do not envy others.
28.	Preserve your income and status.
29.	Remember that imagination breeds fear.
30.	Be a realist, not an idealist.
31.	Your sound judgment will benefit many.
32.	Be in harmony with nature and society.

33.	Retreat gracefully to safer ground.
34.	Honor your obligations to friends.
35.	Gain respect by sincerity.
36.	Do not arouse jealousy by boasting.
37.	Be loyal to your family and friends.
38.	Be kind to the less fortunate.
39.	Look before you leap.
40.	Forget past mistakes and follies.
41.	Charity should start at home.
42.	Fate is on your side.
43.	Avoid motivation by petty desires.
44.	Now is the time for care and reason.
45.	Seek harmonious relationships.
46.	Fear nothing. Advance your interests.
47.	Correct your errors as you progress.
48.	Have the courage of your convictions.
49.	Be guided by tradition.
50.	This unsafe period will soon pass.
51.	Great changes are needed.
52.	Fortune favors the wise.
53.	Concentrate on the solid facts.
54.	You have talents. Make the most of them.
55.	A problem shared is a problem halved.
56.	A still tongue makes a wise head.
57.	Do first things first.
58.	You will soon be a happy achiever.
59.	Now is the time to analyse yourself.
60.	No one can do all things well.
61.	Be suspicious of those in authority.
62.	Content yourself with small aims.
63.	Do nothing previously untried.
64.	All will go well for you.

THEORIES ABOUT THE I CHING

A number of theories have been put forward to account for the manner in which the *I Ching* makes predictions which have an accurate and astonishing relevance to our affairs.

C. G. Jung explained the functioning of the *I Ching* by what he called "the law of sychronicity," which suggests that similar events are occurring at one and the same time throughout the universe, and influence each other to some degree, though generally only very remotely. This is a kind of "lateral cause and effect," where influences are mutual and instantaneous, and not components in a series proceeding from the past into the future. But this is a speculative matter. Nevertheless, one should bear in mind that Jung was at the top of his profession, so his theory may not be entirely without substance.

Perhaps Jung's theory could explain coincidences as being events occurring in unison because they are mutually linked, but in a way of which we have no cognizance. Many people seem to have had that odd feeling – a kind of sixth-sense reaction – that something is amiss, but have not been able to detect anything in a purely physical sense.

It does seem that the compilers of the *I Ching* have made an effective use of auto-suggestion, which is a mental process by which people withdraw some of the information contained in their own subconscious, providing answers to their own questions. Prompted by a single word, a whole train of thoughts, often very revealing, may be set in motion.

Oh God! that one might read the book of fate

Henry IV
William Shakespeare

LOTTERY NUMBERS

In using the *I Ching* to make predictions, the Chinese use the stems of the yarrow (milfoil) plant. But this is only traditional, and it is an over-complicated procedure. Equally effective results can be obtained with six coins. Proceed as follows:

1. Take six coins of any denomination, shake in the hand or in a cup, and then arrange in a row as in the diagram below.

H T H T H H   38

2. Build a hexagram by regarding a head (H) as yang (positive), or a complete line, and a tail (T) as yin (negative), or a broken line. The first coin gives the line at the top of the hexagram, the second coin gives the second line down, and so on.

3. Locate the three top lines of the hexagram in the horizontal row at the head of the table on page 135. Then locate the three bottom lines of the hexagram in the vertical column on the left of the table. Two imaginary lines will intersect in the square containing the hexagram number. This is your first lottery number. In the example shown here, it is 38. If this happens to be more than the highest number in the lottery (in the British National Lottery, for example, numbers over 49 would be of no use), ignore it and repeat the processes 1, 2 and 3.

4. Repeat processes 1, 2 and 3 to select five more numbers. If the same number occurs more than once, use the first number, and make another selection to replace the second number. Thus, if the numbers selected were 6, 12, 52, 6, 30 and 41, you would ignore 52 and the second 6, and then replace them with two more selections.

The diagram below shows another example.

T T H H H H   34

Coin predictions, requiring one throw of five coins, can be used to answer questions about examination results, prospects in romance or marriage, legal cases, trading prospects, job applications, health, lotteries, etc. The results, again using the head as yang and the tail as yin, are interpreted on a six-point scale, as follows:

5 yang	excellent, wonderful, joyous
4 yang, 1 yin	good, promising, quite happy
3 yang, 2 yin	fair, satisfactory, not bad
2 yang, 3 yin	moderate, poor, unsmiling
1 yang, 4 yin	very poor, bad, sad
5 yin	hopeless, disastrous, groans

Of course, there are other methods for selecting lottery numbers. One could use the fortune sticks, as described opposite, to determine the *I Ching* hexagrams.

One could also employ the same technique that is used in raffles. Each of the numbers 1 to 49 is written on a small slip of paper. The slips are folded, placed in a hat and then thoroughly shaken. Six of the folded slips are drawn from the hat. The numbers on these are the selection for the lottery.

There are those who think that their good fortune in a lottery is influenced by the animal governing the year in which they were born. But this would really be expecting too much of fate.

FORTUNE STICKS

Then to the rolling Heav'n itself I cried,
Asking "What Lamp had Destiny to guide
Her little Children stumbling in the Dark?"
And—"A blind Understanding!" Heav'n replied.

Rubáiyát of Omar Khayyám
Edward Fitzgerald

In China, fortune sticks are a popular device for making predictions.

A set of fortune sticks as used in Buddhist temples is 40, 75 or 100 in number, held in a round container. The sticks are made of bamboo, and each is numbered. The prediction-seeker shakes the container, pointing it toward the altar, until a single stick separates from the others and falls to the floor. The medium then finds the numbered prediction – among those in a list of numbered predictions – which corresponds with the number on the stick.

Most people would argue that it is quite impossible to make an accurate prediction by the random selection of a stick. But no selection is ever random, though it is true that, in this case, neither the medium nor the fortune-seeker is aware of the exact nature of all the causes of the effect which is the fall of a particular stick – the size, weight, number and positions of the sticks, the fortune-seeker's decision to consult a medium, and so on.

The medium employs this technique for three main reasons. It creates an aura of mystery, which impresses the client. After all, this is business: it is a lottery-type selection, which attracts many customers, for the Chinese are inveterate gamblers. The selected prediction

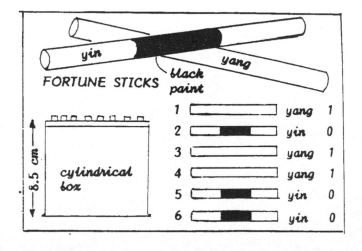

provides a convenient talking-point. The medium will astutely modify a prediction to suit the needs of clients, who will probably be told what they want to hear.

It is easy enough to make a set of fortune sticks which can be used to select the hexagrams of the *I Ching*. All you need are 13 feet of thin dowel rod (which can be obtained from a DIY shop) and some black paint. Saw the rod to make 4-inch sticks. Paint the central 1¹⁄₂ in of each of 25 sticks black. Leave the remaining 24 sticks unpainted.

An unpainted stick represents a complete line of a hexagram, which is yang, or positive, symbolized by the element five, and is 1 in the binary system of numbers. A painted stick, which has a painted "space," represents a broken line of a hexagram. It is yin, or negative, symbolized by the element water, and is 0 in the binary system.

There are 25 yin sticks but only 24 yang sticks. This means that a yin stick has a slightly better chance than a yang stick of being selected. This arrangement is due to the Chinese belief that yin, though passive, is slightly superior to yang, which is active. Water extinguishes fire!

Find a suitable cylindrical container for the sticks. It must be made of an opaque material and be about 3.3 inches high. Obviously, in making selections, it must not be known beforehand which sticks are yin, and which are yang.

To select a hexagram, proceed as follows. Take a stick from the container, and use it as the first line, which is at the top, of the hexagram. Then take another stick from the container. This will be the second line – that is, second from the top – of the hexagram. Carry on in this way until six sticks have been taken from the container, and the hexagram is completed. An example is shown in the diagram above.

Return the six sticks to the container and you will be ready to select another hexagram.

Sages do not have a fixed mind. They share their minds with others. They improve what is good, and also improve what is not good.

Tao Te Ching

DREAMS

Fanatics have their dreams,
wherewith they weave a paradise for a sect.

"The Fall of Hyperion" John Keats

Dreams have always had much significance for those who dabble in the occult, but they can be only of a limited value for divinatory purposes, for dreams are generally soon forgotten.

It may be that day-dreams have more significance than those which occur during sleep, for they are the tool of those richly imaginative people who achieve great things in the aesthetic arts; though, in fairness, it must be said that dreams are also the refuge of those who wish to escape from the harsh realities of life. Dreams rooted in idealism or a love of power have led to religious sects and political groups which have done much damage to society, indicating that excessive imagination can be dangerous. But we all indulge in day-dreaming at some level, whatever our talents or emotional make-up, and it is then that we enter into a world of things that might be, and so plan for a better future.

The dreams which occur in sleep have less significance today than they did in ancient times, when people were much more superstitious. It was dreams which led to beliefs in a spirit world and an afterlife, for sleep was regarded as the brother of death. They were good or bad omens, and a nightmare was a terrifying experience for a superstitious person. The interpretation of dreams was a favorite device of the soothsayers. In the Bible, there are many references to dreams. It is astounding just how much was supposed to have been achieved by nocturnal visions.

In this respect, the people of ancient China were no different from any other ancient race. It was the commonly held belief of the Chinese peasantry that, during a dream, the soul escaped from the body, and was then able to travel to all parts of the world. But, if it did not return, the body lacked control and died, though the soul continued to live somewhere, as a wanderer. Allied with this belief is the one which requires a hole to be made in the skull of a deceased person to allow the soul to escape and be free from the constraints of a useless body. It was also believed that, if these wandering souls are not appeased by offerings of food and suchlike, they would do evil.

The fears and superstitions associated with dreams should be dispelled by a scientific explanation. One part of the brain operates in much the same way as the memory of a computer, recalling those thoughts and sensations associated with past events. During sleep, when the brain is not in full operation, this recall is rapid and mixed, and sometimes has the character of fantasy with a wide variety of sensations – unusual, pleasant, puzzling or frightening, as with a nightmare – and tends to be more visual than aural.

Dreams indicate past events, but past events are sometimes a guide to the future, for human conduct tends to be repetitious. The pictures below are examples of how, in ancient lore, the visual content of dreams was interpreted.

PALMISTRY

Palmistry, which is more properly called chiromancy, was first practiced in India and China about 3,000 years ago. It is still practiced in the rural areas of China, though it is generally not taken as seriously now as it was in former times. During the Middle Ages in the West, it was a popular device for making predictions, but it is now regarded with much scepticism.

SOUND FACTS

As is usually the case with prediction-making devices, palmistry contains elements of sound fact as well as those of superstition. For example, the Taoists in ancient China used fingerprints as a means of identifying people, and few would dispute the value of fingerprints.

What is more, even without the refinements of the palmist's techniques, a hand will provide some information about its owner. A rough and calloused hand is likely to be that of a person engaged in heavy manual labor, whereas a soft and delicate hand will suggest an opposite indication.

THE AIMS OF PALMISTRY

Palmistry has two main aims: to provide an accurate appraisal of a person's character; and to indicate his or her future in terms of romance, marriage, career prospects, and so forth.

To achieve these aims, the palmist takes account of the shape of a person's hand and the lines on its palm.

THE SHAPE OF THE HAND

An ancient system of palmistry classifies hands as four main types. These, and what they indicate, may be briefly stated as follows.

1.
Short, squarish, strong: practicality, masculinity, courage, domination.

2.
Square, strong, spatulate fingers: quick wit, intellect, deviousness, imagination.

3.
Short fingers, long palm: moodiness, impulsiveness, extroversion.

4.
Thin fingers and palm: femininity, dreaminess, introversion.

THE CELESTIAL HAND

The fingers of the hand and their fleshy pads, called mounds, are named after celestial bodies, as the diagram shows. Their indications are as follows:

MERCURY COMMUNICATION

Sun	emotional stability
Saturn	prudence
Jupiter	wealth
Venus	romance
Mars	aggression
Moon	emotion

The size of the fingers and the mounds – big or small – indicates the size – extensive or limited – of their characteristics.

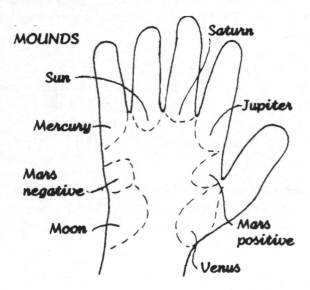

THE LINES ON THE HAND

The main lines on the palm of the hand and the characteristics they indicate are as follows:

Head	intelligence, emotions
Heart	sensuality, romance
Life	vitality
Fate	career
Health	resilience
Sun	recognition
Venus	lasciviousness

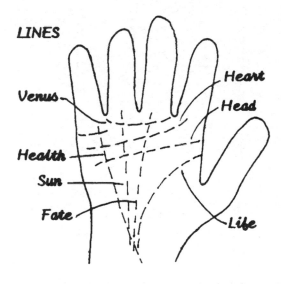

LINES

A gap in a line indicates a problem with its characteristic. The thickness of a line indicates the intensity of its characteristic. There are other lines, but of much less significance.

PHYSIOGNOMY

Physiognomy is the study of a person's facial appearance as a means of determining personality and mood. As a means of divination, it has been practiced in the countries of both East and West since ancient times.

The Taoists of ancient China regarded physiognomy as a useful device in the *tao* of supremacy. They believed that an instinctive anticipation of future events, particularly those in the near future, is reflected by some of the 108 positions on a person's face.

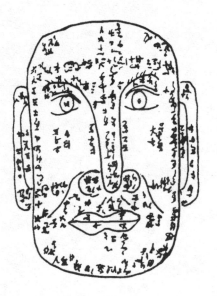

Taoist Face "Map'

The original was drawn about 2500 B.C.

MOOD

Physiognomy generally provides an accurate guide to a person's mood. We laugh or smile when happy or amused, scowl or glare when angry or startled, and when we look surprised, the chances are that we are surprised. What is more, it is usually quite obvious that people are trying to hide their mood when they are poker-faced. In fact, it is difficult for anyone to conceal their true feelings completely by adopting a certain kind of facial expression.

The movements of a person's eyes and lips are the best indicators of mood. Wide-open eyes indicate surprise, pursed lips displeasure, a broad grin amusement, and so on.

LIPS AND EYES

PERSONALITY

A fair face a foul heart
Proverb

Our basic features are inherited, but the influences of our environment and experiences will mold our features. For example, if we are subjected to constant worry, we may develop an anxious and hunted expression, perhaps with wrinkles, which may become almost permanent. If our life is always easy and happy, we may develop a benign expression.

However, looks are sometimes deceptive, and with some people looks, as well as speech, belie their true nature.

FACIAL FEATURES

It is the common wonder of all men,
how among so many million of faces,
there should be none alike.

Religio Medici Sir Thomas Browne

It does seem to be the case that no two persons, not even identical twins, are exactly alike in their features; and so, if a person's inherited features are an indication of character, as physiognomists claim, no two persons are exactly alike in their character.

A person's features and what they indicate may be briefly stated as:

Pronounced forehead	thoughtfulness
Short forehead	impulsiveness
Pronounced middle face	physical endurance and common sense
Square chin	obstinacy and wilfulness
Pointed chin	discontent
Oval chin	artistic tendency and love of pleasure
Dimpled chin	sensuality

DIVINATION

Physiognomy is of limited value as a divinatory technique, for it could hardly provide an exact indication of a person's fate. On the other hand, it can provide an exact indication of a person's character, which could be some indication of the nature of their future. It may be reasonable to suppose, for example, that a morose and unintelligent person is likely to be less successful than a good-tempered and intelligent person.

Assessing people

Students of physiognomy claim that a person's facial appearance is a reliable guide to his or her character. But there could be some doubts here. It is true that a person's face may have a recognizably angry, sad, happy, scornful or querulous expression, and that if this expression is habitual it may give insights into the person's character. However, it is doubtful whether true personality can be judged from the shape of the chin or the size of the nose. Therefore it may be tempting to believe that a person's behavior is the best guide to his or her personality.

Certainly, a wise man does not always judge by appearances, for we all know that appearances are sometimes deceptive. Nor does he believe everything he hears, for some people have a great talent for dissembly, misrepresentation, deviousness or downright fabrication. Therefore it must often be the case that "actions speak louder than words," and not always true that "seeing is believing."

In this connection, a valuable lesson is contained in a story about an anxious father attempting to give advice to his somewhat thoughtless son. This is the dialogue:

Father	I don't much care for your mate Wilfred. Why do you associate with him.
Son	Because he's my best friend.
Father	Ask him to lend you ten pounds and you'll find out that he's not.
Son	Oh, he's all right. He's a smart lad. Everybody likes him.
Father	Fine feathers do not make fine birds.

Clearly the father is worldly-wise and aware that fine words are not always matched by fine deeds. The compilers of the *Tong Sing* were also aware of the weaknesses of human nature and have provided some examples of those actions which may enable us to judge people. Thus, a person who has frequent fits of ill temper, usually without justification, may be assumed to be aggressive and moody. Yet one could not come to this conclusion about a person who is normally placid but quite unexpectedly has a fit of rage. He may be moody, or even filled with hate and boiling with discontent, for some people are very adept at hiding their true feelings. A single action may not be a reliable guide to character, and so, in making judgments of this kind, one must be observant and discerning. Human nature is very complex and only those of great perspicacity can fathom its depths.

Some examples of actions and the conclusions which may be drawn from them are:

Observation Li Chen always drives at high speeds in a fast and expensive car.

Conclusion Li Chen is rich and vain, and possibly also reckless and arrogant.

Observation Mo Ti is intelligent, observant, hard-working and well-informed.

Conclusion Mo Ti will be successful in all his endeavors.

Observation Zheng Fong is pale, listless and nervous. She has sleepless nights and no appetite.

Conclusion Zheng Fong is sick or in love.

Observation Zhang Di is aggressive, arrogant, boastful, ill-mannered and without much knowledge.

Conclusion His only friend will be his mother.

Observation Chan Zhu values his friends and always keeps his promises.

Conclusion Chan Zhu will always have friends.

EARTH MAGIC

"Earth magic" is a term in popular use in reference to the Chinese term *fung shui*, or *feng shui*, but it is partly a misnomer, for *fung shui* is a common-sense and rational attempt to understand and control the physical influences of the environment, but no magic is involved. Perhaps the term magic is used in this connection because some of the people of the West are inclined to take the quite mistaken view that *fung shui* is no more than superstition.

Fung shui is not directly employed for divinatory purposes. On the other hand, those who do not take heed of its warnings could become subject to influences that destroy their chances of a safe and healthy future; and one of the main benefits of divination is the principle that to be forewarned is to be forearmed.

In the Chinese view, a person's position in relation to a building or some aspect of the terrain, such as a hill or a valley, may result in an influence, physical or psychological, which could be detrimental or beneficial. If it is the former, it is said to be bad *fung shui*; if it is the latter, it is good *fung shui*.

Sometimes, these influences can be easily understood – and prevented – where necessary. A house built at the top of a high hill will be exposed to winds and other adverse weather conditions, and a house

built on marshy ground near a river will be liable to flooding and subsidence. These are examples of bad *fung shui*. But a house built on a hillside facing south will have the best weather conditions, and so its occupants will have good *fung shui*.

However, the causes of *fung shui*, whether good or bad, are not always readily discernible, though it may be quite obvious that they do exist. The foul air near a stagnant pond could cause diseases, and the shadow cast by a large building could have a psychologically depressing effect. Sunshine, and its accompaniment of warmth, is comforting both physically and psychologically.

Although we in the West may regard *fung shui* with some suspicion and disdain, we do prefer to live in a house whose living-room windows face south (in the northern hemisphere), take a holiday where there is always plenty of sunshine, and not live in a house overlooking a cemetery, which could be most depressing.

There are many examples of environmental conditions, both man-made and provided by Mother Earth, which influence us for good or ill, but whose effects may not be immediately obvious or accurately measurable. They include the ocean tides, climatic conditions, the configuration of the land – river, lakes, mountains, etc. – the gravitational force of the earth, air pollution, contaminated water, nuclear-energy installations, the earth's magnetic field, and so forth.

People living in houses situated above granite formations are liable to exposure to radon, which can cause lung cancer. Radon is a radioactive gaseous element which is formed when radium disintegrates. This is an example of bad *fung shui* for which there is no apparent cause. It helps to promote the belief that misfortunes are due to evil spirits.

Clearly, to have good *fung shui*, and so be healthy and safe, one must not be in the wrong place at the wrong time.

Cultured and capable people
draw on their own resources,
but small-minded and
incapable people draw on the
resources of others.

Lunyu

HOME AND BUSINESS

Those people who have made a proper study of *fung shui* will appreciate the importance of ensuring that one's living, working and leisure locations are favorable to one's health and well-being. This is largely a common-sense approach to dealing with the environment, yet in the West it is often ignored. Even in big cities where there is no shortage of material wealth there are unhealthy slums and noisy, dirty and uninspiring workplaces.

The Chinese, however, take *fung shui* seriously. The *Tong Sing* provides some helpful information about managing the home and running a business, because the Chinese recognize that an ill-managed home or badly run business can lead only to sadness and discontent, or even depression and despair.

In managing the home, one must think in terms of warmth, light, ventilation, sanitation and other physical factors, and a little forethought in this regard will prevent much misery later on.

The home can be kept warm efficiently and economically by insulating the roofs and windows and choosing the right kind of heating equipment. Outside cold-water pipes should be lagged. Double glazing, however, may lead to inadequate ventilation, which is one of the causes of coughs and colds during the winter months. As an alternative, there is much to be said for a four-poster bed for keeping warm at night, because the air between the walls and the curtains around the bed provides an excellent insulation.

It is important that the home should be bright and adequately lit. To that end, rooms should be decorated with paint and paper which are warm and bright. Mirrors could be positioned so that they reflect light from the windows into dark corners. Given the choice, sensible people will live in a house whose living-room windows face south (north, if they are in the southern hemisphere) in order to obtain the maximum amount of sunshine.

Adequate ventilation is necessary for the health of the occupants. We do need oxygen, and a lack of it makes us feel drowsy, if nothing worse. Ventilation also prevents dampness, which causes decay and unpleasant smells. In this connection, it is wise to have the damp course checked periodically.

Needless to say, the house should be kept clean and tidy. Where there is dirt, there may be disease. Apart from that, an untidy house and garden are eyesores and unpleasant to be in.

But the *Tong Sing* is concerned more with behavior in the home than with the home itself and provides a set of rules designed to protect its occupants. The first of these, which may not appeal to everyone, is to rise at daybreak and then sweep out the front and back yards of the house. This is not very far removed from the English proverb "Early to bed and early to rise makes a man healthy, wealthy and wise." Certainly one should not miss out on sleep, nor fail to make the most of the hours of daylight.

The rules could be written as tables of *dos* and *don'ts*. A man is advised not to employ handsome servants; otherwise he may lose his wife. Clearly the ancient compilers of the *Tong Sing* had no illusions about human nature. But their advice is wide-ranging: one should be ready to help a neighbor, lock all doors before retiring, ensure that one's children attend school, listen to good advice, be patriotic and love wisdom. At the same time one is advised to abstain from greed, gluttony, excess in drinking alcohol, cheating in business, wasting food, love of money, extravagance, envy, arrogance, favoritism, idle gossip, treachery, boastfulness and over-optimism.

When it comes to running a business, the *Tong Sing* is more concerned with moral issues than with the practicalities of trading, and it inveighs strongly against dishonesty of any kind. This is sound advice, for though a dishonest trader may profit in the short term, in the long term his bad reputation will not allow his business to prosper.

The *Tong Sing* points out that trade creates wealth and that this means more mouths can be fed. It also advises that the trader must be trustworthy, patient, cheerful, polite, industrious and careful in working. Moreover, he must not be argumentative, aggressive, quick-tempered or unhelpful.

Numerology is the study of the mystical significance of numbers, and it should not be confused with mathematics, which is the scientific study of numbers, space and quantity and their applications in engineering and physics. But, valuable as numbers are, do they have any mystical significance?

THE MAGIC OF MATHEMATICS

Mathematics is sometimes defined as the language of sizes, which is not unreasonable, for it is mainly concerned with sizes in distance, mass, time, area, etc. These can be generally expressed by formulae such as "equal to," "more than" and "less than."

However, mathematics is concerned with other relationships, and our uneducated forebears must have been impressed by the way in which mathematicians could juggle with symbols and produce spectacular results as if by magic. The manipulations involving unknown quantities expressed as algebraic symbols $(x + y = z)$ may have helped to prompt the belief that numbers have an occult significance.

This is not a belief to be despised, for some of the sages of ancient China discovered that any number, whatever its size, could be expressed by two symbols – 1 and 0 – which, as we have seen, are the basis of the binary number system and the principle of the electronic computer.

THE MYSTICAL VALUE OF NUMBERS

It was the common belief in ancient China, as it was in the West, that certain numbers have a mystical or occult significance. In the West, 3 and 7 were thought to be lucky because the former is associated with the Holy Trinity, and the latter with the Heptateuch (the first seven books of the Old Testament). Thirteen was thought to be unlucky. To avoid superstitious fear, there was no thirteenth regiment in the army of imperial Russia (though some of the soldiers of the fourteenth regiment may well have been dismayed when they found out that their regiment was really the thirteenth). In China, there is a preference for even numbers because, being exactly divisible by two, they yield pairs which are assumed to be complementary opposites on the yin-yang principle. Sixty-four is a popular number in China, for it is the top number in the range of hexagrams in the *I Ching* (see page 133). Moreover, it is divisible by 2, as are its submultiples:

$64 \div 2 = 32, 32 \div 2 = 16, 16 \div 2 = 8, 8 \div 2 = 4, 4 \div 2 = 2, 2 \div 2 = 1.$

DESTINY NUMBERS

Some people believe that a person's destiny is associated with a certain number. An easy way to find a destiny number is as follows:

1. Add the day of birth to the month of birth.
2. Add the year of birth.
3. Add the figures in the total achieved by the last step.

So, for a person born on 15 December 1934, the stages are:

1. 15 + 12 = 27
2. 27 + 1934 = 1961
3. 1 + 9 + 6 + 1 = 17 – the person's destiny number

For 26 September 1984, the stages are:

1. 26 + 9 = 35
2. 35 + 1984 = 2019
3. 2 + 0 + 1 + 9 = 12 – the destiny number

LUCKY 7 AND 8

If you ask a Westerner to select a number between 1 and 12, the chances are that they will choose 7. It could be that, for religious reasons, they regard 7 as lucky, but it is more likely that the explanation is psychological . Consciously or subconsciously, people try to achieve randomness by avoiding what is orderly and seeking what is incongruous, though randomness cannot be achieved by deliberation. The stages would be on these lines:

1. The term "between" suggests numbers which are not at the ends of the range of numbers, so 1, 2, 11 and 12 are not selected.

This leaves a choice of 3 4 5 6 7 8 9 or10.

2. 5 and 10 are round numbers and decimal, so they are not selected. This leaves 3 4 6 7 8 or 9.

3. 4, 6 and 8 are even and orderly, so they are not selected.

We are down to 3, 7 or 9.

4. Of the three numbers 3, 7 and 9, 7 is in the middle – away from the ends – so 7 is selected.

But a Chinese person faced with the same choice would not select 7. His thinking could be as follows:

1. Avoid the numbers at the ends, leaving 4 5 6 7 8 9 or 10.

2. Avoid the odd numbers – they are bad! This leaves 4 6 8 or 10.

3. Of these, only 4 and 8 are multiples exclusively of 2 – a good thing. So the choice is reduced to 4 or 8.

4. 8 is nearer the middle of the range than is 4, so 8 is selected.

LOTTERIES

Most lotteries, whether conducted on a large scale by a national government or as raffles by charities, operate on the principle that a winning number or set of numbers is selected at random. But the numbers are no more than labels – they do not indicate quantities, and so they have no mathematical significance and could be represented, though less conveniently, by letters of the alphabet, colors or pictures.

For national lotteries, many people select destiny numbers or dates of birth as their "lucky numbers"; others make a deliberate attempt at a random choice, which is influenced by psychological factors. But, in fact, one number is as good as another, and a combination of 1, 2, 3, 4, 5 and 6, stands as much chance as 6, 8, 19, 23, 42 and 51.

What are the odds?
The mathematical content of any lottery is in the odds. Thus, if a church sells 1,745 raffle tickets, numbered 1 to 1,745, and there is only one prize, the odds against a purchaser of a single ticket winning the prize are 1,745 to 1. If he buys 5 tickets, the odds are 1,745 to 5, that is 349 to 1.

In a national lottery, the odds against winning are astronomical – many millions to one, in fact. Punters who pay £100 (that is, buy a hundred tickets) have slightly better odds than those who pay £1; but, on the other hand, they have considerably increased their chances of losing money. With a lottery of this size, the odds against winning are so great that the punter who pays £1 stands almost as good a chance as the person who pays £100 or more.

A gambler should always ask the question: what are the odds?

CHARMS

Of course, it is not enough just to make a prediction. If what is predicted is evil, unsatisfactory or undesirable in some other way, one must take appropriate action to mitigate its effects. In ancient China, this was usually done by means of a charm, which may be defined as a device which has magical power to ward off evil and be a good influence. A charm often took the form of a book or a ring.

The use of charms is not peculiar to China. It is common enough in the West, where people hang up horseshoes or wear bracelets to which are attached small trinkets and other amulets. However, the practice was much commoner and taken much more seriously in ancient times, when people were more superstitious than they are today. In the story of King Arthur, the sword Excalibur is a talisman.

It is very doubtful whether charms have any physical effect, but many people have a great capacity for self-deception and do genuinely feel better if they are wearing something which they believe will bring them good fortune. Needless to say, most of the good fortune accrues to the purveyors of charms, who do very well out of the superstitious.

Charms have always played a prominent part in Taoism and Buddhism, but more so in the latter. In recent years, owing to the Chinese government's attempts to eradicate fraud, Buddhist monks exercise great caution in using charms and now insist that the benefits are mainly psychological.

A commonly used charm is the *Tong Sing* itself. It may be placed under the pillow of a sick person, or under the abdomen of a pregnant woman who is in distress. Each copy is provided with a red ribbon or string so that it can be hung where it will do the most good – and red is a lucky color.

A Pa Kua mirror is another common charm. It consists of a small mirror with a frame of wood, plastic or other suitable material on which are carved or painted the eight trigrams of the Pa Kua (see page 62). It is believed that the mirror reflects evil back to its source.

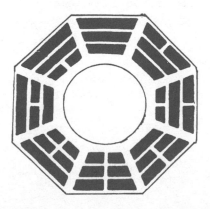

Most charms are written. But if they are to be fully effective they must have been written by an astrologer, a diviner, a Taoist or Buddhist monk or some other professional in the occult field. This is usually done in a room where incense has been burnt. The charm or spell is written in red ink on yellow paper. Red because, again, it is a lucky color, and yellow because it is the imperial color, suggestive of authority.

Some charms begin with the word *Chen* which means "to repress" or "to conquer"; it is used to reduce chaos and produce harmony. Others begin with *Ch'ih*, which means "to command" and is used in charms intended to combat illness. A few charms begin with *Cheng*, meaning "first." In Taoist literature, this denotes the Tao, the principle of universal harmony. From this it is apparent that the essential function of a very potent charm is to combat those forces which cause chaos and threaten harmony.

Charms are thought to be more effective if they are associated with lightning. This is achieved by lengthening and bending the final stroke of the principal character to make a lightning symbol. The reason for this can be found in the creation story. According to tradition, a bolt of lightning shattered the darkness of the primeval chaos, from which heaven and earth emerged, so releasing yin and yang, the creative forces of life and the universe. The Thunder God is concerned with harmony and purification. He strikes down all those who threaten the cosmos, or divine order.

When a charm has been written, the paper is burnt and the ashes mixed with water. This liquid is then drunk or sprinkled where it is needed or is likely to have the most favorable effect.

The greatest influence of charms comes from Taoism and has been in operation since ancient times. Charms are mentioned in *Ku Wei Shu* or "Old Mystery Books," which were written about A.D. 100, and which also mention Yao and Shen, two of the legendary emperors, and Yu the great, founder of the Xia dynasty (2100–1600 B.C.).

Another great influence is the Taoist writer Chang Taoling, also known as Chang Tian-shih or "Heavenly Master Chang," who was born in A.D. 35 and founded a medical school at Kiangsi. He would require a patient to write out all the sins and failures in his life and then, holding the list in his hand, wade out into a river, where he would be cleansed of his sins. This, no doubt, explains the popularity of written charms.

TELLING FORTUNES WITH TEA LEAVES

And now, I pray thee, Hetty dear,
That thou wilt give to me,
With cream and sugar soften'd well,
Another dish of tea.

The Life of Samuel Johnson James Boswell

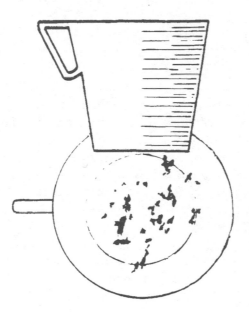

The Chinese have various divinatory systems and forms of indoor entertainment, but it seems that tasseography, or the art of telling fortunes by means of tea-leaves, is not one of them. But some of the Chinese in Hong Kong, where there is a strong British influence, may have engaged in this pursuit.

TASSEOGRAPHY

Tasseography is a very convenient way of telling fortunes, for the equipment required – just a cup and a few wet used tea leaves – is usually to hand, and the tea leaves cost nothing, for they are a waste product.

The innovation of tea-bags has caused a decline in the telling of fortunes by tasseography, a pastime that was extremely popular during the nineteenth century. If you want to tell fortunes by reading tea leaves, you must revert to brewing tea in the old-fashioned way, that is, by using loose tea.

Tea fortunes

The unseen chain of events – or series of cause and effect, as scientists would call it – which caused a few sodden and dilapidated tea leaves to be deposited at the bottom of a teacup bears no relation to the chain of events which has decided the fate of any person, even the one who has been using the teacup in question.

Furthermore, the supposedly mystic message which derives from the configuration of tea leaves at the bottom and on the sides of the cup is essentially a product of the fortune-teller's skill and imagination in an entertainment-type art. Therefore, the telling of fortunes by tea leaves should be regarded as a post-prandial or post-elevenses amusement, and little more.

The equipment

All that is needed for tasseography is a blend of tea with large leaves – they are more easily seen – and plain white cups, for the tea leaves and the patterns they make may not be visible enough against a dark or colored background. Many of the blends of tea produced for the British market consist of broken leaves and the pieces are often so small that they are little more than dust, like the tea in tea-bags, and not effective for tasseography. However, there are some fermented, full-leaf teas from China which, being black and consisting of whole leaves, are ideally suited to fortune-telling and may be crushed to produce the size of particle required.

The procedure

The person whose fortune is to be told should leave a little tea at the bottom of the cup, swirl it around, then gently pour off the liquid, leaving the leaves on the bottom and around the inside of the cup.

The interpretation

If one gazes at the deposited tea leaves for some time, and uses more than a little imagination, the groups of leaves will have shapes, or will appear to have shapes if the gaps are filled in, some of which may be interpreted as follows:

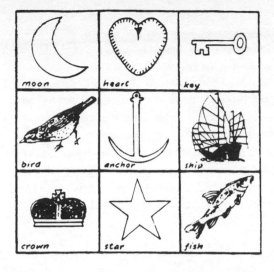

moon   heart   key

bird   anchor   ship

crown   star   fish

Airplane/airship promotion, prosperity

Anchor journey ending in happiness

Arch profitable meeting

Arrow happy love affair

Balloon as for aeroplane

Beehive industry brings prosperity

Bell good news is on the way

Bird good luck is imminent

Book seek advice about problems

Bottle social activity will increase

Butterfly your lover will be fickle

Cannon expect a big surprise

Chain more effort at work is needed

Clock important meeting to be expected

Crescent good news about money

Cross bad news or a crisis

Crown promotion is likely

Cup fuller social life to be expected

Dart as for arrow

Dice avoid reckless behavior

Envelope immediate good news

Face changes for the better

Fish good news from a distant place

Flag good luck is coming

Foot good news will come slowly

Gate changes are on the way

Hammer more effort will bring success

Harp Happiness with love and wealth

Hat minor danger or problem

Hatchet be careful with money

Heart great excitement to come

Hook as for arch

Horse good news will come quickly

Key burglary or mystery is likely

Knife quarrels in the offing

Ladder promotion or some other benefit

Mountains minor problems lie ahead

Ring success in affairs of the heart

Road promotion or wealth will come quickly

Scales guard against erratic behavior

Ship travel to a distant place

Square trust only honest people

Star good fortune is certain

Trees improvement in lifestyle

Triangle windfall is very likely

Trumpet beware of damaging gossip

Umbrella guard against foolish conduct

Wings as for bell

Windmill hard work will bring wealth

Other signs

Many other signs are possible, and some imagination and intuition are needed to interpret these. Size may indicate intensity. Thus, a small arrow can indicate a happy love affair, but a large arrow can indicate an ecstatic love affair. Literal interpretations are not essential – a violin could be interpreted as "beware of dishonesty," not as "good music is likely." (This is because a violin is sometimes called a fiddle, and "fiddling" is a slang term meaning swindling or cheating.)

Incomplete or misshapen signs may cause doubt and confusion. Discretion and common sense are needed to complete such signs. Thus, A could be a hatchet, a hammer or a pick; B could be a hatchet with a broken handle, or a flag with a broken staff; C could be a corkscrew or a gimlet.

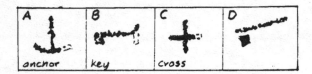

A sign may be a single leaf or a group of leaves. In diagram D, the large single leaf could be identified as a flag or a square if taken by itself, but it could be regarded as the blade of a hatchet or a key if it is considered to be a part of the adjoining row of small leaves.

Signs may be combined. Thus, an arrow and an envelope taken together could give "good news of a happy love affair."

Timing events

The approximate time of a predicted event may be indicated by a simple scale, as this diagram shows. A sign at the bottom of the cup refers to an event which is two or more years in the future. A sign near the rim refers to an event which is ahead by a month or so, and a sign on the side to an event about one year ahead.

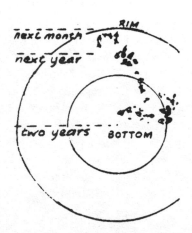

TEATIME

In Britain, and many other countries in the Western world, "tea" refers to a meal taken between the hours of four and six in the afternoon, at which tea is usually served. In China, however, teatime is any time – at each meal, between meals when one feels thirsty, and when visitors call. But, even so, and rather surprisingly, not as much tea is drunk in China as in Britain, where the tea consumption is equivalent to four cups per person per day, just behind the Irish, who drink more tea per capita than any other country in the world.

WHAT IS TEA?

Tea as a beverage is an infusion of the leaves of the tea plant, *Camellia sinensis*, a small evergreen shrub with shiny, laurel-like leaves and white flowers of a waxy appearance.

Before tea reaches the consumer, it is subjected to a series of delicate and complicated processes – plucking, withering, rolling, fermenting, drying, grading, and packing in airtight chests, for tea deteriorates very quickly. It is then shipped to destinations in various parts of the world, where it is tested by tea-tasters before the various grades are blended to produce the kinds of tea required by particular markets.

A GOOD CUP OF TEA

> But hear, alas! this mournful truth,
> Nor hear it with a frown,
> Thou canst not make the tea so fast
> As I can gulp it down.

Samuel Johnson

A number of factors are involved in making a cup of tea: the blend, freshness and quality of the leaf; the freshness, hardness and temperature of the water; the initial temperature of the teapot; the time allowed for infusion, etc.

But what constitutes a good cup of tea and the proper manner of brewing tea is a matter of opinion. Tastes vary considerably. The Chinese do not take milk or sugar in their tea, but the people of Tibet and the nomadic peoples to the north and in the west of China add milk, and even butter, to their tea, though it is added to the water in the pot in which the tea is being brewed.

TEAS IN CHINA

Six kinds of tea are consumed in China:

Green unfermented green leaves which produce a pale yellow and slightly astringent infusion.

Red fermented, producing a strong infusion, but much less popular than green tea.

Black fermented black leaves which produce a reddish infusion with a strong flavor.

Oolong semi-fermented with the flavor of green tea and the strength of red.

Brick mixed teas pressed into a block, and popular with Russians, Tibetans and the nomadic tribes in the north of China.

Flower-scented good quality green tea mixed with dried fragrant flowers, such as jasmine, rose and chrysanthemum.

Camellia sinensis

Green tea

In China, green tea is the kind generally served with a meal, always being drunk plain and weak and sipped at any stage. This is the way to make green tea.

Warm a teapot of 1³/₄ pints capacity, add 3 teaspoons green tea, fill with boiling water, allow to stand for at least 3 minutes, and decant the infusion slowly into Chinese-style cups (small, without handles and preferably of porcelain, if only for the sake of appearances), making sure that the tea solids remain in the pot. Do *not* add milk or sugar. Add hot water to the cups if the tea is too strong.

This tea may be kept warm in a metal or earthenware pot over a small flame, or in a vacuum flask, but it must be served within 24 hours from the time it was made.

Lemon tea

This is a most refreshing drink when one has acquired a taste for it.

Warm a teapot of 1³/₄ pints capacity, add 2 teaspoons black tea, fill with boiling water and stand for 2 minutes.

Thinly slice a lemon, drop two slices into each of several heat-resistant glasses, and pour the tea into the glasses, making sure that the tea solids remain in the pot. Add sugar to suit the taste.

THE MEDICINAL PROPERTIES OF TEA

In China, tea is consumed as a mild stimulant, an aid to the digestion and a refreshing drink.

Tea contains caffeine, theophylline and theobromine, which stimulate the central nervous system and assist in relaxing muscles, and also polyphenols and a few of the B-complex vitamins. Polyphenols, or tannin, give tea its flavor, but an excess of them, which happens when tea is over-infused, is not beneficial.

The Chinese consider that green tea aids digestion, improves vision, calms the nerves, stimulates the brain, strengthens the arteries, disposes of excess fat, clears phlegm, counteracts poisons, destroys micro-organisms, tones the kidneys and controls diarrhoea. They also consider that too much strong tea can damage the alimentary canal and nervous system.

"Red tea fungus," which is made by growing yeast in an infusion of red tea with sugar added, is used in Chinese folk medicine to treat constipation, strengthen the liver and kidneys, inhibit the ageing process, reduce blood pressure and increase resistance to toxins. It might also help to prevent cancer.

THE HISTORY OF TEA-DRINKING

Tea-drinking originated in China during the time of the Qin dynasty (221–206 B.C.), becoming widespread in the north of China and the valley of the Yangtze at the time of the Han empire (206 B.C.–A.D. 220), and assuming much importance in the Tang period (618–907). Buddhist monks did much to popularize tea, which they cultivated on the vast estates attached to their monasteries. They claimed that it kept them awake during their meditations. They instituted tea-drinking ceremonies as part of their religious rituals.

By the end of the twelfth century, tea-houses had become established all over China, and tea-drinking was avidly fostered by scholars, poets and the nobility.

THE TEA-HOUSES OF CANTON

During the time of the Qing (Manchu) dynasty (1644–1911), the Chinese tea-houses began to provide tasty snacks as well as tea, and they became meeting places for all sections of Chinese society. But the tea-houses of Canton, a major port in the south of China, developed on somewhat different lines. They specialized in the provision of cheap meals for ordinary people, working men in particular. The simple but savory items on their menus, such as prawn and meat dumplings, steamed buns, spring rolls and wonton (sometimes called "Chinese ravioli"), known collectively as dim sum, became extremely popular.

TEA LEGENDS

It could be that some of these legends contain elements of fact.

According to one of these legends, the emperor Shen Nong, who taught the Chinese the arts of agriculture and medicine, had a transparent abdomen, so he was able to follow the movements and notice the effects of the food and drink that had entered his body. He observed that tea cleaned out his bowels, so he recommended it as a medicine.

There was an occasion when some leaves, blown by the wind, fell into the pot in which the emperor's drinking water was being boiled. He was so pleased with the flavor imparted to the water that he ordered the cultivation of the tree whence these leaves had come.

Buddha cut off his eyelids so that he should not be disturbed in his meditations. A tea plant grew where each eyelid had fallen.

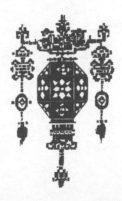

TEA TIPS

The following tea-making tips may be helpful, though to the tea enthusiast they may seem to be pointing out the obvious:

1

Do not use water which is stale from standing or from previous boiling.

2

Use soft water, but not artificially softened water. Hard water makes the tea cloudy, and artificially softened water makes it muddy. Naturally soft water, filtered water or peaty water makes a good cup of tea.

3

Use a teapot of the right size. One cannot make a large amount of tea – enough for six persons, say – in a small teapot.

4

Do not allow the tea to stand too long. Over-infusion produces tannin, which is astringent and unpleasant in taste.

5

If milk is to be added, use fresh non-creamy milk. Sour or creamy milk floats about as unsightly lumps on the surface of the tea.

6

If sugar is to be added, use granulated sugar. Caster sugar and brown sugar taste too sweet, almost sickly, in tea.

ENGLISH-STYLE TEA

This recipe will provide a good cup of tea which will suit the tastes of most British people, and also those Chinese in Hong Kong who prefer to take tea in the English way.

Fill a kettle with cold water fresh from the tap, and proceed to heat. Warm a teapot by standing it in a warm place or by rinsing it out with hot water. Add 1 small teaspoon tea of your choice per person. As soon as the water boils – and no later – take the pot to the kettle, and pour the water into the pot, allowing ¼ pint water per person, stand in a warm place or under a cosy for 3 minutes, give a good stir, pour through a strainer into cups, and add milk and sugar to taste.

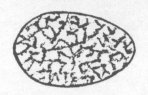

MARBLED EGGS

The Chinese use black tea in making marbled eggs, or porcelain eggs, as they are also called – an unusual snack to be eaten with a cup of tea.

For 4 persons, you will need 8 eggs, 3 tablespoons black tea, 2 tablespoons dark soy sauce and 1 teaspoon salt.

Place the eggs in a large saucepan, add 3½ pints water, bring to the boil, and then simmer for 10 minutes. Remove the eggs and place them in a dish of cold water. Do not throw away the water in which the eggs have been boiled.

When the eggs are cool, remove them from the water and tap the shell of each egg with the back of a spoon until the whole shell is covered with a network of cracks.

Return the eggs to the saucepan of water in which they were boiled, add the tea, soy sauce and salt, bring to the boil, and then simmer for 30 minutes. Turn off the heat and allow the eggs to cool in the liquid.

Remove the eggs from the cold liquid and gently detach the cracked shells. On each egg, there should be a handsome weblike pattern with the appearance of weathered marble or porcelain.

Cut the eggs in halves or quarters and serve as an accompaniment to other cold dishes, or as a garnish for a hot dish.

If not required immediately, the eggs can be stored, unshelled and in the liquid, preferably in a refrigerator, for up to 2 days. Remove the shells immediately before serving.

FESTIVE EGGS

The above recipe can be used to create eggs for festive occasions. Use less tea and replace the soy sauce with natural pigments. Here are some suggestions: tomato purée, scarlet; beetroot juice, pink or crimson; blackberry juice, mauve; blackcurrant juice, pale blue; mushy peas, pale green; cocoa, fawn.

Success will depend on the quantities used and your skill and patience as an experimenter.

CHINESE COOKING

Chinese meals differ greatly from Western-style meals, and their characteristics are determined to some extent by such factors as the economy, climate and traditions of China, but mainly by the conviction that a sound diet is the key to health and a long life.

The main features of the Chinese diet may be briefly summarized as follows:

1

The Chinese diet is beneficial in three ways. It is highly nutritious, health-giving and superbly appetizing.

2

The Chinese cook has three main concerns: best ingredients, correct preparation and effective presentation.

3

The Chinese diet is mainly vegetarian, and most meals contain no more than ten per cent meat, the main sources of protein being beans, cereals, eggs, fish, poultry and just a little pork.

4

Meals are made appetizing by harmonious blending of complementary opposites in color, flavor, texture and fragrance: dark with bright, sweet with sour, smooth with lumpy, etc.

5

Individual dishes are balanced on the yin-yang principle: cooked with uncooked, acid with alkaline, fish with cereal, and so on.

6

The two main classes of food are the *fan* and the *cai*. The former, which is yin, consists of cereals and vegetables, and the latter consists of meat, fish and spicy items. *Fan* literally means "cooked grain." It is filling, satisfying, easily digested and not irritating. It absorbs the excess grease and acids in the *cai*.

7

Much variety ensures that one does not consume too much of what is harmful, nor too little of what is beneficial.

8

There is a preference for fresh ingredients.

9

Ingredients are generally shredded, diced or thinly sliced to create a greater surface area so that they are more easily blended, cooked and digested.

10

The main method of cooking is stir-frying. This ensures that the ingredients are cooked quickly, and so the nutrients are sealed into the food and are not destroyed.

11

Another common method of cooking is steaming. It has two advantages. The food will not burn or be overcooked, for it cannot attain a temperature which is higher than that of boiling water (212°F). Its soluble nutrients are not lost by being dissolved in the water, as would be the case if it were boiled.

12

The cooking methods used in the West – baking, roasting, etc. – are also used in China, but on a much smaller scale. Oven cooking is quite uncommon.

13

Soups are generally prepared by slow simmering in a *saguo*, which is an earthenware pot glazed on the inside.

14

Wooden ladles, earthenware cooking pots, porcelain spoons and dishes, wooden or plastic chopsticks and bamboo steamers are preferred to metal cutlery and cooking vessels. The Chinese are aware that the acids in food react chemically with metals, often with unhealthy effects.

15

Some ingredients, such as shark's fin and bear's paws, are of an exotic character, and some have valuable medicinal properties.

16

There is no neglect of attractive presentation – napkins, finger-bowls, jars of flowers, murals, joss sticks, etc. – for the Chinese are aware that it is not only food which whets the appetite.

17

The main courses are supplemented with tea, which is a mild stimulant and an aid to the digestion.

18

Basically, a Chinese meal for a family contains three or four main courses. An extra course is provided for each additional diner. Thus, a meal for ten people will contain twelve or more courses.

19

Foods which are damaging to the health are kept at a minimum or avoided altogether. They include synthetic additives, red meat, animal fats, refined sugar, eggs that are not well cooked, salt, chocolate and other confectionery, unwashed vegetables and fruits, and stale and tainted food.

THE DRAGON'S KITCHEN

To the ruler, people are heaven:
to the people, food is heaven.

Chinese Proverb

The Chinese employ a wide variety of cookery techniques, and they are not without complications. For example, there are four main ways of stir-frying, three ways of steaming, and many ways of cutting food into small pieces. Therefore, the reader who aspires to proficiency in Chinese cooking should obtain a Chinese cookbook and make a thorough study of its contents. The following information could be helpful in this respect.

THE THREE-IN-ONE RULE

By tradition, the seven essentials in a Chinese household are firewood, tea, salt, oil, rice, soy sauce and vinegar. When buying ingredients in common use, it is sensible to buy in bulk, of the best quality and at the lowest price.

THE WOK

Of all the tools that are available to the culinary artist, the wok is surely the most versatile. It may be used for stir-frying, deep-frying, shallow-frying, sautéing, boiling, simmering, steaming, braising and poaching. Only a small quantity of oil is required for deep-frying; and two different items may be fried at the same time, one deep and one shallow.

Choosing a wok

Woks come in various sizes. For a family of four or five persons, a wok about 14 inches in diameter is suitable.

For slow simmering or cooking large quantities, when the wok has to stand unattended for long periods, a two-handled wok is to be preferred. It is easier to lift a heavy device with two handles than with one. But for stir-frying, a one-handled wok is preferable, for the cook can hold the wok with one hand, and the slice or other utensil with the other hand.

Woks are made of iron, stainless steel or aluminium. An iron wok is considered to be the best because it is the most robust and holds the heat well.

Heating a wok

When a wok is used in the traditional way, its rounded bottom is pushed into the glowing embers of a charcoal, wood or coal fire. When heated on a gas cooker, it must be supported on a stand. It is possible to buy a flat-bottomed wok which can be heated directly, without a stand, on the ring or plate of an electric cooker. One must take great care when deep-frying, for a spillage of oil could result in a serious fire.

Seasoning a wok
A new wok needs to be seasoned. To do this, thoroughly scrub the inside of the wok with detergent and hot water, rinse it well, dry it, add 2 tablespoons cooking oil, heat and rub over the inside with kitchen paper to form a thin coat of oil. Continue to heat for 10 minutes, pour off the oil and repeatedly wipe the inside with kitchen paper until it is clean and shiny. This needs to be repeated if the wok becomes rusty through lack of use. A wok with a non-stick surface does not need to be seasoned.

OTHER UTENSILS
A Chinese cook can prepare a wide range of dishes, from the simplest to the most gorgeously elaborate, with very few utensils. In general, a Chinese kitchen will contain a wok, strainer, cleaver, chopping block, rolling pin, teapot, all-purpose knife, roasting pan and meat/fish slice and two steamers – one large and one small – chopsticks, earthenware cooking pots, wooden and porcelain ladles and spoons and various bowls and dishes. A mortar and pestle, which may be purchased at a pharmacy, is a most useful addition to a kitchen. It is used for crushing and grinding garlic, ginger and other spices.

With a cleaver and an all-purpose knife, a Chinese cook can perform all the cutting operations required in a kitchen.

DIM SUM

Those items known collectively as dim sum are now a well-established part of the dietary life-style of all Chinese, not only in China but throughout the world. They are also a regular feature of Chinese restaurant menus in the West and have developed into a sort of Oriental brunch. The following are all quick and easy to prepare at home.

WONTON WITH CHICKEN FILLING

**24 purchased wonton skins or
  8oz noodle paste
6oz mushrooms
1 tablespoon sunflower oil
12oz cooked chicken
2 spring onions
pinch of salt
pinch of pepper
¹/₄ teaspoon sugar
1 tablespoon light soy sauce
1 egg yolk
vegetable oil for deep-frying**

If home-made noodle paste is used, roll it out thinly on a lightly floured board and cut to make 24 skins, each 3in square.

Chop the mushrooms coarsely and stir-fry in the sunflower oil for 2 minutes.

Chop the chicken, onions and fried mushrooms very finely, add the salt, pepper, sugar and soy sauce, mix well and divide into 24 equal portions.

Put one of the portions on each skin, fold in the same way as a turnover and seal the edges with egg yolk. Deep-fry in hot oil until golden, drain well and serve immediately.

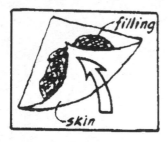

WONTON WITH PORK FILLING

Follow the previous recipe, but replace the chicken with 10oz cooked lean pork, and the mushrooms with 8oz mixed vegetables: cooked peas, carrots, green beans, spinach, bamboo shoots, water chestnuts, celery, broccoli, tomatoes, bean sprouts, peppers, etc. If tomatoes, bean sprouts and peppers are used, they must not be precooked.

STEAMED DUMPLINGS WITH PORK FILLING

12oz cooked pork
2oz lean bacon
1 egg
2oz mushrooms
2 spring onions
1 slice fresh ginger
¹/₂ teaspoon sugar
pinch of salt
pinch of pepper
¹/₂ teaspoon sesame oil
1 tablespoon light soy sauce
3 teaspoons rice wine/sherry
24 wonton skins, purchased
or home-made

Mince the pork and bacon, beat the egg and finely chop the mushrooms, onion and ginger. Mix all the ingredients together thoroughly and divide into 24 equal portions.

Put one of the portions on the center of each skin, fold up the edges to make a bag-shaped container and press the bottom against a lightly floured board to make a flat base. The top may be left open – some people like to see the contents – or sealed by gathering up the edges.

Pack the dumplings closely together in a single layer on a sheet of greaseproof paper and place in a steamer. Stand the steamer on a rack in a large wok/pan containing 3in water, bring to the boil, cover, turn down the heat and steam gently for 25 minutes. It may be necessary to do this in several batches.

OPEN

SEALED

STEAMED DUMPLINGS WITH CHICKEN FILLING

Follow the previous recipe, but replace the pork with 12oz cooked chicken and the bacon with 2oz cooked ham.

CHILLI OIL

Chilli oil can be used as a dip-in sauce with wonton, dumplings and many other Chinese dishes.

¹/₄ pint peanut or sunflower oil
1 tablespoon fresh red chillies

Heat the oil in a wok or pan until it begins to smoke. Remove from the heat, add the chillies, allow to cool and pour into a suitable container. Strain after 2 days.

CHINESE-STYLE BREAD BUNS

1 teaspoon baker's yeast
8oz plain flour
4 tablespoons sugar
2 tablespoons olive oil

Stir the yeast in ½ pint warm water and add to the flour, together with the sugar and oil. Knead well, cover with a moist cloth and leave to stand for 2½–3 hours.

After the dough has risen to twice its size, reknead, shape into a long roll and cut into 10–12 pieces of equal size. Shape into buns and stand in a warm place for 15 minutes so that the dough rises again.

Steam for 15 minutes and serve.

WESTERN-STYLE BREAD BUNS

Western-style bread is becoming increasingly popular in China.

Proceed as in the previous recipe but, instead of steaming, brush with beaten egg, sprinkle with sesame or caraway seeds and bake in a hot oven until golden brown.

Serve cold, cut in half, buttered and with a sandwich filling: boiled egg, sliced tomato, grated cheese, cooked ham, brawn, roast chicken, etc. Or serve uncut and unbuttered with a spicy meat, chicken or fish dish.

PRAWN CRACKERS

Prawn crackers consist of a paste compounded of prawn meat, starch, sugar and salt.

1 pint peanut oil
3oz prawn crackers

Heat the oil in a large wok/pan until hot. Drop one cracker into the oil. If it puffs up and floats to the top immediately, the oil is hot enough. Otherwise, wait for a time, and then test again. Deep-fry the crackers in batches – a handful at a time.

When all people dislike something, it should be examined. When all people like something, it should be examined.

Lunyu

SPRING ROLLS

8oz lean pork/ham
3 spring onions
1 green pepper
6oz bean sprouts
4oz peeled cooked prawns
1 tablespoon peanut oil
1 teaspoon salt
1/2 teaspoon brown sugar
1 teaspoon light soy sauce
1 teaspoon dark soy sauce
1 tablespoon dry sherry
1 teaspoon sesame oil
8oz flour
1 egg
vegetable oil

Mince the pork/ham, finely chop the onions, thinly slice the pepper, trim, wash and drain the bean sprouts, and chop the prawns.

Stir-fry the pork/ham, prawns and vegetables in the peanut oil for 1 minute at high heat. Add the salt, sugar, soy sauces, sherry and sesame oil, stir-fry for a further 3 minutes and leave to cool.

Mix the flour, egg and 1 pint water together, and beat well to make a smooth batter. Lightly grease a wok/pan and make 12–15 pancakes, cooked on one side only.

Divide the filling into the same number of portions as there are pancakes. Put a portion in the center of a pancake, fold the nearest edge (A) to the center, fold in the sides (B and C), roll up and seal the final edge (D) with a little water.

Make the other pancakes in the same way. Deep-fry at high heat for about 15 minutes, turning over occasionally to ensure even cooking, drain and serve.

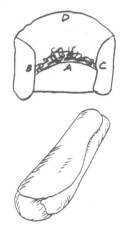

WHEAT CAKES

8 oz plain flour
2 tablespoons
  peanut oil

Knead the flour with 1/2 pint hot water. Roll out the dough thinly and cut out 20 2-inch diameter rounds. Brush 10 rounds with oil, and press the other rounds on top, sandwich fashion. Roll each "sandwich" to make a larger 5-inch round. Place each round in turn in a lightly oiled wok or non-stick frying-pan with a tight-fitting cover and fry over low heat for 3 minutes on each side.

Stack the cakes on a plate, separating them with greaseproof paper so that they do not stick together.

PEKING STYLE
THE CUISINE OF
CHINA'S CAPITAL CITY

China is a country of immense size with many different regions, most of which have their own traditional dishes and style of cooking. Dim sum, for example, is a component of the Cantonese style of cuisine.

REGIONAL STYLES

The characteristics of the regional styles of cuisine are largely determined by local conditions in regard to geography, climate and social customs.

Although most Chinese restaurants, especially the high-class ones, generally provide dishes cooked in the various regional styles, most will be in the styles of Peking (Beijing) and Canton (Guangzhou). This is understandable, for Peking is the capital city of China, and so it takes the lead in matters of fashion, including the culinary style. Canton, a large city and port in the Guangdong province, is regarded as the capital of the south of China.

THE PEKING STYLE

The Peking style of cuisine, which is sometimes called the northern style, employs strongly-flavored dishes, and a greater quantity and variety of meat is eaten than in the south. Wheat, maize and millet eaten as bread, pancakes, dumplings and noodles constitute the staple diet. It owes many of its characteristics to the influence of the cooks at the imperial court.

But, in fairness, it must be said that many Chinese regard the Cantonese style as the true *haute cuisine* of China, for it could well be that its exotic character is due to the influence of the talented cooks of the imperial court who fled from Peking to Canton when the Ming dynasty was overthrown in 1644.

PEKING DUCK

This is a great delicacy, the recipe for which was devised by the cooks in the imperial kitchens. It is prepared from ducklings which are bred for the purpose. They are fed on a rich diet of cereals during the few weeks prior to being slaughtered. After being coated with malt sugar and roasted in special ovens, which burn wood, the ducks have a brown, crispy skin, moist flesh, little or no fat and an aromatic fragrance.

**1 large duck,
fresh or frozen**

If the duck is frozen, thaw it out completely. Wash, and then dry with a cloth.

2 spring onions

**2 slices fresh
ginger**

Finely chop the onions and ginger, and cut the lemon into thin slices without removing the peel.

1 lemon

**3 tablespoons
dark soy sauce**

**¼ pint dry
sherry**

**¼ pint chicken
stock**

Put all the ingredients except the chicken stock into a large wok or pan, add 2 pints water, bring to the boil and then simmer for 20–25 minutes. Pour this mixture over the duck a little at a time and several times until it is completely coated. Then hang the duck to dry in a place that is cool and airy, placing a pan beneath it to catch the drips. This drying process could take 12 hours or more.

Place the duck, breast upward, on a rack in a roasting pan, adding the chicken stock to absorb the fat drips, put into an oven preheated to 475°F and roast for 15 minutes. Then reduce the heat to 350°F and continue to roast for a further 70 minutes.

Allow to stand for 10 minutes, carve into small pieces and arrange on a warm plate. Serve immediately with wheat cakes ("Chinese pancakes"), spring onions and a small dish of hoisin sauce as a dip.

PEKING FISH

Sole or plaice is suggested for this recipe because both are readily available in the West. However, sea bass, trout and monkfish are also often recommended for Westerners attempting Chinese fish recipes, and it is worth experimenting with other fish, both freshwater and marine.

1 lb sole/plaice
salt
pepper
1 egg
cornstarch
1 spring onion
2 slices fresh ginger
4 tablespoons peanut oil
3 teaspoons white wine
3 tablespoons chicken stock
1 teaspoon sugar

Cut the fish into 3 inch x 1 inch strips, rub with salt, sprinkle on pepper, and allow to stand for 30 minutes.

Mix the egg and 1 tablespoon cornstarch with just enough water to make a runny batter. Coat the fish pieces with the batter.

Finely chop the onion and ginger. Heat the oil in a wok/pan, add the onion and ginger, stir-fry over medium heat for 1 minute, remove and allow to cool. Place the fish pieces in the wok/pan so that they are laid evenly. Sauté over low heat for 1 1/2 minutes each side, remove from the heat and drain off the oil.

Mix 2 teaspoons cornstarch with just enough water to make a smooth paste. Make a sauce by mixing together the wine, stock, sugar 1/4 teaspoon salt and cornstarch paste. Pour this sauce evenly over the fish, sauté for 1 minute, turning the fish pieces over in the sauce, transfer to a warm dish and serve immediately with all the sauce.

QUICK-FRIED LAMB

The Chinese consume very little red meat, but some lamb is consumed in the north of China, where the barren terrain and colder climate are more suitable for grazing sheep than for growing crops.

12 oz leg of lamb
10 spring onions
1 clove garlic
1 tablespoon light soy sauce
2 pinches black pepper
1/2 teaspoon salt
3 teaspoons cornstarch
1 tablespoon rice wine/dry sherry
4 tablespoons peanut oil
3 teaspoons sesame oil
1 tablespoon wine vinegar

Remove any fat from the lamb and slice very thinly. Chop the onions and crush the garlic.

Mix together the soy sauce, pepper, salt, cornstarch, wine and 1 tablespoon peanut oil. Add the lamb and onions to the mixture, and marinate for 1 hour.

Heat 3 tablespoons peanut oil in a wok/pan until very hot, add the garlic, lamb and onions, stir constantly for a few seconds, and then add the sesame oil and vinegar. Stir well and serve very hot.

FRIED CHICKEN LEGS

1 egg
1 teaspoon salt
2 teaspoons cornstarch
12oz small chicken
  drumsticks
vegetable oil for deep-
  frying
2 spring onions
2 tablespoons peanut oil
1 tablespoon light soy
  sauce
3 tablespoons chicken
  stock

Separate the egg. Beat the white until frothy, add the salt and 1 teaspoon cornstarch, and mix together. Dip the drumsticks in the mixture, allow to stand for 15 minutes, and then deep-fry until tender.

Chop the onions and stir-fry in the peanut oil at high heat for about 20 seconds, add the drumsticks and the remaining ingredients, and cook at medium heat for 4–5 minutes. Transfer to a warm dish and serve immediately.

Colors blind their eyes, sounds deafen their ears, flavors spoil their palates, the chase and the hunt craze their minds, and greed makes their actions harmful. And so the sage will avoid extremes.

Tao Te Ching

Take-away meals are essentially simple and inexpensive dishes designed to please the gourmets – and gourmands! – of the Western world. Rapidly prepared and without a high degree of elaboration, they do bear some resemblance to the national dishes of China, but cannot be expected to include the exotic food served in a high-class restaurant in Peking or Canton.

A take-away meal does not normally contain the large number of courses of a traditional Chinese meal. It generally consists of two courses, of which one is an egg, meat, fish or poultry dish, and the other is based on a cereal, such as rice or noodles. French fried potatoes – or chips – are often provided as an alternative to the cereal dish. Commonly used vegetables include bean sprouts, bamboo shoots, water chestnuts, mushrooms, onions, peppers and tomatoes.

Chopsuey and curry dishes are the most popular take-away meals in the West. Other popular dishes are chow mein, which is a noodle dish, and fuyung, which is an omelette. But these are prepared with many variations, and so there need be no monotony in eating take-away style.

CHOPSUEY

Chopsuey is of very humble origin. The word chopsuey is an Anglicized version of the Chinese word *zacui*, which is the name given to the boiled hotchpotch of left-overs from restaurants which, until quite recent times, was distributed free of charge or sold cheaply to poor people, such as beggars, laborers and rickshaw men. Chopsuey, then, began its career as a despised makeshift.

PORK CHOPSUEY

8oz cooked pork
1 clove garlic
2 slices fresh ginger
1 tablespoon cornstarch
4 tablespoons peanut oil
2lb mixed cooked vegetables as
  available
1/4 pint meat/chicken stock
1/4 teaspoon salt
1 teaspoon sugar
2 tablespoons dark soy sauce

Mince or thinly slice the pork, crush and chop the garlic, finely chop the ginger and mix the cornstarch with enough water to make a smooth paste.

Heat the oil in a wok or pan, add all the ingredients and stir-fry over fierce heat for 2 minutes, and then over gentle heat for a further 5–10 minutes.

CHICKEN CURRY

8oz cooked chicken
1 clove garlic
6oz mixed cooked vegetables
2 teaspoons cornstarch
3 tablespoons peanut oil
$^1/_2$ teaspoon salt
2 teaspoons mild curry powder
1 teaspoon sugar
1 tablespoon light soy sauce
4 tablespoons chicken stock

Dice the chicken to make 1-inch cubes, crush and chop the garlic, chop the vegetables, and mix the cornstarch with enough water to make a smooth paste.

Add the oil to a wok or pan, heat until very hot, add the chicken and vegetables and stir-fry for about 2 minutes. Add the remaining ingredients and cook for a further 4–5 minutes, stirring constantly to make sure that all the sauce is absorbed.

Serve immediately. If this dish is not hot enough, use more curry powder – or a stronger variety.

RICE

There are many varieties of rice – black, aromatic, glutinous, long-grain, etc. – and they have a number of uses: as a vegetable, in dessert dishes, and in making wine and vinegar.

In China, where rice is the staple crop, no part of the rice plant is wasted. The seeds or grains are eaten, the straw is woven into hats, mats, shoes and bags, the husks are used as cattle feed, and the roots are burnt to make a fertilizer.

Westerners who try their hand at Chinese cooking are often uncertain about the correct way to prepare and cook rice, so the following notes may prove useful.

GROWING RICE

Rice is grown in all those parts of the world where the conditions, natural or man-made, are favorable to its growth, as in China, Japan, Malaysia, the United States and Italy.

RICE

There is a variety of rice, requiring little water, which can be grown on land that is dry, sloping and well-drained. It is called upland rice. But most varieties require plenty of water. These are called lowland rice, and they thrive best in the wet alluvial soil on the shores of lakes and the banks of rivers. Ideal conditions for growing rice are found in the fertile river valleys in the south of China, where there is more than one growing season, so that several crops of rice may be harvested during the year.

SELECTING RICE

It is important to select the variety of rice which is appropriate for the dish in preparation. Both long-grain and short-grain rice are used in those vegetable dishes which are an accompaniment to meat, fish or poultry, but the long-grain is usually preferred. Short-grain rice should not be confused with the pudding rice used in the West. The other varieties are used on a smaller scale in special dishes, such as snacks and desserts.

It is advisable not to use pudding rices, precooked rices, and those "easy-to-cook" rices which are intended to save time in preparation and make life easier for the cook, for they do not generally give good results with Chinese-style dishes.

PREPARING RICE

Rice must be washed thoroughly before use, for undesirable foreign bodies are sometimes present. To do this, put the rice that is to be cooked into a large bowl. Fill it with water, swirl the rice around with a spoon or your hand – a clean hand! – and then carefully pour off the cloudy water. Do this several times until the water is clear.

COOKING RICE

Rice is cooked in three ways: boiling, steaming and stir-frying. Boiling is the easiest method, but the Chinese prefer it to be steamed, which gives the best results. Fried rice, which is a means of using up left-over boiled rice, is more popular in the West than it is in China, where it is regarded as an extra to be eaten at the end of a meal, and not an integral part of the meal.

BOILED RICE

The newcomer to Chinese cooking generally asks two very relevant questions about boiling rice: How much water should I use? How do I prevent the rice becoming gluey?

Chinese cooks use a rule-of-thumb method, or perhaps we should say a "rule-of-finger" method, to estimate the correct amount of water to be used. They dip a finger into the rice, and add water until it reaches the level which, from past experience, they know to be correct. A simpler method for the novice when boiling rice in ordinary quantities in a wok, saucepan or cooking pot, is to cover the rice with water to about 1inch above the surface of the rice. Rice becomes gluey if it is overheated or too much water is used.

In measuring the rice, 3oz per person provides a generous helping. A breakfast cup of rice is adequate for four persons.

Wash 12oz long-grain rice, drain, put into a heavy pan or pot, cover with about 1inch water and boil for about 15–20 minutes, stirring occasionally to prevent sticking, until most of the surface water has evaporated. Cover the pan/pot with its lid, which must be tight-fitting, and then cook very slowly over the lowest possible heat for a further 15–20 minutes. The rice cooks in the steam from the remaining water, so do not remove the lid or the steam will escape.

Sowing rice

STEAMED RICE

Small quantities of rice can be cooked in a traditional-type steamer, which is a bamboo box with holes in its bottom and lid; but the boiled rice as prepared above is semi-steamed, and is quite satisfactory for most purposes.

FRIED RICE

To achieve success in preparing fried rice, these three rules should be observed.

1. Use boiled rice that is cold or quite cool, and which, if not freshly cooked, has been stored in a refrigerator.
2. Do not add soy sauce to fried rice. It makes the rice too salty and gives it a dingy appearance.
3. Make sure that the oil is hot and that there is not too much of it; otherwise, the rice becomes greasy and stodgy.

2 tablespoons peanut oil
1 lb boiled rice
$\frac{1}{2}$ teaspoon salt
pinch of black pepper
2 eggs

Heat a wok or pan until hot, add the oil and continue to heat until very hot. Add the rice, salt and pepper and stir-fry over high heat for 5 minutes. Beat the eggs until smooth, pour on to the rice in a thin stream, constantly stirring, and then stir-fry at gentle heat until the eggs are set.

When fried rice is prepared as a dish in itself, and not as an accompaniment to another dish, it can be enlivened by the addition of small amounts of other ingredients, such as precooked pork, chicken and vegetables.

*The superior man reduces
what is excessive and
increases what is deficient,
so bringing about equality.*

I Ching

EIGHT TREASURES RICE

This traditional dessert dish is known to the Chinese as *bo bo fan*.

1oz each walnuts, chestnuts, blanched almonds/lotus seeds
2oz each stoneless dates, glacé cherries, raisins/sultanas/currants, mixed glacé fruits, mixed candied peel
3 teaspoons peanut oil
8oz rice
3oz brown sugar

Immerse the walnuts and chestnuts in boiling water, and then skin them. Chop the nuts, dates and glacé cherries. Oil the inside of a large pudding bowl with a little of the peanut oil.

Mix all the ingredients, together with 2 tablespoons water, put into the bowl, press down firmly and cover with greaseproof paper or aluminium foil, securing with thin string. Place the bowl in a wok or pan containing enough water to reach half-way up the bowl. Boil gently for 50 minutes. Do not allow the wok/pan to boil dry. Unmold and serve hot.

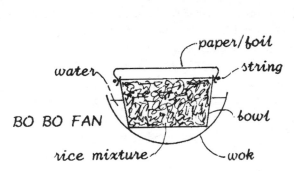

water — paper/foil — string — bowl — wok — rice mixture — BO BO FAN

NOODLES

Noodles or Chinese pasta take second place to rice in the cereal component of the diet of the Chinese. They also have some historical significance.

Noodles were invented about 2,000 years ago. The first of the Chinese emperors to sample the new dish was Wang Mang, who reigned for only 14 years, during the early part of the Han dynasty (206 B.C.–A.D. 220).

This invention improved the diet of the poor, whose meals had been mainly composed of an unexciting combination of boiled wheat and rice grains and soya beans.

Noodles occupy quite an important place in Chinese tradition, for they are symbolic of strength and longevity. They are always served at New Year, wedding and birthday feasts.

Noodles are made mainly from wheat or rice flour, though some are made from mung beans and soya beans. They are in various shapes and sizes – flat or round, and in sticks, threads or sheets. They may be hard or soft, fresh or dried, and with or without the addition of egg. Lye water (potassium carbonate solution) is sometimes added to prevent them going mouldy in a hot and humid climate.

Noodles possess some important advantages. They are inexpensive and economical in use, for nothing is wasted, and the dried types keep so well that they can be stored almost indefinitely without deterioration. In the north of China, they are a useful stand-by for the winter months, when fresh vegetables are not readily available. They are quickly and easily cooked and have the same sort of versatility as rice.

People are generally surprised to learn that pasta products – noodles, spaghetti, lasagne, macaroni, ravioli, etc. – and rice dishes, such as risotto, which we think of as being typically Italian, did not originate in Italy but in China.

It is said that Marco Polo introduced pasta to his native Venice when he returned from China in 1295.

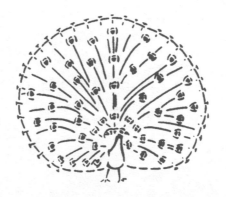

BOILED NOODLES

8oz wheat noodles, fresh or dried

If the noodles are fresh, boil them in about 1³/₄ pints water for 3–5 minutes until soft. Drain and serve.

If they are dried, follow the manufacturer's instructions on the packet; otherwise, boil them in 1³/₄ pints water for 4–5 minutes until soft. Drain and serve.

Noodles may be precooked and stored in a refrigerator for up to about 2 hours until they are required for stir-frying or adding to other dishes. They should be put into a bowl and covered with a plastic bag.

FRIED NOODLES

Fried noodles are sometimes called plain chow mein, for that is what they are: noodles stir-fried as in a chow mein dish but without the addition of meat, fish or vegetables.

**8oz egg noodles
1 tablespoon peanut oil**

Boil the noodles, following the procedure in the previous recipe, and drain well. Heat a wok or pan, add the oil and noodles, stir-fry over medium heat for 2–3 minutes, and serve immediately.

CHICKEN NOODLE SOUP

**1³/₄ pints chicken stock
8oz egg noodles**

Put the stock and noodles into a wok or pan, boil for 4–5 minutes and serve at once. Add salt to taste.

CHINESE CHOICE

Things sweet to taste prove in digestion sour

King Richard the Second
William Shakespeare

The Chinese do not consume large quantities of desserts and confectionery, for they regard sugar, particularly refined sugar, as an unhealthy item of diet if taken in excess. Their choice would generally be fresh fruit or a spicy dish rather than a sweet dish. They have a great liking for those savory snacks called dim sum, which loosely translated means "fill a space."

However, it must not be thought that the Chinese do not have any dessert dishes. On the contrary, they have some delectable ones, but these are generally served only on festive occasions.

ALMOND CREAM

1oz gelatine
1pint milk
2 tablespoons sugar
1 teaspoon almond essence

Put 4 tablespoons water into a pan, add the gelatine and heat but do *not* boil. Stir constantly until the gelatine dissolves.

Heat ³/₄ pint water, add the milk, sugar and almond essence, and stir until the sugar has dissolved. Add the gelatine, stir again, pour into a shallow dish, allow to cool and set. Cut into bite-sized pieces and store in a refrigerator until required.

CARAMELIZED WALNUTS

8oz shelled walnuts
4oz sugar
vegetable oil for deep-frying
2 tablespoons sesame seeds

Blanch the walnuts by boiling in water for 10 minutes, drain, dry on kitchen paper, coat in sugar and leave to dry out thoroughly, which will take several hours.

Deep-fry the walnuts in batches for about 2 minutes over moderate heat until the sugar melts and they are golden. Remove with a strainer, sprinkle with the sesame seeds, and lay in a heat-proof dish to cool.

BANANA FRITTERS

3 eggs
1oz flour
2 teaspoons cornstarch
6 large bananas, slightly underripe
vegetable oil for deep-frying
10 tablespoons sugar syrup

Separate the egg whites, and mix them with the flour and cornstarch and just enough water to make a smooth batter.

Peel the bananas and cut them at an angle to make pieces about 1¹/₂ inches long. Dip in the batter, deep-fry, about 6 at a time, until golden, drain well and transfer to a warm dish.

Warm the sugar syrup, pour on the fritters and serve immediately.

PINEAPPLE FRITTERS

Proceed as for banana fritters, but replace the bananas with 1 ½lbs pineapple chunks or rings. If rings, cut into quarters, and dry well on clean kitchen paper.

DATE CAKES

8oz dates
8oz rice flour

Stone the dates, warm to soften, add the rice flour and knead to make a soft dough. Roll out to ¼ inch thickness, cut into small shapes and cook in a steamer for 5 minutes. They are very appetizing when served with almond cream.

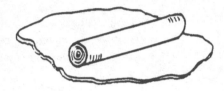

*Sages know themselves, but do
not admire themselves.
Sages take care of themselves,
but they do not exalt
themselves. They choose the
former and avoid the latter.*

Tao Te Ching

BEVERAGES

Water, water, everywhere,
Nor any drop to drink.

The Rime of the Ancient Mariner
S. T. Coleridge

The beverages available to the Chinese are more limited in range than those commonly found in the West, and they do not include chocolate and milky drinks. For the Chinese, the main drinks are boiled water, tea, fruit juices and soup. Wine is regarded as something of a luxury, but the consumption of coffee and beer is on the increase, the most popular beer being a lager produced by the brewery at Qingdao, which is a legacy of the German occupation of that port at the end of the nineteenth century.

FRUIT JUICES

Many so-called fruit drinks in the West contain little real fruit juice, and consist mainly of water and such ingredients as sugar, citric acid, artificial sweeteners, coloring, flavoring and carbon dioxide gas.

The Chinese, however, prefer to use real fruit juice and unrefined sugar or the actual sugar cane. The sugar cane is boiled in water for several hours until all the sugar is extracted, and then the fruit juice is added according to the individual taste.

Here, the Chinese have plenty of scope, for there is an abundance of fruits of all kinds in China, especially in the south, including oranges, lemons, grapefruits, peaches, cherries, plums, melons, apples, bananas, pears, grapes, pineapples, litchis, loquats, kumquats, mangoes, pawpaws and kiwi fruits.

RAINBOW WATER

$^1/_2$ **cucumber**
8 red cherries
2 slices melon
1 apple
1 orange
2 slices lemon
6 grapes, green or black
4 large plums
1 sprig fresh parsley
icing sugar

Core and peel the fruits where necessary, chop them into small pieces and put them, together with the parsley, into a jug of $3^1/_2$ pints capacity. Fill the jug with boiling water, allow to stand overnight, add sugar to taste, and then store in a refrigerator until required.

SOUPS

Soups are generally the most delectable and exotic components of a Chinese meal. They are also of value medicinally, for herbal medicines are usually administered in soups.

Unlike a Western-style soup, which is thick and heavy and almost constitutes a meal in itself, a Chinese-style soup is thin and light and is consumed as a beverage rather than as a substantial course, though it is likely to be highly nutritious.

The ingredients in a Western-style soup are integral parts of it, whereas a Chinese-style soup consists of a basic stock to which other ingredients are added almost as an afterthought. For example, a Western tomato soup is red; but, in a Chinese tomato soup, the tomatoes are cooked quickly and separately and then added to the stock, where they float on the surface. The soup therefore remains pale in color.

CHICKEN STOCK

The stock for a Chinese soup is usually made from chicken. The liquid in which chicken has been boiled could be used as stock; otherwise, one could proceed as follows:

1lb chicken remnants, cooked or uncooked – bones, backs, feet, wings, necks, gizzards, etc.
1 slice fresh ginger
2 spring onions
1 small clove garlic
¼ teaspoon salt
pinch of sugar
pinch of black pepper
¼ teaspoon dried parsley
½ teaspoon soy sauce, light or dark

Clean the chicken remnants, put them in a large wok or pan, cover with 2½ pints water, simmer gently, and skim off the scum without disturbing the stock. Do *not* allow the stock to boil.

Slice the ginger into very thin strips, chop the onions finely, crush the garlic clove, and add them, together with the other ingredients, to the stock. Simmer over low heat for 3 hours, replacing the water lost as steam. Strain the stock so that it contains no debris.

Stand to cool, and then skim off any fat on top.

If a larger amount of stock is required, increase the quantities in the proportions of 6oz chicken remnants to each 1 pint water.

PRAWN AND EGG-FLOWER SOUP

1 spring onion
6oz peeled cooked prawns
½ teaspoon light soy sauce
½ teaspoon salt
2½ pints chicken stock
2 eggs

Chop the onion and prawns finely, add them, together with the soy sauce and salt, to the stock, heat but do *not* boil, and simmer gently for 2 minutes.

Beat the eggs well and slowly pour into the soup to produce thin flower-effect shreds.

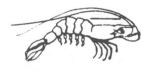

WATER

People take a wide variety of drinks, and for a wide variety of reasons: as a stimulant, soporific (sleep-inducer), aperient, appetizer or a means to quench the thirst. But the main reason for drinking is that it provides the water which the body needs. Water is not a food, for it contains no nutrients, but it is vital to our existence. This is why the Chinese, who are as sensible in their drinking habits as they are in all else, attach much importance to the intake of pure water; they do not despise it, even though it is the humblest and cheapest of drinks.

In China, it is the general practice for all water intended for drinking, whatever its source, to be boiled. It is a practice that we should follow in the West, for the water available on tap is not always as potable as the authorities would have us believe, and the sparkling spring water which comes to us in attractively-labeled bottles may contain, in addition to mineral salts that are beneficial to the health, pathogenic micro-organisms, which are damaging to the health. In fact, spa water may be less safe to drink than tap water. However, boiling does not destroy those poisonous chemicals which occur where water is contaminated by fertilizers and suchlike.

Boiled water makes a good start for the day if it is drunk before breakfast, for it offsets the dehydration which has occurred during the night.

WINES AND SPIRITS

In China, wines and spirits are generally reserved for special occasions. The Chinese never drink on an empty stomach, so food is always served with wine. Excessive drinking is regarded with disfavor, but wine is regarded as a health remedy if it is taken in moderation. Li Shizhen (1518–1593), the eminent Ming physician, wrote of wine: "A beautiful gift from heaven which, if taken moderately…brings joy and disposes of melancholy." Most Chinese wines are made from rice, but a few are made from wheat, millet and various fruits.

MEDICINAL WINES

Chinese folk remedies include hundreds of medicinal wines, which are made by steeping herbs in wine or spirit for several months (see individual recipes for the varying lengths of time, but be prepared to be patient). The alcohol acts as a stimulant and extracts the active ingredients and facilitates their absorption into the bloodstream.

Medicinal wines are very potent, so they must be taken with great care. Generally, the daily dosage must *not* exceed 3fl oz, and they must *not* be taken for a period of more than three months, which must be followed by a rest period of at least one month before the treatment is resumed. They must *not* be taken by a pregnant woman, nor by anyone with one of the following conditions: poor digestion, common cold, influenza, heart condition, weak constitution, cancer.

CHRYSANTHEMUM WINE

This wine is taken as an aperitif or a nightcap. It clears the head, improves the vision and inhibits the ageing process. But it should *not* be taken by anyone with hypertension.

2oz white/yellow chrysanthemum flowers
1 pint rice/white wine
3oz refined sugar

Detach the stems from the flowers and put all the ingredients into a large clean jar. Cover, seal and store in a cool, dry, dark and undisturbed place. After 12 months, strain the wine, discarding the flowers, and store for another 12 months before drinking.

DANDELION WINE

Proceed as for chrysanthemum wine, but replace the chrysanthemum flowers with 2oz dandelion flowers.

The Chinese take this wine as an aperitif and to relieve headaches, influenza and constipation. No more than two small glasses should be drunk daily.

FIG WINE

This wine is a remedy for constipation, exhaustion, anemia and hypertension. It has a tonic effect on the stomach and intestines. Two small glasses per day is the maximum dosage.

peel of a large lemon
6oz dried figs
1 pint rice/white wine
1¹/₂oz refined sugar

Finely chop the lemon peel and enclose it in muslin. Put all the ingredients – do not wash the figs – together with the lemon peel in muslin, into a large clean jar, cover, seal and store where cool, dry, dark and undisturbed. After a month, dispose of the lemon peel. Reseal and store again. After five months, dispose of the figs. Store for one year before drinking.

WOLFBERRY WINE

3oz dried wolfberries (*Lycium chinense*)
1 pint rice/white wine
3oz honey

Do not wash the berries. Put all the ingredients into a large clean jar, cover, seal and store in a cool, dry, dark undisturbed place. After 12 months, strain the wine. It is now ready for drinking. This wine is an ageing-inhibitor and a panacea for many ills, including kidney disorders and diabetes. It improves male virility. One small glass per day is the maximum dosage.

PEACH WINE

This wine is drunk as an appetizer and a blood cleanser and to relieve constipation. Two small glasses per day is the recommended dosage.

5 unripe peaches
1 pint rice/white wine
1½ oz refined sugar

Quarter, but do not wash, the peaches. Put all the ingredients into a large, clean jar, cover, seal and store where cool, dry, dark and undisturbed. After 9 months, strain and put into a clean bottle.

OTHER WINES

Other commonly used medicinal wines include persimmon wine and red date (jujube) wine, which are made in a way similar to those above.

HEALTH
AND
MEDICINE

CHINESE HEALTH FOODS

中國健康食物

To be healthy,
eat the Chinese way!

In the West, a sharp distinction is made between medicines and health foods. The former are regarded as non-nutritious substances with specific remedial properties, whereas the latter are regarded as foods which, in addition to being nutritious, have health-giving or medicinal properties, and include such items as vitamin supplements, food concentrates and organically-grown fruit and vegetables. In China, there is no sharp distinction, and medicines often have the character of foods and vice versa. Furthermore, in China, medicines are usually administered as special ingredients in soups and other dishes.

Fruit is a most important item of a healthy diet, as the Chinese know well. It provides roughage, sugars in their most easily assimilable forms, minerals and vitamins A and C; as fruit is usually eaten raw, the vitamins are not destroyed by cooking. Fresh fruit should always be washed before it is eaten if there is any possibility that it may have been contaminated by pesticides.

Figs are soft, pear-shaped, many-seeded fruits, which are eaten fresh or dried. They are very nutritious and rich in iron and vitamin C – the "sunshine vitamin." They are also a good source of natural sugar. Medicinally, they are consumed as a dessert or in soups as a laxative and a treatment for conjunctivitis, hemorrhoids and halitosis. If raw figs are eaten daily over a long period, they will improve the digestion and the complexion – but it is likely that there will be some frequent visits to the toilet.

Haws are the small red fruits of the hawthorn, of which there are several species. Those used in China, both as a health food and as a medicine, contain vitamin C, and are added to soups and stews and confectionery. The haws of British species may be used similarly. In medicine, the Chinese take haws as a stomachic and digestive. They are a treatment for pain in the scrotum, postnatal abdominal pain and diarrhoea. They dilate veins and arteries, reducing blood pressure, and dissolve deposits of cholesterol in blood vessels.

Blackberries are the fruits of the bramble, of which there are many species. They are succulent, sweet and blue-black in color. They are rich in iron and vitamin C, and are much relished as a dessert. The Chinese use the unripe berries medicinally as an astringent, a tonic for the kidneys and a treatment for poor vision, impotence, spermatorrhoea, incontinence, bed-wetting and premature ejaculation. *Rubus coreanus* is the species generally used for this purpose in Britain.

Kanlans, or Chinese olives, *Canarium album*, are not related to the European olive, *Olea europaea*. They are small, oily, pale yellow, plum-shaped fruits, which are used as an antipyretic and an astringent, and to reduce inflammation. They are considered to be a good remedy for seafood poisoning. European olives are somewhat larger than kanlans, and yellow-green when unripe, and black when ripe. Their oil, which is used in cooking and medicine, is very nutritive. Being unsaturated, it is easily digested and has no harmful effects. In fact, it has been said that olive oil can be consumed without ill-effects by people with gastric or duodenal ulcers.

Mandarin oranges, and indeed oranges of any kind, should be included in the diet as a source of vitamin C. The Chinese dry and store the peel as a standby. It contains vitamins A and C and those of the B-complex. It is used as an expectorant and as a digestive and stomachic to relieve dyspepsia, flatulence, nausea, vomiting and abdominal pain. The seeds, ground into a powder, are used as an analgesic.

Bananas are flavorsome and of exotic appearance. Commonly eaten as a dessert in both China and the West, they are very nutritious. They are rich in protein, carbohydrate, minerals and vitamins. They also provide roughage and are easily digested. They are a valuable health food, and physicians sometimes prescribe them for certain illnesses, especially those of children and elderly persons.

Citrons are similar to lemons in appearance, but larger, less sour and thicker skinned. A source of vitamin C, they are used as a tonic food and as a treatment for indigestion, bronchitis, coughs and asthma. For indigestion, they are boiled with chicken or pork to make a soup. For coughs and bronchitis, they are steamed with sugar and honey and eaten once daily until the symptoms subside. For asthma, they are dried and then combined with some of the other herbs which are used in treating asthma, such as apricots and coltsfoot.

Vegetables have the same kind of dietary importance as fruit. They provide roughage, minerals and vitamins, though vitamin C is not predominant. They do not contain large quantities of sugar, but in some, such as peas, beans and yams, there is an abundance of starch. Green leafy vegetables contain all the minerals except iodine, and all the vitamins except D and K. However, vitamin K is contained in tomatoes. An ample intake of vegetables is a positive aid to health, and the real benefit of vegetables to the Chinese is that they consume them in much larger quantities than do people in the West, so ensuring a sufficiency of dietary fibre.

Soya beans yield a wide selection of food products: sauces, pastes, bean curds of various kinds, meat-substitutes, soya-bean milk, bean sprouts, etc. Yet, strangely enough, the unprocessed beans, whether cooked or uncooked, are indigestible and their nutrients are not easily assimilated. Rich in protein, vitamin A, B-complex vitamins, iron, calcium, starch and fibre, they are highly nutritious and, weight for weight, contain more protein than any other plant or animal product, and twice as much protein as beef.

Carrots, of which there are many varieties, come in different shapes and sizes. They are highly nutritious, being rich in vitamins and minerals. Their bright orange color is due to the presence of the pigment carotene, which is also present in green vegetables, but is masked by the green pigment chlorophyll. They are a good source of vitamin A, which is essential to growth, the functions of the skin and cells, and the health of the eyes. Night-blindness is one of the symptoms of deficiency in vitamin A. Carrots are present in most Chinese herbal soups.

Bamboo shoots are commonly served in Chinese take-away restaurants. They can be purchased in cans, making them simple to prepare and cook. Canned bamboo shoots are young and tender, so they are easily digested. They contain small amounts of carbohydrate, protein, minerals, vitamin C and B-complex vitamins, but their chief merit is that they provide bulk, which breaks up fat in the bowel, and gives texture and homogeneity to meat dishes. They absorb liquids, ensuring an even meaty flavor, though little meat may be used.

Onions, and also shallots, leeks and chives, are closely related to garlic and have similar medicinal properties, though they are less potent. They are mildly antiseptic, good for the complexion and aperient in their effects. If they are a regular part of the diet, there should be no constipation and fewer pimples. Onions and garlic are good for rheumatism, and their juices can be applied to insect bites and stings.

Legumes, which include peas, runner beans, peanuts and soya beans, are plants with pod fruits. They come next to the cereals in nutritional importance, and are very rich in protein, starch, minerals, vitamins and dietary fibre. In a purely vegetarian diet, they are regarded as a good substitute for meat. People who feel they have need of an aphrodisiac could do well to eat more beans.

Dandelions are relished as a vegetable in China, whereas in the West they are more frequently despised as a troublesome weed. They are rich in vitamins and iron and other minerals. Their bitter-tasting leaves add zest to salad dishes. During both the World Wars, the Germans used dried dandelion roots as a coffee substitute. The dandelion has medicinal properties, and any part of it may be used as an antipyretic and to reduce swellings.

Sweet potatoes, or batatas, are native to the Pacific slopes of South America, but they are now grown in all parts of China, where they are firmly established as the third most important food crop, after rice and wheat. Heavy-cropping, highly nutritious and deliciously flavored, they are a most useful adjunct to the diet of the Chinese. Their roots are farinaceous, and so are very rich in carbohydrate. They are also easily digested. These days, they are readily obtainable at many food stores in the West.

Parsley is used in Chinese dishes, especially those prepared in the West, as a substitute for coriander. It is rich in iron, magnesium, calcium, vitamins A and C and vitamins in the B-complex group, and so is a useful addition to any dish. Its pungent and distinctive flavor makes it valuable as a garnish or an ingredient in salads. It has medicinal uses, being of benefit to the kidneys, stimulating the digestive system, preventing and relieving rheumatism and clearing the complexion. It may be used as a dressing for sore eyes and as a poultice for sprains.

Fungi grow very easily and in great profusion in the hot wet regions of South China. As a result they are consumed in larger quantities and in greater variety in China than in the West. They are a boon to the Chinese, for many have valuable medicinal properties, though a few are poisonous. By contrast, many Westerners have never tasted any fungus other than the common mushroom, *Agaricus campestris*. However, this has its merits, too. Though it contains few nutrients, it provides roughage, is easily digested and contains minute traces of chemical substances which benefit the health.

Winter mushrooms, which are obtainable at Chinese grocery stores in the West, have a blackish-brown leathery appearance. They are always purchased in the dried state, and need to be well soaked before use. When cooked with meat, they provide a highly nutritious and perfectly balanced meal. They are rich in vitamins, especially those in the B-complex, of which vitamin B_{12} is predominant. They are a tonic for the nervous system, and help prevent cancer and anemia. They also reduce hypertension (high blood pressure) and give some immunity against viruses and epidemic diseases generally.

Nuts are a prominent feature of the Chinese diet, and those commonly consumed include sweet almonds, bitter almonds, cashew-nuts, chestnuts, gingko nuts, peanuts, pine nuts and walnuts, as well as lotus, pumpkin and sesame seeds. All are very rich in protein. Weight for weight, peanuts contain more protein than does beef steak. Nuts tend to be indigestible, but the Chinese cook them to break down the tough fibres. Bitter almonds should be avoided, for they contain prussic acid (hydrocyanic acid), which is a poison.

Coconut milk is the colorless, sweetish sap that fills almost the whole of the inside of the unripe nut at the center of the fruit of the coconut palm, *Cocos nucifera*. It makes a pleasant, thirst-quenching drink. As the nut ripens, the milk assumes a whitish appearance, and, though it does not have the same nutritional value as cow's milk, it may be used as a healthy alternative for those who, for dietary reasons, are restricted in their intake of cow's milk.

Ginger is one of the cheapest of the spices, and it is used extensively by the Chinese. It is generally called root ginger, though the so-called root is actually a rhizome, or swollen underground stem. It owes its medicinal properties to the presence of a volatile oil, phenols and alkaloids. Fresh or dried, it is warming, pungent, antiseptic and stomachic. It stimulates the circulation, dissolves phlegm and promotes perspiration. It is a remedy for colds, chills, coughs, nausea, vomiting, colic, spasms and travel sickness.

Barley is a staple food in the north of China, where the climate is too cold for growing rice. As with all cereals, it is rich in carbohydrate, protein, calcium, phosphorus, niacin and thiamine. Barley flour is made into bread; and malt, which is sprouting barley grains, is used together with yeast and hops in brewing. Beer makes a good nightcap, and any yeast it contains has an aperient effect. Barley water, made by steeping barley grains in water, is a mild diuretic, a treatment for loss of appetite, a general tonic during pregnancy and, needless to say, a refreshing drink.

*To know things unconsciously is good,
but to pretend to know what you don't
know is sickness. To avoid sickness, one
must be aware of the sickness of sickness.*

Tao Te Ching

Abalone, a marine mollusc abundant in the coastal waters of South China and California, but in other parts of the world generally available only in cans, is a source of protein, a little fat, minerals and vitamins. It also provides salt and iodine in a natural form. It is boiled with lean pork to make a soup which is consumed as a treatment for a poor liver condition, of which the usual symptoms are giddiness, headaches and insomnia. This soup is also a remedy for fevers and tuberculosis. Cooked together with a pig's bladder, abalone is a traditional treatment for women's ailments.

Shellfish, whether they are crustaceans, such as crabs and lobsters, or molluscs, such as oysters and mussels, are a source of protein, polyunsaturated fat, sea salt, niacin, thiamine, vitamin A and phosphorus, iodine and other minerals. They are easily cooked and digested, and they confer the same benefits as marine fish. They can relieve those with goiter, asthma or nervous and mental disorders. "More seafood and less meat" could be a watchword for those who value their health and peace of mind.

Fish liver oil contains a great concentration of health-giving substances – among other things, vitamins A and D and a number of polyunsaturated fatty acids, which are known collectively as Omega 3. For many years in the West, proprietary brands of cod-liver oil, flavored with orange juice and malt, have been used to provide energy and resistance to illness, and salmon oil, which is cheaply available in capsule form, is now becoming popular as a source of polysaturated oils and vitamins A and D.

Poultry is rated very highly by the Chinese, their favorites being duck, chicken, goose and pigeon. These birds are sources of fat, protein and B-complex vitamins, and their flesh is usually white, soft-textured and more digestible than that of mammals. They are generally precooked by boiling to remove excess fat. Chicken stock is the basis of many of the Chinese medicinal soups. The Chinese fully utilize the offals: liver, intestines, gizzard, crop, feet, kidneys, etc. The liver is a source of iron, vitamins A and D and folic acid. It is useful in the treatment of anemia.

Eggs from both domestic birds and wild birds of many kinds – geese, ducks, hens, pigeons, pheasants, quail, etc. – are consumed by the Chinese, who contend that, since an egg contains all the nutrients required for the growth of the embryo of a bird, it must also contain most of the nutrients required by the human body. In fact, it contains chiefly body-building substances: much protein, a little fat, vitamins A, B_2 and D, calcium, phosphorus and iron. But eggs are susceptible to infection, so they must be purchased fresh, not undercooked and not consumed to excess.

Pork offal is much valued in China for its nutritional and medicinal properties, and is not regarded as the waste products of butchering, fit only to be a poor man's meal, as it often is in the West. Liver contains iron, vitamins A and D and a little glycogen (animal starch). It is good for anemia. Kidneys are a source of vitamin A. The brain is rich in phosphorus, as is all nervous tissue. The heart is cooked as an ingredient of soup, which is consumed as a mild sedative.

Game, which include rabbits, hares, deer, boar, pheasants, quail, wood pigeons and wild duck, are much favored in China as dietary items, and rightly so, for their flesh is healthier than that of domestic animals. The diet of wild animals is more varied and more natural; and, as they range freely and hunt for their food, they have plenty of exercise, do not eat too much and therefore do not become fat and listless. Also, the sickly animals soon become prey to other animals, so that it is only the healthy ones which survive and breed, producing more healthy animals – a good example of the survival of the fittest!

Vinegar is essentially a very dilute, 3–6 per cent, solution of ethanoic acid – what was called acetic acid prior to the introduction of the current system of nomenclature in chemistry. It is an irritant, and yet, for reasons which are somewhat obscure, the physicians of China assure us that it is a most desirable item of diet. Certainly, it is an internal antiseptic: micro-organisms are not likely to survive in a sweet-and-sour sauce. Also, there is some evidence that vinegar reduces blood pressure. As the Chinese are rarely wrong in matters of diet, vinegar may perhaps be regarded as a health food.

There are many Chinese dishes which, by virtue of their ingredients or mode of preparation, have valuable health-giving or remedial properties.

WHITE RICE PORRIDGE

A porridge of rice may be used medicinally as an effective and natural treatment for constipation, diarrhoea, nausea, loss of appetite, flatulence, hangovers and other conditions which result from over-indulgence in food or drink.

8 tablespoons rice
1 tablespoon chopped
  orange peel

Put the ingredients into a wok/pan, add $1^3/_4$ pints water, and boil vigorously until the porridge has a milky appearance. Serve boiling hot, and consume in gentle sips. This is a nourishing dish for invalids and elderly people.

SWEET-AND-SOUR SAUCE

Because of its antiseptic properties, sweet-and-sour sauce is a valuable item of diet. Home-made sweet-and-sour sauce is preferable to that which may be purchased at a grocery store.

1 slice fresh ginger
1 tablespoon cornstarch
6 tablespoons wine vinegar
1 tablespoon soy sauce
2 tablespoons brown sugar
1 tablespoon tomato
  purée/ketchup
$1/_4$ pint chicken stock
pinch of salt
large pinch of pepper
1 tablespoon marmalade

Finely chop the ginger, and mix the cornstarch with just enough water to make a smooth paste. Blend all the ingredients together in a wok or pan, bring to the boil, stirring all the time, and simmer for 2 minutes until translucent.

This sauce can be bottled and stored in a refrigerator until required. If a larger amount is needed, increase the quantities of the ingredients in proportion.

SWEET-AND-SOUR CRISPY NOODLES

Noodles are a good source of protein, carbohydrate, calcium, iron and other minerals for athletes and growing children. The vinegar in the sweet-and-sour sauce has internal-antiseptic properties.

2oz cooked lean pork
10 tablespoons sweet-and-sour sauce (see page 211)
8oz egg noodles
vegetable oil for deep-frying

Thinly slice the pork. Heat, but do not boil, the sauce in a small pan for about 2 minutes, and keep hot.

Put 3$^1/_2$ pints water into a wok/pan, bring to the boil, add the noodles, continue to boil for 10 minutes, and then drain well.

Deep-fry the noodles in hot oil until crispy and golden, drain well, serve in a warm dish and top with the pork slices and sauce according to taste.

ONION SOUP

This dish is warming in cold weather and has a gentle laxative effect.

1 tablespoon cornstarch
2 slices fresh ginger
2 pints chicken stock
2 onions
1 teaspoon salt
pinch of black pepper

Mix the cornstarch with just enough water to make a smooth paste. Add this, together with the ginger, to the stock, bring to the boil, stirring well, and simmer for 5 minutes.

Finely chop the onions, add them, together with the remaining ingredients, to the stock, stir and simmer for 10 minutes. Serve immediately.

BRAISED FISH WITH PINEAPPLE

Two or three meals of oily fish each week could reduce the possibility of defects of the heart and circulation.

2lb whole bass/trout
2 teaspoons salt
1 small can pineapple
2 spring onions
$^1/_2$ teaspoon ground ginger
2 teaspoons peanut oil
1 tablespoon light soy sauce

Cut and wash the fish, scrape off the scales, but do not remove the head, tail and fins. Put into a wok or pan, cover with cold water, add the salt, bring to the boil, cover and simmer for 5 minutes. Place the fish in a large shallow dish.

Chop the pineapple and onions, put into a small pan, together with the pineapple juice and other ingredients, heat gently, stir, pour over the fish and serve at once.

Martial artists will need plenty of rice, noodles and other energy and growth foods in their diet.

Kung fu

功夫

TARO STARCH JELLY

This highly nutritious energy-giving dish is very suitable for elderly people and invalids with an impaired digestion.

6 tablespoons sugar
4 tablespoons taro starch
(available at a health food shop
or a Chinese grocery store)

Put the sugar and taro starch into a large heat-resistant dish, add 1³/₄ pints boiling water, stir vigorously and set aside to cool.

Consume when a cold jelly has formed. It can be eaten hot, but it is less appetizing that way.

PORK WITH PEANUTS

The Chinese generally stew peanuts with pork, which renders them more digestible and eliminates the phytic acid they contain. Phytic acid inhibits the absorption of calcium, magnesium, zinc and iron.

4oz mushrooms
2 spring onions
2oz white cabbage/ Chinese leaves
1 clove garlic
1lb lean pork
1 teaspoon salt
3 tablespoons peanut oil
1 tablespoon light soy sauce
1 teaspoon cornstarch
1 tablespoon rice wine/sherry
¼ pint chicken stock
8oz shelled peanuts

Wash the vegetables, slice the cabbage and mushrooms, crush the garlic, chop the onions and shred the pork.

Sprinkle the onions with the salt, stir-fry in 1 tablespoon peanut oil for 3 minutes and drain.

Mix the pork, soy sauce, cornstarch, garlic and wine/sherry, and stir-fry quickly in 2 tablespoons peanut oil in a separate wok or pan for 2 minutes. Add the stock, peanuts, onions, mushrooms and cabbage and cook for 2–3 minutes. Serve immediately.

猪

SALMON SOUP

This soup is nutritious, health-giving, appetizing and inexpensive.

2 large salmon heads
2 spring onions
3 tomatoes
2 thin slices fresh ginger
1 teaspoon light soy sauce
¹/₂ teaspoon salt
pinch of black pepper
¹/₂ teaspoon coriander seeds
1 teaspoon sesame oil

Clean and wash the salmon heads, chop the onions, quarter the tomatoes, and immerse in 2¹/₂ pints water in a wok or pan. Add all the remaining ingredients, bring to the boil, and then simmer slowly for 2 hours, replacing the water lost as steam.

To serve, slowly decant or strain the liquid, leaving the debris behind.

GINGER AND ONION SAUCE

This dip-in sauce for meat and poultry dishes combines the aperient effect of onions with the carminative effect of ginger.

3 spring onions
3 slices fresh ginger
2 teaspoons salt
1 teaspoon light soy sauce
4 tablespoons peanut oil

Finely chop the onions and ginger, and mix them together with salt and soy sauce in a pan. Heat the oil in a wok/pan until it is smoking, and then pour it on the mixture in the pan. After a few seconds of sizzling, the sauce will be ready for use. It should be used at once, for it does not store well.

DIETARY REMEDIES

Allow your food to be your medicine, and your medicine your food.

Hippocrates

The following dietary remedies, most of which are of ancient origin, have been derived from the folklore of China.

ACNE

An infusion of $^1/_{10}$oz flowers of the peach, *Prunus persica*, or almond, *Prunus amygdalus*, in 1 pint water, consumed daily, is considered to be an effective treatment.

ANEMIA

Chopped raw pig's liver and winter mushrooms help combat anemia (but not pernicious anemia) if consumed as ordinary items of diet. Winter mushrooms need to be stood in cold water for some time before they are steamed, stir-fried or added to soups.

Fig wine also counteracts anemia. The recommended daily dosage is two small glasses.

ANXIETY

Raw carrots and lettuce have a soothing effect. Also effective is an infusion of $^1/_{30}$–$^1/_8$oz leaves and flowers of camomile *Matricaria chamomilla*, in 1 pint water, to be consumed in three separate parts on the same day.

ARTHRITIS

Cinnamon tea sometimes gives relief. This is made as an infusion of $^1/_{15}$–$^1/_6$ oz bark of Chinese cinnamon, *Cinnamomum cassia*, in 1 pint water to be consumed in three separate parts on the same day.

For cold arthritis of the feet, steep 1oz sage in rice wine or gin for about two weeks. During cold weather, drink a little each day.

For warm arthritis, drink an infusion of $^1/_3$–1oz of purslane, *Portalaca oleracea*, in 1 pint water.

ATHLETE'S FOOT

Add 1 pint vinegar and several crushed garlic cloves to a large bowl full of hot water. Immerse the feet in this liquid for about 30 minutes. Repeat this process until the condition is cured. This may take a long time.

BAD BREATH

Chew a few leaves of peppermint or the peel of a mandarin orange.

BRONCHITIS

Finely chop 1 pear, 4 fresh water chestnuts and 1 slice of a fresh lotus rhizome, and steep them in pint hot water for about 1 hour. Drink the liquid slowly over a period of one day.

CATARRH AND SINUS DISORDERS

Consume a stew of lean pork, orange peel, coriander, ginger and white pepper.

CHILLS AND COLDS

Make a decoction of a mixture of $1/2$oz of each of finely chopped *cong bai* ("Chinese spring onion'"), ground cinnamon, dried ginger and honey or brown sugar by adding them to 1 pint water and reducing to $1/2$ pint of liquid by boiling. Sip this liquid slowly and occasionally over a period of one day. Repeat this process until the cold or chill is alleviated.

COMPLEXION

The complexion can be improved by nourishing the skin. To do this, chop 3oz mushrooms and stir-fry them with 8oz soya bean sprouts and 1oz sesame seeds or $1/2$ teaspoon sesame oil. Serve with noodles or rice. Prepare and consume this dish as often as possible if there is to be a pronounced effect.

CONSTIPATION

Some remedies are fig wine, stewed pears and bananas eaten cold with honey, and 1oz finely chopped walnuts with $1/2$oz honey, also eaten cold.

COUGHS

Add a dessertspoon of honey to 1 pint warm water, stir and sip gently. This also has a soothing effect on a sore throat.

DEBILITY

Pig's feet cooked in black rice vinegar is a remedy for debility and some other conditions, including blood clots, poor circulation, flatulence and irregular bowel movements. For mothers during the postnatal period, it increases lactation and alleviates tension.

Ingredients: 4 eggs, 4 pig's feet, 2oz green ginger, 1 pint black rice vinegar (from a Chinese grocer), 1 teaspoon salt, 3oz sugar.

Boil the eggs hard and shell them. Wash the feet, burning off the bristles with a candle flame, and scrub and rinse them. Soak the ginger in boiling water, scrape off the skin, crush slightly and fry without oil in a wok or pan until dry and fragrant. Put the vinegar into an earthenware pot, add the salt, ginger and sugar, bring to the boil, cover and simmer for 40 minutes. Add the feet, bring to the boil, cover and simmer gently for 3 hours. Add the eggs, marinate for 8 hours, and then serve at room temperature.

DEPRESSION

An effective treatment is a tea made by infusing a mixture of 1oz crushed wheat grains and ^{1}/$_3$oz roots of Chinese liquorice, *Glycyrrhiza uralensis*, and adding ^{1}/$_3$oz honey or brown sugar.

DIARRHEA

Make a tea by infusing 2 tablespoons each of powdered ginger and green tea in 1 pint boiling water. Sip gently.

FEVERISHNESS

Simmer winter melon with black mushrooms, shellfish and pork, chicken or pigeon for several hours. Consume as a soup.

FLATULENCE

Chew the seeds of the mandarin orange.

GASTRITIS AND STOMACH ACIDITY

Add 8 tablespoons white rice and 3 slices fresh ginger or the peel of half a mandarin orange to 1 pint water, and then simmer gently until a sticky and milky liquid is formed. Sip the liquid gently, preferably while still hot. Avoid acid, spicy and fried food.

GIDDINESS

Boil abalone with lean pork, and consume as a soup.

HEMORRHOIDS

Simmer 4oz rice and 1oz each of walnuts, almonds, sesame seeds, pine nuts and peach kernels in 3^1/$_2$ pints water. Consume as a soup.

HAIR LOSS AND GREYING

Finely chop a carrot, an apple and a quarter of a lemon, add 1^3/$_4$ pints boiling water, and allow to stand until cool. Consume the whole of this liquid on the same day.

HANGOVER

Make an infusion of 6 haws (the fruits of the hawthorn) in 1 pint boiling water. Sip gently.

Also, consume plenty of liquids, particularly meat and fish soups, to replace the potassium and sodium salts lost by perspiration.

INCONTINENCE

Steam a pig's bladder with dried hops, and consume as an ordinary item of diet.

INFLUENZA

An infusion of one of the following, slowly sipped, is helpful:

> **Dandelion, all parts, $^1/_3$–1 oz**
> **Garlic, 3 cloves**
> **Onion, bulb, $^2/_3$–1 $^1/_3$oz**
> **Marigold, flowers, $^1/_{10}$–$^1/_3$oz**
> **Corn mint, leaves, $^1/_{15}$–$^1/_8$oz**
> **Chrysanthemum, flowers, $^1/_8$–$^1/_3$oz**

LIBIDO

To strengthen the sexual organs and improve the libido, stir-fry a mixture of 2oz each of longan fruits, *Euphoria longan*, black sesame seeds, black dates (jujubes) and chopped walnuts which have been softened by steeping. Serve with boiled rice or noodles.

MORNING SICKNESS

Add 2oz sliced fresh ginger to 1$^3/_4$ pints water, bring to the boil, simmer for 10 minutes, and then sip gently.

WRINKLES

Include generous amounts of soya bean sprouts in the diet.

WORMS

The inclusion of musk pumpkin, *Cucurbita moschata*, and garlic in the diet helps to prevent or eliminate worms.

To eliminate pin-worms (threadworms) consume a decoction of $^1/_6$oz peel of pomegranate each day for 8 days.

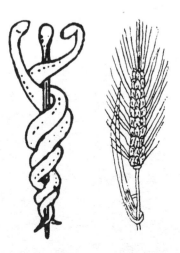

HEALTH HINTS

Rule youth well, for age will rule itself.

Proverb

For most people, it is possible to live to a great age, and be healthy and youthful in the process, by following the keep-fit rules listed below. Though fitness and youthfulness are highly desirable aims which can be achieved by adopting the right techniques, they cannot be guaranteed, for the unexpected can always happen.

These rules are quite simple, and putting them into practice need not be a time-consuming process.

1

Consult a physician at once if you have doubts about your health, for prevention is better than cure.

2

Treat minor ailments immediately so that they do not have a chance to develop into conditions which are acute or chronic or even incurable.

3

Think young in all that you say and do.

4

Adopt the Chinese diet. Failing that, ensure that your meals are balanced and varied, and consume more vegetables, fruit, cereals and fish, and less red meat, animal fats, sugar, salt and foods containing synthetic additives.

5

Supplement your diet with Chinese-style health foods and tonic medicines, including ageing inhibitors; but do this only occasionally, not on a regular basis.

6

Do not eat or drink too much or too little.

7

Every day, consume one garlic clove, preferably fresh, crushed and chopped.

8

Every day, before breakfast, take a big drink of water which has been boiled.

9

Take up a gentle form of the martial arts, such as tai chi chuan. Failing that, take a long and gentle walk twice daily.

10

Every day, do some deep breathing in clean air – if you can find some clean air – before an open window in the early morning and late evening.

11

Be moderate and regular in all that you do – diet, alcohol, exercise, rest, sleep, sex, work and play – to prevent illness, injury and social friction.

12

Avoid the vices of smoking, drug-taking, gambling and casual sex.

13

Work with, not against, nature. Avoid unnatural acts.

14

Be clean personally and in handling food, but do not become a hygiene crank, for that would not help your body, though it could upset your mind.

15

Worry less, laugh more and do not miss out on sleep.

16

Avoid stressful situations as far as possible.

17

Consult the *I Ching* when you have a problem. Its great wisdom may help you.

18

Meditate when you have a problem. This is best done in bed where, alone and undisturbed, you will be able to think deeply, and also fantasize to give your mind a "holiday."

19

Give yourself good *fung shui* by ensuring that your living, working and leisure conditions are favorable to your health and well-being.

20

Keep a check on your heart by measuring your weight and blood pressure occasionally.

THE GOLDEN RULE

You will find that life will be much easier for you and the people around you if you abide by Confucius' "golden rule": *What you do not want done to yourself, do not do to others.* And always keep in mind his five cardinal virtues: wisdom, justice, honesty, benevolence and propriety.

HEALTH RULES FOR THE ELDERLY

Those who have had a long and healthy life do not want their twilight years to be marred by minor ailments and other adverse conditions which could easily be prevented. The following rules, which are simple and mainly to do with diet, will help:

Do not eat too much meat, too much salty food, too much sweet food, too much spicy and fine food, too fully and too quickly.

Do not drink unboiled water and too much alcohol.

Do eat on time, keep active, smile and be cheerful, and get your sleep.

TCM

Traditional Chinese medicine, for which TCM is the usual abbreviation, is the oldest and finest system of medicine in the world. Its main features are as follows.

KEEPING FIT

TCM is based on the assumption that good health is not simply the absence of illness, but a state of fitness in which a person is full of vigor and purpose or, to use a Western idiom, "fighting fit and glowing with health."

Someone who is in a normal state of health can keep fit by having regular exercise, fresh air, a balanced and varied diet, moderate habits, some knowledge of those herbal medicines and other forms of therapy which may be used in the treatment of minor ailments, and enough common sense to consult a physician if he or she should become seriously ill or have doubts about their health.

THE CHINESE PHYSICIAN

Chinese physicians not only provide remedies for illnesses but also give advice and treatments to prolong the lives of patients and maintain them in a state of youthful vigor. In this endeavor, they pay particular attention to the vital organs, blood, climatic conditions and humors.

PREVENTION

In one way or another, TCM provides preventive or curative treatment or some degree of alleviation for all the ills to which the human flesh is heir. The emphasis is on prevention, which makes sense, for many of the illnesses which are virtually incurable, such as those of the heart and circulation, can generally be prevented by a little forethought in matters of diet, exercise, personal habits and a judicious use of herbal medicines and remedial exercises. It is no accident that there is a low incidence of cancer and diabetes in China.

The human body may be likened to an automobile. Both require fuel of the right quality, regular maintenance and more than a little loving care, and will deteriorate if over-worked or allowed to be completely idle. If damaged, neither will be as good as it was originally.

ALLOPATHY

TCM is allopathic, as is Western medicine, by and large. Allopathy is a system of medicine by which a treatment is applied to induce a condition which is opposite in nature to that caused by the illness. Do we in the West not apply the same principle when we "starve a fever and feed a cold"?

*Treat hot illnesses with
cooling medicines,
and cold illnesses with
warming medicines*

The Pharmacopoeia of Shen Nong

In TCM, all illnesses are broadly classified as yin or yang. As one might expect, yin medicines are used to treat yang illnesses, and vice versa, so maintaining the bodily harmony. Yang illnesses are positive and tend to manifest themselves with vigor and hotness, whereas yin illnesses are negative and tend to manifest themselves, but less clearly, through weakness and coldness.

NATUROPATHY

To some extent, TCM is a naturopathic procedure. Naturopathy is a system of medicine in which the body is encouraged to heal itself by diet and physical methods so that there should be no need to resort to drugs. It has many specialized techniques, which include physical and breathing exercises, hydrotherapy and massage. Naturopathy attempts to find the underlying cause of an illness and treat that cause, rather than merely trying to suppress or alleviate the symptoms.

HOMOEOPATHY

There is no homoeopathy in TCM.

ANATOMY

The common names of the bones indicated are as follows: *mandible* jaw-bone, *cervical vertebrae* neck-bones, *clavicle* collar-bone, *scapula* shoulder-blade, *sternum* breastbone, *humerus* upper armbone, *vertebral column* backbone, *pelvis* hip-bone, *radius* and *ulna* lower armbones, *carpals* wrist-bones, *phalanges* toe-bones and finger-bones, *patella* kneecap, *femur* thigh-bone, *tibia* shinbone, *fibula* calf-bone, *tarsals* ankle-bones.

The bones most likely to be fractured are the skull, clavicle, scapula, humerus, vertebral column, radius, ulna, carpals, femur, patella, fibula and tibia.

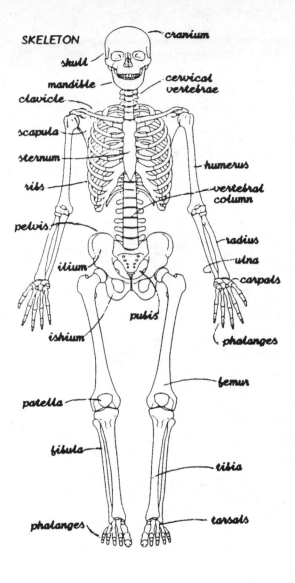

SKELETON

cranium
skull
mandible
cervical vertebrae
clavicle
scapula
sternum
humerus
ribs
vertebral column
pelvis
radius
ilium
ulna
carpals
pubis
ishium
phalanges
femur
patella
fibula
tibia
phalanges
tarsals

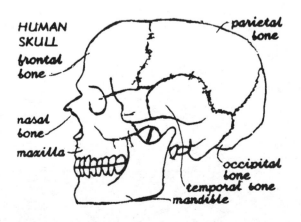

HUMAN SKULL

parietal bone
frontal bone
nasal bone
maxilla
occipital bone
temporal bone
mandible

THE VITAL ORGANS

There are 12 vital organs in Chinese medical theory. Six are hollow and yang, and six are solid and yin. They are arranged in corresponding pairs, each of which is associated with an element, emotion, climate, season, direction, taste, sound, color and planet.

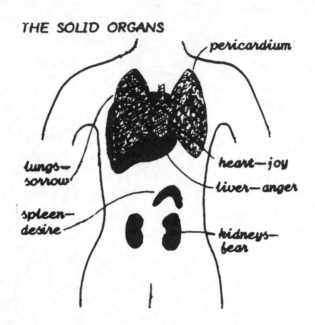

THE SOLID ORGANS

pericardium

lungs—sorrow

heart—joy

liver—anger

spleen—desire

kidneys—fear

Heart and small intestine
fire, joy, hot, summer, south, bitter, laughter, red and Mars.

Lungs and large intestine
metal, anxiety, dry, autumn, west, pungent, weeping, white and Venus.

Liver and gall-bladder
wood, anger, windy, spring, east, sour, shouting, green and Jupiter.

Spleen and stomach
earth, concentration, moist, midsummer, center, sweet, singing, yellow and Saturn.

Kidneys and bladder
water, fear, cold, winter, north, salty, moaning, black and Mercury.

THE SOLID ORGANS

lungs	sorrow
spleen	desire
kidneys	fear
liver	anger
heart	joy

THE HOLLOW ORGANS

Small intestine	joy
Large intestine	anxiety
Gall-bladder	anger
Stomach	concentration (desire)
Bladder	fear

One should note that the pericardium (or heart-constrictor), which is solid, and the triple-warmer, which is hollow and has three openings in the bowel, are not organs in the Western sense of the term. For most practical purposes, they can be disregarded.

THE ELEMENTS

The five elements of Chinese philosophy are fire, earth, metal, water and wood. But they are purely symbolic, and are not real fire, real earth, etc. They are used as convenient labels for concepts and principles, just as scientists in the West use Greek and Roman letters to represent principles and unknown quantities. In TCM, they are used in diagnosis to show the relationship between organs, viscera and symptoms.

Fire	heart, small intestine, blood, endocrine glands, hot.
Earth	spleen, stomach, muscles, damp.
Metal	lungs, large intestine, skin, dry.
Water	kidneys, bladder, bones, cool.
Wood	liver, gall-bladder, nerves, windy.

The relationships between the vital organs and the elements can be shown by a diagram in which the outside arrows indicate the generative, or positive (yang) cycle of elements, and the inside arrows indicate the suppressive, or negative (yin) cycles.

ELEMENT CYCLES

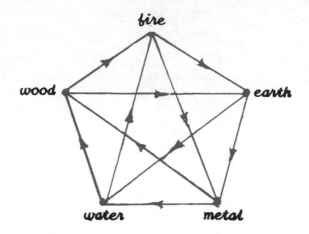

One notices that there is a resemblance to real things.

In the generative cycle, also known as the mother-to-son rule, fire generates ash, or "earth"; earth yields metals from its ores; metal becomes liquid, like water, when it is heated; water encourages the growth of those plants which contain wood; and wood produces fire when it burns.

In the suppressive cycle, which is also known as the victor-and-vanquished rule, fire melts metal, metal cuts wood, woody plants break up the earth, water is absorbed by earth, and water extinguishes fire.

CLIMATIC CONDITIONS

The body is affected by climatic conditions, but Chinese physicians believe that climatic conditions can occur within the body. They are described as the "six excesses" – wind, cold, summer-heat, dampness, dryness and fire.

THE FOUR HUMORS

QI	essential life force – from air
XUE	blood
JING	vital essence (energy)
JIN YE	body fluids – from food and medicine

CIRCULATION OF THE BLOOD

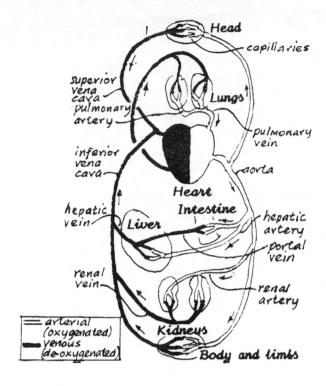

THE SEVEN GLANDS OF TAOISM

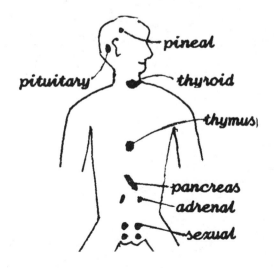

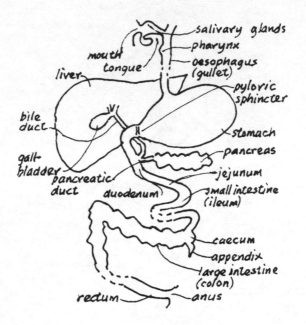

The small-minded man thinks that small acts of
virtue are insignificant in the good they do, and so
he refrains from performing them, and that small
acts of wickedness do little harm, and so he does
not abstain from performing them. The result is
that his wickedness becomes so great that it
cannot be concealed, and his guilt becomes so
great that it cannot be pardoned.

I Ching

HERBAL MEDICINES

Herbal medicines constitute one of the main components of TCM, as they did in Western medicine before being largely superseded by the manufactured, and mainly synthetic, medicines produced by the major drug companies.

Herbal medicine as practiced in China has such a good reputation that Chinese herbal medicines are now obtainable in most parts of the world, catering not only for the Chinese communities in the large cities in both East and West, but also for the needs of non-Chinese people in the West who, during recent years, have acquired a liking for Chinese herbal remedies.

THE ORIGIN OF HERBAL MEDICINES

Chinese herbal medicine began over 3,000 years ago, as an offshoot of the culinary arts, when it was first noticed that some plants were not only safe to eat but also had beneficial effects in other ways. Those found to be poisonous, causing nausea, diarrhoea, drowsiness or even death, were avoided. At a later stage, it was noticed that some plants had specifically beneficial effects: some relieved sickness, some eased pain, some had a stimulating effect, and so on. And some of the poisonous plants which had initially been ignored were applied externally to destroy skin infections or soothe aching limbs, or were taken internally in small amounts as purgatives or emetics.

THE ADVANTAGES OF HERBAL MEDICINES

Herbal medicines have a number of advantages. They are natural, generally non-addictive and without any unpleasant side-effects. Many herbal medicines have the same or similar properties, and so, if a patient develops an allergy to a particular medicine, his or her physician can usually prescribe a more suitable alternative. Chinese physicians have such a vast repertoire of herbal medicines at their disposal that they try one medicine after another until they find one that will effect a cure or a high degree of alleviation. However, herbal medicines are slow-acting and must be taken over a long period if they are to be truly effective. On the other hand, cures brought about by herbal medicines tend to be permanent.

COLLECTING HERBS

Medicinal herbs which are indigenous to China will generally need to be purchased from a Chinese pharmacy. But some of those in popular use are also available at a Chinese grocery store. Many can be collected from the field and garden. Pick those which are dry, clean and growing in unpolluted places, bearing in mind that certain species are protected and that it is illegal to pick them. Do not wash the herbs.

Some poisonous plants, such as the foxglove and deadly nightshade, have attractive fruit or flowers – they look good enough to eat! – and some totally different species are of a similar appearance. Therefore, to avoid mishaps, it is important to identify plants correctly. A good flora guide, such as *The Concise British Flora in Color*, by W. Keble Martin, can be helpful in this respect. Do *not* eat any part of a plant unless you are quite sure that it is safe to do so.

A few herbs can be used immediately in their fresh state, but most need to be dried and stored for later use. To do this, place them on clean cloth or paper, and keep them in a dry, airy and dark or shaded place until they become dry and brittle.

Dried herbs can be stored whole or ground, but the hard parts – seeds, roots and bark– will generally need to be ground. Do this with a mortar and pestle (which may be purchased at a pharmacy). Store them in cardboard boxes, paper bags or dark-glass jars to protect them from sunlight. Do not use cans or plastic bags, in which the herbs could ferment. They should keep in a good condition for six to eight months. Fresh herbs can be stored in a deep-freeze.

USING HERBAL MEDICINES

Dosages of most Chinese herbal medicines are generally not critical, and so they may be added to soups, stews, salads and other food dishes, or, where appropriate, administered individually and specifically by one of the following methods.

Infusion Prepare in the same way as tea by pouring 1 pint boiling water on to $^{1}/_{20}$oz – or the prescribed weight – dried herb, and allowing to stand for 10–15 minutes. If the fresh herb is used, double the weight.

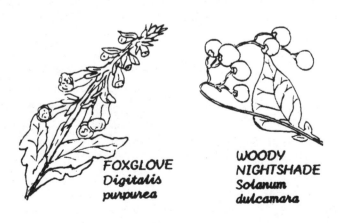

FOXGLOVE
*Digitalis
purpurea*

WOODY
NIGHTSHADE
*Solanum
dulcamara*

Decoction First prepare an infusion, and then bring to the boil and simmer for 10–15 minutes to lose water as steam, and to reduce the liquid to about one third of its original volume, thereby increasing the concentration. This method is preferable when preparing extracts from seeds, bark and other hard parts.

Pills When unpleasant to the taste, herbs may be ground, mixed with a binder and rolled into pills, which are swallowed whole, so bypassing the mouth. In the West, the usual binder is edible wax or gum tragacanth (gum arabic). In China, it is honey, which is much more pleasant.

SOME POINTS TO NOTE

1. Aqueous solutions, that is, solutions made with water, such as infusions and decoctions, are assimilated more readily than dry solids.
2. Most infusions and decoctions may be sweetened with honey or unrefined sugar.
3. Generally, medicines must *not* be consumed with alcohol, for it may negate their therapeutic effects, and is sometimes dangerous.
4. In using proprietary brands of medicines, follow the manufacturer's instructions.
5. Some symptoms are misleading, so ensure that an ailment is correctly diagnosed.
6. Do-it-yourself medicine can be risky. Where there is the slightest doubt, consult a physician.
7. A medicine meant for external use may be harmful if taken internally.

DOSAGES

A normal dosage in a Chinese pharmacopoeia – and as it is to be understood here – is the average daily requirement, by weight, of the dried herb, and not that of the fresh herb used in making an infusion.

In making an infusion or decoction, the amount of water used is a matter of taste, but it is usually sufficient to add 1 pint water to ½oz dried herb or 1oz fresh herb. It is also usual for the infusion or decoction to be divided into three equal parts, one to be taken every eight hours – early morning, midday and late evening.

However, prescriptions vary, and so, though ½oz is the accepted normal dosage for many herbal medicines, other quantities must be used where required and as specifically indicated by a physician's prescription or some other authoritative statement.

MAGIC MEDICINES

I know a bank whereon the wild thyme blows,
Where oxslips and the nodding violet grows.

A Midsummer Night's Dream
William Shakespeare

For those who aspire to a long and healthy life of youthful vigor, the Chinese have a wide range of health foods and herbal medicines, whose efficacy is often exaggerated, but which, nevertheless, are almost magical in their effects as ageing-inhibitors, blood-cleansers and tonics to improve the general health and complexion. Some of these medicines are listed and briefly described below.

Honey safer than refined sugar and synthetic sweeteners; good source of energy; nutritive

Asiatic ginseng *Panax ginseng* ageing-inhibitor; aphrodisiac; blood-cleanser; tonic

American ginseng *Panax quinquefolium* as Asiatic ginseng

Siberian ginseng *Eleutherococcus senticocus* as Asiatic ginseng

Royal jelly (made by bees) tonic; treatment for stress and run-down conditions

Dang shen *Codonopsis tangshen* as Asiatic ginseng but less potent

Garlic *Allium sativum* blood-cleanser; antibiotic

Onion *Allium cepa* as garlic but less potent

Shallot *Allium ascalonicum* as garlic

Leek *Allium porrum* as garlic

Chive *Allium schoenograsus* as garlic

Wolfberry *Lycium chinense* ageing-inhibitor; tonic

Ginger *Zingiber officinale* antiseptic; stimulant; digestive

Dandelion *Taraxacum officinale* blood-cleanser; antipyretic

Red tea fungus (hongcha jun) yeast grown in a red-tea infusion with sugar added; ageing-inhibitor; said to prevent cancer

Parsley *Petroselinum crispum* digestive; blood-cleanser

Sage *Salvia officinalis* tonic; blood-cleanser; mild antiseptic

Hawthorn *Crataegus monogyna* digestive; reduces hypertension by dissolving cholesterol

Hop *Humulus lupulus* tonic; digestive; sedative

Stinging nettle *Urtica dioica* tonic; blood-cleanser

Purslane *Portulaca oleracea* laxative; tonic

Self-heal *Prunella vulgaris* tonic; blood-cleanser

Thyme *Thymus vulgare* eradicates wrinkles

Coriander *Coriandrum sativum* blood-cleanser; ageing-inhibitor

Chrysanthemum *Chrysanthemum morifolium* sedative; lowers blood pressure

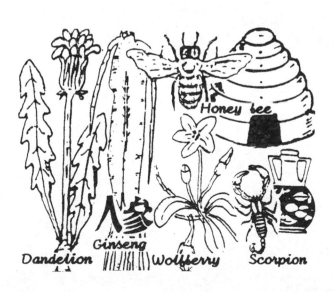

Dandelion   Ginseng   Wolfberry   Scorpion   Honey bee

In TCM, most dosages are non-critical, but, as a matter of safety, the above medicines should be administered within the prescribed limits.

MEDICAL LEGISLATION

Most countries have laws which govern the distribution, sale, preparation, testing and prescribing of medicines, whether herbal or not. In Britain, the distribution of narcotics is strictly controlled, the collecting of near-extinct herbs is severely limited, and medicines which could have harmful effects may only be prescribed by registered medical practitioners.

When using medicines of any kind, including those obtainable "off-prescription" and generally regarded as safe, one should take no risks. It is also important to ensure that one is not behaving unlawfully. Under the terms of the Medicines Act 1968, certain medicines cannot be prescribed by anyone other than a registered medical practitioner, and when they are so prescribed, the permitted dosage must not be exceeded.

ANIMAL-DERIVED MEDICINES

A few Chinese medicines are derived from animals: scorpions, centipedes, earthworms, sea horses, cicadas, ass hide, rhinoceros horn, stag horn and tiger bones. Generally, they are said to owe their efficacy to the presence of male sex hormones.

THE SECRET OF YOUTH

Age, I do abhor thee; youth, I do adore thee.

Venus and Adonis
William Shakespeare

It is possible for almost everyone to have a long and healthy life and achieve an old age characterized by youthful vigor. In this respect, the Chinese have been remarkably successful and, by more than 3,000 years, have anticipated the view of some modern medical scientists that the human life-span could be extended to between 110 and 120 years.

THE ART OF LIVING

In China, it is not uncommon for an elderly woman to have the physique and facial features of a woman in her fifties, and for a woman in her fifties to have all the youthful bloom of a girl in her teenage years. What is their secret?

They owe their success to the fact that they have mastered the art of living. For the Chinese, this means being as healthy as one can, for as long as one can, and living as contentedly as one can – health, longevity and peace of mind.

THE CHINESE SECRET OF YOUTH

The Chinese reduce the rate at which the body deteriorates with age, and so maintain some degree of youthfulness, by means of a balanced and varied diet, moderate exercise, personal hygiene, moderate habits, health foods, preventive medicine and social harmony.

A balanced and varied diet, including health foods, helps to prevent deterioration of the bodily organs by starvation, malfunction or infection.

Moderate habits, including moderate exercise, ensure that the muscles and other organs are not misused, overused or under-used.

Personal hygiene keeps the skin in a healthy state and prevents the spread of infection.

Preventive medicine precludes or delays the onset of illness. All illnesses and injuries, even when thought to be cured, have physical or psychological after-effects which encourage ageing, if only to a small degree. Important components of TCM are those medicines and health foods which delay or inhibit the ageing process.

Social harmony helps to prevent stress and nervous disorders, which encourage ageing.

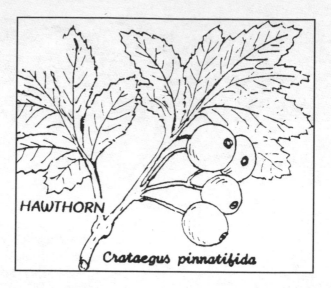

HAWTHORN

Crataegus pinnatifida

THE CAUSES OF AGEING

The causes of ageing include a slowing down of the production of hormones, a weakening of the immune system so that the body becomes less resistant to disease, the general wear and tear due to accidents and illness, a lifetime of physical exertion and stress, and exposure to pollution and the sun's ultraviolet rays, together with obesity, unsound diet, lack of exercise and sleep, overuse of drugs, and immoderate habits generally. Constant neglect of the health may cause premature ageing.

A GOOD COMPLEXION

It is sometimes the case that a person with an unprepossessing complexion will feel youthful and be healthy, even though facial features may be marred by acne scars, wrinkles or discolored teeth. But, in general, the condition of the skin is an indication of the condition of the body. Clear eyes, white teeth and an unblemished skin are among the hallmarks of health and youth. It is possible, as the Chinese have demonstrated, for elderly women to have a genuinely youthful and beautiful appearance without the aid of cosmetic preparations.

Chinese physicians contend that a healthy skin and a good complexion are largely determined by the health of the body, and the bloodstream in particular, for therein lie the hormones, or "vital essences," as the Chinese describe them, which control many of the activities of the body. The blood also contains those toxic wastes which cause skin eruptions, painful joints and aching muscles. Elimination of waste from the bowel by a diet high in fibre, and from the blood by a diet high in medicinal herbs, may do more for the health and beauty of the skin than cosmetic preparations which clog the pores and destroy the natural protective oil.

CARE OF THE SKIN

Taking care of the skin is easy if one adopts the Chinese diet, for it has in-built components which are beneficial to the health of the skin. But, if one's diet is in the Western style, one should avoid too much pasta, white bread and flour, pastries and cakes, biscuits, chips and other fried foods, refined sugar, canned fruits and soups, soft drinks, confectionery and butter and other animal fats On the other hand, the diet should include

wholegrain bread and cereals, honey, fish, chicken, eggs, molasses, garlic, avocados, carrots, parsley and spring onions.

An adequate amount of exercise will also help to maintain the skin in a healthy condition.

PERSONAL HYGIENE

Personal hygiene helps in the attainment of a good complexion. Attention should be given to features other than the skin, such as the hair, eyes, ears, nose, teeth and finger-nails.

Tired-looking eyes may be due to the eyestrain caused by too much reading, watching television and working in poor light.

Bad breath is caused by infections and upsets of the teeth, mouth, nose, throat, lungs and stomach. If the condition persists, medical advice should be sought. Otherwise, it can be treated with a mouthwash, such as an infusion of sage.

HAIR CARE

The only care the hair really needs is a once-weekly wash and a varied diet to ensure a good supply of nutrients. Oily skin and hair have a variety of causes, which include unsuitable cosmetics, stress and some kinds of oral contraceptives.

Permanent baldness is usually hereditary, but other factors may be involved – stress, poor circulation and inadequate diet. Temporary baldness may be caused by anemia, deficiencies in the thyroid hormones, contraceptive pills, antibiotics, steroids, scalp infections and excessive use of shampoos.

SKIN DISEASES

Some diseases and defects of the skin, such as warts and dermatitis, may have external causes, and may be spread by contact. But many, such as acne, eczema, psoriasis, wrinkles and baldness, have internal causes.

HYGIENE

Hygiene could be briefly defined as the principle of maintaining health by cleanliness, which is as important to the Chinese as it is to the people of the West, except that the methods used by the Chinese derive from many centuries of medical wisdom. They are not riddled with restrictive and pointless regulations, nor influenced by political correctness, keep-fit enthusiasts or food faddists.

There are many weaknesses in the hygiene crusade which has swept across Europe as part of the "green revolution," four of which spring immediately to mind: too much washing of the skin, especially with soap and cosmetic preparations, destroys the natural oil which is there for its protection; the detergents and disinfectants which are now so widely and intensively used may do more damage than the microbes they are

intended to destroy; the body is not able to develop its own immunity to disease if it is not allowed to make some contact with the micro-organisms which cause disease; manufacturing processes, including the introduction of preservatives and other chemicals which are meant to make food safe could destroy some of the tiny traces of substances vital to the health.

One could add that some of the measures taken in the interests of hygiene are more aesthetic than medical. A doctor's white coat may be no more germ-free than an undertaker's black one.

It is useful to remember that all micro-organisms, including those which cause diseases, multiply rapidly where there is moisture, warmth and a supply of nutrients. This means that, in the interest of food hygiene, a kitchen should be kept as cool and as dry as possible. It should also be regularly cleansed in order to remove dirt, grease, stale food, etc., which contain nutrients for micro-organisms.

The same common-sense thinking should be applied to personal hygiene. A toilet seat recently vacated is usually warm, moist and fouled, if only slightly, by excreted substances, which makes it an ideal place for the breeding and transmission of micro-organisms.

Wild animals occasionally succumb to disease, but they are generally remarkably fit, even though they do not take a regular bath, brush their teeth, use a flush toilet, apply cosmetic preparations or abide by hygiene regulations, because their diet is sound and their exercise is adequate. This suggests that we are often prone to illness because of our unhealthy lifestyle, and it supports the Chinese view that a person in a sound state of health, and who takes the trouble to strengthen his vital organs with preventive medicines, should be able to throw off most infections, particularly those of a minor nature.

We in the West sometimes weaken our resistance to infections by those very same methods we design to protect our health. In matters of hygiene, our approach should retain a sense of proportion. To take one pertinent example: in using a synthetic antiseptic fluid to deal with micro-organisms, we eradicate not only those which are harmful but also those which are harmless or even useful. This interference with the balance of nature can have unfortunate consequences. In this situation, the Chinese use garlic, which is a natural and selective antibiotic that destroys only the harmful flora. Western hygiene freaks may do well to follow the Chinese example.

MANIPULATION

The Chinese have an excellent system of herbal medicine, but they also have other systems of therapy, such as massage, acupuncture and remedial exercises, which involve movement and manipulation. One of the greatest advances in Chinese medicine was the realization that many illnesses can be prevented, cured or alleviated by treatments which are non-medicinal.

Some of these manipulative techniques can be performed effectively and safely only by a Chinese physician or a trained operator. While people in a normal state of health may feel that they have no need of some of these treatments, they may benefit from an occasional course of massage or acupuncture as a means of relaxation. Those sceptics who take a course of acupuncture are often pleasantly surprised by the outcome.

REMEDIAL EXERCISES

Two of the most effective systems of non-medicinal therapy are the physical and breathing exercises which derive from Taoist philosophy. Some encourage relaxation, games and meditation, which are good for mental health; some are keep-fit exercises intended for people in a normal state of health and who wish to remain so; and some are designed to prevent, cure or relieve specific conditions therapeutically, including many which are regarded in the West as incurable or intractable. It is surprising – and comforting – to learn that the Chinese can sometimes cure such difficult conditions as asthma, arthritis and emphysema by means of therapeutic exercises and without recourse to medicines.

CALLISTHENICS

Callisthenics, which are gymnastic exercises designed to achieve both physical and mental health, together with some elegance of movement, are performed by the Chinese not only to keep fit but also as a form of therapy for a wide range of ailments. Since these exercises generally involve co-ordination of the mind and body, they are particularly effective in treating disorders which are closely associated with the emotions, such as hypertension, depression and insomnia. They have been developed from the Taoist exercises, which have close associations with the martial arts.

TAOIST THERAPY

All Taoist thought and practice is based upon the sound assumption that a man's health, vitality, general well-being and prolongation of life depend on consumption and movement – in other words, diet and exercise. Movement, say the Taoists, has three components – mental activity, bodily activity and sex – but there can be no movement without *qi*, or "vital energy," which derives from food, drink and air. See pages 65–66.

MASSAGE

There are various systems of massage, including shiatsu and reflexology. But, in recent years, there has been a tendency for them to borrow from each other. The orthodox system used in the West relaxes, stimulates and invigorates the mind and body, improving circulation, relieving depression and tension, and treating migraine, insomnia, sinusitis and hypertension. It achieves this mainly by toning the blood, nerves and muscles, and helping the body to assimilate food and eliminate waste products. Athletes and others engaged in strenuous activity benefit considerably from massage, for it assists in drawing off those toxic wastes which cause stiffness of the muscles. However, it must not be used as a treatment for persons with varicose veins, thrombosis, phlebitis or a fever. In fact, when a person has a severe illness, professional medical advice should be sought before applying massage.

Massage could be regarded as "exercise in reverse." By improving the circulation of the blood and toning the muscles and other organs, it provides the same benefits as exercise, but the energy is expended *by* the environment, as represented by the masseur, and not *against* the environment, as is the case with exercise. In other words, the work is done by the masseur, not by the subject. It could be said to be the lazy person's way of taking exercise. It is of particular benefit to elderly people who, for one reason or another, cannot take exercise.

CALLISTHENICS

TRADITIONAL CHINESE MASSAGE

Tui na, or traditional Chinese massage, provides benefits similar to those of the systems of the West, but the techniques are simpler and more direct. They clear waste and blockages in the meridians, stimulate circulation of the blood and *qi*, loosen stiff joints and muscles, and increase stamina and resistance to disease.

Tui na is mainly used in combination with acupressure or acupuncture to treat a wide variety of ailments, which include sprained joints, pulled tendons, arthritis, cramp and premenstrual tension.

REFLEXOLOGY

Reflexology is a system of foot massage believed to have originated in China about 5,000 years ago, but it is now very much a Western development. It is not one of the prominent systems of TCM. Its essential principle is that massaging certain parts of the feet, called reflex areas, produces a curative or alleviative response in those parts of the body which correspond to the stimulated areas. However, these so-called reflexes are not the same as the reflexes, or involuntary movements, produced by the nervous system.

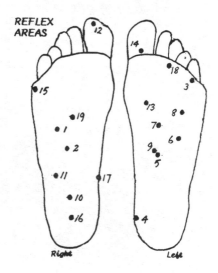

REFLEX AREAS

Right   Left

Examples: 1. Liver 2. Gall-bladder. 3. Ears 4. Bladder 5. Kidneys 6. Spleen 7. Stomach 8. Lungs 9. Adrenal gland 10. Ileum 11. Colon 12. Brain 13. Heart 14. Neck 15. Shoulders 16. Sciatic nerve 17. Spine 18 Eyes 19. Solar plexus

SHIATSU

Shiatsu is a Japanese system of massage and manipulation which is similar to acupressure in that stimulation is applied to hundreds of acupoints, or *tsubos*, as the Japanese call them. However, while only the fingertips are used in acupressure, the fingers, thumbs, knuckles, palms, elbows and even feet are used in shiatsu.

ACUPUNCTURE

Acupuncture is a system of therapy in which the brain, nervous system and vital organs are stimulated by the insertion of fine, stainless-steel needles into the acupoints, or vital-energy points, on the body. There are more than 800 acupoints, but only about 150 are in common use.

This stimulation, achieved by rotating the needles to produce a tingling, tightly-twisting sensation, has specific remedial effects on the organs to which the acupoints relate, and a more generalized effect in improving vitality by unblocking, increasing or decreasing the flow of *qi*, so correcting any yin-yang imbalances. It is essentially a painless procedure, and is usually followed by a pleasant feeling of heaviness and relaxation. The needles must, of course, be properly sterilized to prevent the transmission of blood-borne diseases, such as hepatitis and HIV.

ACUPRESSURE

Acupressure is a combination of massage and acupuncture techniques in which the fingertips are used instead of needles to exert pain-relieving

STONE-AGE ACUPUNCTURE

pressure on the acupoints, which are generally, but not always, the same as those used in acupuncture.

MOXIBUSTION

Moxibustion, similar to acupuncture and acupressure in its effects, uses a glowing wick instead of needles or fingertips as the source of stimulation for the acupoints. It is an effective treatment for menstrual problems, but it must be carried out by a qualified practitioner.

EAR ACUPUNCTURE

Ear acupuncture, which has been practiced in China for many centuries, is based on the principle that there are points on the outer ear which correspond to the organs of the body, and that by stimulating certain points, the corresponding organs will be so affected that any conditions associated with them will be cured or relieved. Ear acupuncture is now used successfully as a treatment for alcoholism and tobacco and drug addiction.

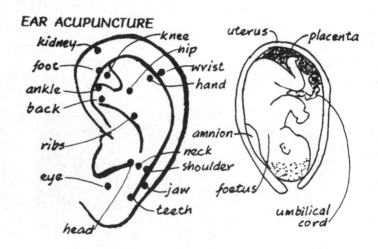

EAR ACUPUNCTURE

kidney, knee, hip, foot, wrist, hand, ankle, back, ribs, amnion, neck, shoulder, eye, jaw, teeth, head, uterus, placenta, foetus, umbilical cord

MERIDIANS

On the body, there are 59 meridians, or *qing lo*, as the Chinese call them. In TCM, they are thought to be more important than the nerves and blood because they are the energy channels which circulate *qi* throughout the body, and illness may be caused if they become obstructed or filled with waste so that the movement of *qi* is impeded. They make up an invisible network which connects all the acupoints, organs and tissues.

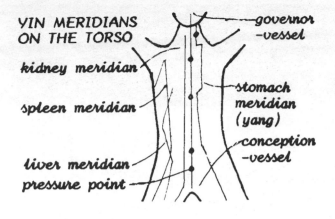

YIN MERIDIANS ON THE TORSO

governor-vessel

kidney meridian

stomach meridian (yang)

spleen meridian

conception-vessel

liver meridian

pressure point

According to the classical theory of TCM, there are 12 main meridians, but modern theory recognizes 14, of which 12 are paired and two unpaired. Each pair contains a yang meridian, connecting with a hollow organ, and a yin meridian, connecting with a solid organ. The diagram shows the yin meridians on the torso. The stomach (yang) meridian is paired with the spleen (yin) meridian. This diagram also shows the unpaired meridian on the front of the body, which links the conception-vessel (sexual organs) to the governor-vessel (brain).

Until recent years, physicians in the West were sceptical about the existence of meridians, and took the view that they are no more than fibres of the central nervous system. But the undoubted success of acupuncture has proved them wrong. The World Health Organisation endorses acupuncture as a treatment for a wide range of conditions.

The most difficult thing in the world is to effect precise communication between two people who are very pleased or two people who are very angry.

Tao Te Ching

SELF-HELP TREATMENTS

Acupressure is easy and safe to self-administer. Try it for any of the following conditions.

FAINTING

Apply the fingernail to stimulate the acupoint on the midline two-thirds of the way up between the upper lip and the nose. If a person faints frequently for no apparent reason, medical advice should be sought.

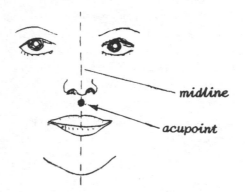

midline

acupoint

HEADACHE

Massage the head reflexes on the big toes.

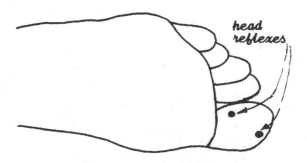

head reflexes

ACIDITY

Massage the acupoints on the furrow between the second and third toes, at the middle of the ankle joint on the front of the leg, and at four finger-widths below the kneecap on the outside of the shin-bone.

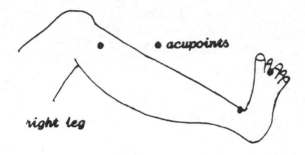

right leg

acupoints

VOMITING

Apply pressure to the point midway between the breastbone and the navel.

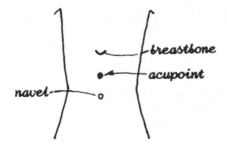

breastbone

acupoint

navel

INSOMNIA

Before retiring, take a leisurely walk, self-massage the body all over, and then massage the *yung chuan* acupoint, which is in the middle of the sole of the foot.

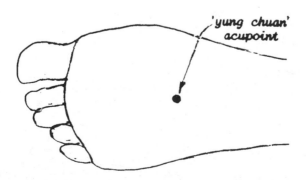

'yung chuan' acupoint

TOOTHACHE

The problem may be due to an abscess, which is commonly caused by toxins resulting from a liver disorder. If this is the case, press or massage the acupoint between the thumb and forefinger.

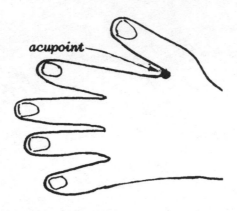

acupoint

INCONTINENCE

Relief is sometimes obtained by applying acupressure upward to the hollow between the Achilles tendon and the inner ankle bone.

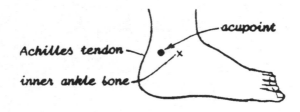

acupoint

Achilles tendon

inner ankle bone

PERIOD PAINS

Firmly massage the acupoint which is four finger-widths below the kneecap and just outside the shinbone.

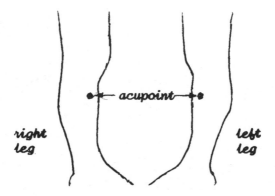

acupoint

right leg

left leg

HYPERTENSION

Place the palms on the outside of the thighs, and then slowly bring them down the legs, outside the knees, over the calves and into the ankles. Do this about 12 times daily. But hypertension is a serious condition, and medical advice should be sought before attempting any kind of self-treatment.

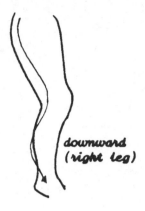

*downward
(right leg)*

VERTIGO

Apply pressure at the point which is about 1 inch below the outer ankle-bone.

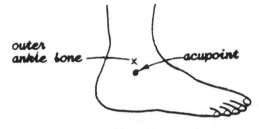

*outer
ankle bone* — x — *acupoint*

MENSTRUAL CRAMPS AND VARICOSE VEINS

Place the palms on the inside of the legs at the ankles, and then slowly bring them up the legs, inside the knees and up the thighs into the genitals. Do this 12 times daily.

*upward
(left leg)*

STAMMERING

Press the acupoint at the bottom of the outside edge of the thumb-nail on either hand. (See diagram above.)

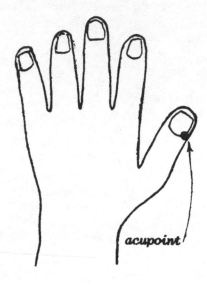

acupoint

TINNITUS

This condition can sometimes be relieved by applying pressure at the point that is about 1 inch in front of the ear, at the top of the cheekbone.

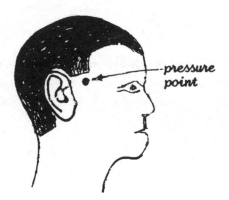

pressure point

EXCESSIVE PERSPIRATION

Firmly press or massage the acupoint which is three finger-widths from the wrist crease and in line with the thumb.

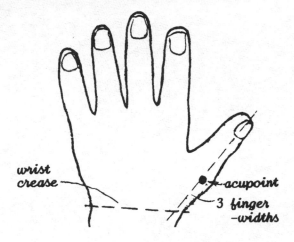

wrist crease

acupoint

3 finger –widths

NAUSEA

1. Press the acupoint between the thumb and forefinger on either hand. 2. With the palm upward, use the same pressure and movement on the point which lies 2 inches from the wrist crease and between the two tendons. 3. Use the thumb to apply pressure and a rotating movement to the region between the tendons of the second and third toes on either foot.

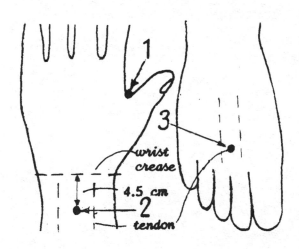

1

3

wrist crease

4.5 cm

2

tendon

THE
CHINESE
WAY OF LIFE

SEX

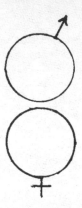

*Men and women are meant
to love and complement each other.*

I Ching

Whatever philosophers may decide about human destiny, nature has
already decreed that our main purpose is to ensure the continuance of
the human race, and, to that end, has provided us with an instinct for
self-preservation and a capacity for procreation.

FORBIDDEN FRUIT

The Chinese have a matter-of-fact attitude toward sex. They do not
regard it as forbidden fruit, but as an activity which is as normal and
natural, and as necessary and desirable, as eating and drinking. It is not
an activity to be degraded by perverted forms of pleasure, nor as a
subject of obscene humor. On the other hand, they do not treat it as
taboo, as people did in Victorian England. They recognize that the sexual
appetite needs to be satisfied, mainly as a matter of health, but they
acknowledge that with sex, as with food, there is a need for moderation
and precaution, for one can have too much – or too little! – of a good
thing. The consequences of unbridled lust or total celibacy can be just as
damaging as those of gluttony or fasting. They also abhor any practices
which are potentially destructive of the stability of the family and the
fabric of society.

SEX AND HEALTH

In Taoist philosophy, sex is one of the three components of movement
(see page 242), made possible by *qi*, which derives from eating, drinking
and breathing. Therefore a good appetite for sex, like a good appetite
for food, is an indication of a sound state of health.

On the other hand, the Taoists in ancient China perpetuated the belief that, for men, sexual intercourse without ejaculation, so conserving the semen, was good for the health and led to a long life.

It is interesting to note that the front unpaired meridian on the body (see page 247) connects the governor-vessel, or brain, to the conception-vessel, or sexual organs, which indicates that the Taoists regarded the sexual urge as a predominant factor in thought. And, no doubt, it is!

SEX AND MARRIAGE

There are those who would say that marriage, with all the formalities of a wedding ceremony, is the proper procedure. But marriage is rarely idyllic; in the West, it is no guarantee of fidelity, and it often fails in one of its main purposes, which is to provide a child with two caring parents. However, marriage seems to work very well for the Chinese, perhaps because they live by the spirit of their Confucian-based moral code, and are not content to abide merely by the letter of the law. Moreover, in China, the family is the basic unit of society.

In this respect, there is much to be said for the system of arranged marriages as practiced in China and other oriental countries, for statistics show that they rarely lead to the abuse of children or end in divorce. The Chinese advocate marriage, not as a sacred institution, but on a secular basis, as a practical way of preventing the spread of disease and providing the security of good parenthood for their offspring. They know that, as a matter of genetics, worthy descendants arise from worthy ancestors, and so the emphasis is more on planned procreation than reckless recreation. Sensible and caring parents will put aside

romantic considerations and discourage their son or daughter from entering into a marriage which could lead to the transmission of hereditary defects and diseases. Because of this concern with the production of healthy offspring, intermarriage between members of the same family is considered highly undesirable.

Clearly, though sexual activity ensures the near-immortality of the human race, wise marriages will help to ensure that it is also healthy.

The Chinese regard contraceptive devices as unnatural, but they accept them as a matter of compromise, for China already has far too many mouths to feed. They have a preference for condoms, which prevent both conception and the transmission of diseases.

APHRODISIACS

Chinese physicians do not favor the general use of aphrodisiacs. They regard them as unhealthy because they make excessive and damaging demands on the body. In any case, if sexual potency is one of the hallmarks of a sound state of health, it follows that a person in a normal state of health should have no need of aphrodisiacs.

It is helpful to consume foods which are particularly nutritious or have health-giving properties. Eggs, artichokes, figs, honey, mushrooms, oysters and cinnamon are often recommended. Cereals and sweet wines are thought to be helpful, but wine does no more than cloud the judgment and diminish the sense of moral responsibility.

There are three herbs which Chinese physicians regard as safe and effective as aphrodisiacs: Asiatic *ginseng (Panax ginseng)*, broomrape (*Crobanche salsa*), horny goat weed (*Epimedium sagittatum*). But medical advice should be sought before taking any of these remedies.

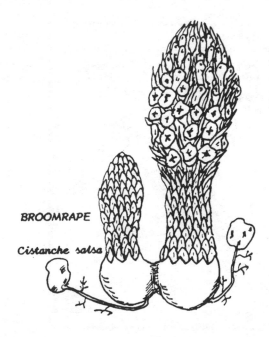

BROOMRAPE

Cistanche salsa

BABY CARE

The birth of a baby is generally a very happy event; and, since babies are such a great source of delight, it is understandable that so much has been said and written about childbirth and baby care. Pregnancy and childbirth are natural and normal occurrences, and should proceed without problems if a few common-sense procedures are adopted.

Before birth, a baby needs a mother who is healthy and sensible, and who is aware that her unborn child will be affected by what she eats, drinks and smokes, and by her ailments and medications. After birth, a baby needs parents who are healthy and sensible, and who will provide love and security, together with a sound diet and the basic creature comforts.

FORECASTING YOUR BABY'S SEX

The Chinese sometimes try to determine the gender of an unborn baby by means – hardly foolproof – of a little verse, which is translated as:

> Seven sevens are forty-nine:
> Add the conception month,
> Subtract the mother's age,
> And add nineteen.
> Odd is a boy, and even is a girl.

To give an example, let us assume that a young woman, aged twenty, becomes pregnant in August. Proceed as follows:

49	start
+8	conception month
= 57	
– 20	woman's age
= 37	
+19	
= 56	An even number – the baby will be a girl.

THE CONCEPTION CHART

A more complex claim of a similar nature is that one can choose the time of conception to produce a boy or a girl, as desired. For this, they use the so-called conception chart.

This chart consists of 336 frames, each of which contains one of two Chinese characters –

男

meaning boy and

女

meaning girl.

The numbers 1 to 12 at the top of the chart indicate the twelve months of the Chinese lunar year, and the numbers 18 to 45 down the left-hand side show the woman's age, which must be calculated in the traditional Chinese way, as explained below.

Whether a woman gives birth to a boy or a girl will be decided by her age and the month when conception occurs, together with some considerations with regard to diet, and providing no mistakes are made. Thus, as the chart indicates, a woman aged 31 who conceives during the fifth month is likely to give birth to a girl. If conception occurs during the ninth month when the mother-to-be is aged 20, the baby is likely to be a boy.

The chart can, of course, deal only in tendencies. Other factors, such as the effects of the menstrual cycle, the time between intercourse and ovulation and the woman's state of health, must be taken into consideration, as must the husband's virility.

CHINESE MONTHS

In addition to the variable lengths of Chinese years (see page 79), calculations must accommodate the differing lengths of Chinese months. In China, the months do not have names as they do in the West. They are simply designated first month, second month and so on. Also, since Chinese lunar months are of varying lengths, some adjustments are made to the number of days in the months. This means that a Chinese lunar year contains 12 months, each of 29 or 30 days. But in using the conception chart it can be assumed that each month has 30 days, which makes a yearly total of 360 days and falls short of the true length of a solar year by $5\frac{1}{4}$ days.

Clearly, the Chinese lunar months do not coincide with the months of the Western calendar, and so those who use the conception chart must ensure that their estimations are based on Chinese lunar months.

To achieve accuracy some calculations are required. For example, assuming a month of 30 days, the Chinese first month for 1997 in the Western calendar ran from 8 February to 9 March (21 days in February and nine in March), and the second month was 10 March to 8 April (22 days in march and eight in April). In 1998 the first month began on 29 January and ran through to 27 February. So it is necessary to do a fresh calculation for each year. An easier route may be to obtain a copy of a current Chinese calendar, stocked by some Chinese grocery stores.

CONCEPTION CHART

	1	2	3	4	5	6	7	8	9	10	11	12
18	女	男	女	男	男	男	男	男	男	男	男	男
19	男	女	男	女	女	男	男	男	男	男	女	女
20	女	男	女	男	男	男	男	男	男	女	男	男
21	男	女	女	女	女	女	女	女	女	女	女	女
22	女	男	男	女	女	女	男	女	女	女	女	女
23	男	男	女	男	男	女	男	女	男	男	男	女
24	男	女	男	女	男	女	男	女	女	男	女	女
25	女	男	男	女	男	男	女	男	女	男	男	男
26	男	女	男	女	女	男	女	男	女	女	女	女
27	女	男	女	男	女	女	男	男	男	男	女	女
28	男	女	男	女	男	女	男	男	男	男	男	女
29	男	女	女	女	女	男	男	男	男	女	女	女
30	男	女	女	女	女	女	女	女	女	女	男	男
31	男	女	男	女	女	女	女	女	女	女	女	男
32	男	女	男	女	女	女	女	女	女	女	女	男
33	女	男	男	女	男	女	女	男	女	女	女	男
34	男	女	男	女	女	女	女	女	女	女	男	男
35	男	男	女	男	女	女	女	男	女	女	男	男
36	女	男	男	女	男	女	女	女	男	男	男	男
37	男	女	男	女	男	女	男	女	女	女	男	女
38	女	男	女	男	女	女	男	女	男	女	男	女
39	男	女	男	男	男	女	女	女	女	男	女	女
40	女	男	女	男	女	男	男	男	女	男	女	女
41	男	女	男	女	女	男	女	男	女	女	男	男
42	女	男	女	女	女	女	女	女	男	女	男	女
43	男	女	男	女	女	女	男	女	男	男	男	男
44	男	男	女	男	男	男	女	男	女	男	女	女
45	女	男	男	女	女	女	男	女	男	女	男	男

AGE

The ages given on the conception chart range from 18 to 45 years, because the latter is the average age for the menopause, after which a woman can no longer bear children, and the former, in the Chinese view, is the most suitable age for a woman to have her first baby.

However, the Chinese way of calculating a person's age is different from that employed in the West. For example, a child born in the West on, say, 1 March 1997 would have been three months old in June 1997 and would not have been one year old until 1 March 1998. In China, a child born on 1 March 1997 would immediately have been assumed to be one year old, and considered to be two years old on the first day of the next Chinese year, that is 28 January, when in fact according to the Western system he would be less than a year old. Therefore it is generally the case that the "true" age of a Chinese woman, in Western terms, is at least one year less than that shown in the conception chart.

Another way of stating these facts is to say that a Western child will always be less than one year old during the year in which it is born, whereas a Chinese child is assumed to be one year old during the year in which it is born. But this creates a strange anomaly. A Chinese child who was born on 27 January 1998, for example, would instantly be regarded as being one year old, but only one day later – because it was the start of a new year– it would have been regarded as being two years old. Yet according to the Western system it was only two days old!

When a Chinese physician was asked for some information about this seemingly odd way of measuring ages, he commented: "The conception chart is of ancient origin and so it follows that the traditional method of measuring ages will be used. But, apart from that, when a child is born, he is already nine months old, assuming that he was not born prematurely."

The way sensible people
relate to the world is to
avoid both rejection and
attachment, and to
treat others justly.

Lunyu

THE GOLDEN MEAN

The Chinese are calm by temperament and of moderate habits, and they try to establish harmony and moderation in all their endeavors, which are two of the reasons why they are healthy and have peace of mind. It must surely follow that people who are not reckless in their habits will be less prone to illness and accidents, and so will be likely to live longer.

In these matters, the Chinese are strongly influenced by the teachings of Confucius and Lao Zi, both of whom advocated a strict adherence to the "golden mean," which is the principle that one should always take the middle way, and so avoid violent extremes of conduct.

But this principle applies not only to human conduct but also to the whole of nature. According to Taoist philosophy, nothing can be completely yin or completely yang, and so there can never be any complete extremes. If it were otherwise, there would be no balance, and all would be chaos (see page 57).

NEI PIEN

In a book called *Nei Pien*, published about A.D. 320, the Taoist scholar Ko Hung wrote about those practices which can damage both peace of mind and physical health.

> Sadness, disquiet, ambition without talent, greed, jealousy, excessive joy, idleness, decrepitude, drunkenness and over-strenuous activity are injuries; and when they have amassed to the highest level, exhaustion and death will soon follow. Therefore, to keep alive, one must not listen, look, sit, drink, eat, work, rest, sleep, walk, exercise, talk or dress too much. Do not overdo the five tastes when eating, for too much saltiness injures the heart, too much pungency injures the liver, too much acidity injures the spleen, too much bitterness injures the lungs, and too much sweetness injures the kidneys.

Clearly, Ko Hung had perceived that there is a relationship between health and moderate habits, and so established an important principle, which went largely unnoticed by the physicians of the West until recent times.

MODERATION AND MORALITY

Tobacco, alcohol, drugs, gambling and casual sex seem to have become established as the five cardinal vices, if not the five cardinal sins, throughout the world. Perhaps gourmandizing should be added to these vices, for more people die from overeating than from under-eating.

Sadly, many of the people of the West tend to adopt an "all-or-nothing" approach, so immoderacy abounds. With many, it is either total self-indulgence or total abstinence.

The Chinese are less rigid in their approach. They see no virtue in greed: on the other hand, they see no virtue in complete self-denial. They have a total abhorrence of drug-taking and promiscuity, but they are less condemnatory of tobacco, alcohol and gambling, and would argue that, if moderation is practiced, the benefits of those pleasures which contain risks might outweigh their ill-effects. As far as the Chinese are concerned, a strict code of morality, of which moderation is an essential component, is vital to a sound state of health and the attainment of a long life.

Chinese morality is to do with such matters as moderation, compromise, harmony, wisdom, justice, benevolence, honesty, propriety, dietary procedures, social etiquette and respect for one's ancestors, and so it is all-embracing and immensely practical.

Chinese physicians have always taken the view that many mental and nervous disorders are due to the way in which we live, and could be ascribed as much to lack of morality as to any overtly medical causes.

PEACE OF MIND

In China, meditation is greatly valued as a means of treating stress and its associated conditions, such as insomnia, headaches and certain skin complaints. It is also regarded as a source of physical relaxation and peace of mind. The person who has peace of mind will eat better, sleep better and generally feel better.

MEDITATION SYSTEMS

There are various systems of meditation, almost all of which, such as yoga, which is a Hindu system, and tai chi chuan, which is Chinese, are of oriental origin. However, these systems are not essential to success, and meditation can be practiced on a do-it-yourself basis.

THE BENEFITS OF MEDITATION

Meditation provides three main benefits. Those who meditate may make a calm and rational appraisal of their situation and, if they have problems, can decide how best to handle them. Or they can focus their thoughts on comforting and pleasure-giving items, as people do when they are day-dreaming and fantasizing, which could provide a short "holiday" for an over-active and troubled mind. Or they may try self-hypnosis, and so, by a colossal effort of will, convince themselves that their affairs are in a much better state, or could be in a better state, than they really are.

PRACTICING MEDITATION

To meditate simply and effectively, one should choose a quiet room where distractions are unlikely, sit upright but comfortably with the eyes open and the hands resting in one's lap, fix the mind on pleasant thoughts, breathe gently and slowly, and then relax so that the shoulders, elbows and feet are loose. One should continue this for 10–20 minutes, ignoring all unpleasant or distracting thoughts which enter the mind. Then, before standing up, one should gently exercise the muscles to prevent giddiness or fainting as a consequence of reduced blood pressure. This procedure can be followed daily for many months.

MEDITATION AND SLEEP

One can meditate in a limited way immediately after retiring by concentrating one's mind on solutions for problems or merely on pleasant thoughts. The warmth and softness of the bed should ensure relaxation. Providing one's problems are not too serious, this is more effective than counting sheep if one has difficulty in getting off to sleep.

HYPNOTHERAPY

Hypnotherapy and its variations auto-suggestion or self-hypnosis can be effective if properly applied. It is a system of therapy by which a person empties the mind of conscious thoughts, and then, by repeating certain words and phrases, plants instructions in the subconscious mind so that the unconscious processes of behavior are steered in the desired direction. Thus, the mind is conditioned to increase the general feeling of well-being.

COUÉISM

This system of self-hypnosis was devised by Emile Coué (1857–1926), a French apothecary. Patients are expected to repeat certain phrases, the best known being "Every day, in every way, I am getting better and better." But his system of therapy is not original, for its techniques are similar to some Chinese meditation exercises.

EXERCISE

*Exercise is bunk. If you are healthy, you don't need it,
if you are sick, you shouldn't take it.*

Henry Ford

Unlike Henry Ford, the Chinese do not underestimate the value of
exercise. In TCM, physical and breathing exercises, together with sound
diet, regulated sex, moderate habits and herbal medicines, are a
fundamental component of preventive treatment.

DIET AND EXERCISE

Exercise helps to ensure that the maximum benefit is derived from food.
It promotes good circulation of the blood, which conveys oxygen and
nutrients to the tissues where respiration occurs, and conveys waste
products to the kidneys and lungs where they are excreted. It is also an
aid to digestion, for bodily movements assist peristalsis, the involuntary
contraction and relaxation of the wall of the alimentary canal. Chyme –
the food that has undergone gastric digestion – is thus kept in motion,
thereby aiding assimilation and preventing constipation.

A little exercise relieves flatulence, or "shifts the wind." However, it is
inadvisable to take violent exercise after a heavy meal, for this puts too
much strain on the heart.

HEALTH AND EXERCISE

Exercise helps to ensure that muscles do not become soft and flabby, and joints do not become stiff. But it must be regular, for what is gained by a short period of exercise is negated by long periods of sedentary living.

Exercise should not be over-strenuous. It is true that moderate exercise removes waste products from the body, but overdoing exercise does more to create waste products than to eliminate them – a fact that is seemingly not known to many athletes.

In this respect, we have something to learn from animals. Cats and dogs run quickly when danger threatens, but most of the time they are still and do not damage their bodies by excessive exertion.

BREATHING EXERCISES

Many centuries ago, during the time of the Zhou (Chou) dynasty (c. 1100–221 B.C.) the *xian*, or "immortals of the mountains," sought seclusion and safety in the mountains. Without interference, they could experiment with herbs and practice the "way of long life," a Taoist concept, which includes the martial arts, meditation, a diet of herbs and breathing exercises. They believed that the mountain mists contained *qi*, the vital energy of life.

Breathing exercises improve the circulation and ensure that the organs and tissues receive an adequate supply of oxygen. They also encourage relaxation and improve the quality of meditation.

TAKING EXERCISE

Although it may seem rather tame in comparison with boxing or football, there is much to be said for a twice-daily walk as a healthy and safe form of exercise. It is one in which young and old alike can indulge. For those to whom a steady walk seems unexciting, martial arts might be a sensible alternative These days there is no shortage of clubs and other organizations where these arts are taught and encouraged.

THE MARTIAL ARTS

Although the martial arts may be used in self-defence the Chinese do not generally practice them for aggressive combat, but as physical exercises which provide pleasure and improve health.

Despite the blood-curdling yells and the rapidity of the movements involved in kung fu films, the martial arts are gentle sports in which all the movements are governed by rules and procedures. There are hundreds of different systems of the classical martial arts, and some have meditative overtones.

TAI CHI CHUAN

Tai chi chuan is a system of gentle exercises derived from tai chi kung fu, and is suitable for both young and old. Its gentle movements are intended to promote mental and emotional awareness as well as

功夫

Kung fu

功夫

Tang-lang

Hsing-I

physical health by correcting imbalances of *qi*. It needs perseverance and the ability to relate mental states to physical patterns. It is a treatment for anxiety and stress, and it stimulates the circulation and tones the muscles. Some of its exercises are performed as a kind of dancing or shadow-boxing. The movements are slow and graceful and indicative of great self-control

KUNG FU

This is a Chinese term which means "skill produced by training." It is used commonly and most specifically to denote the Chinese martial arts; but can be applied to any skill that has been learned, such as carpentry and embroidery. The literal translation of martial arts is *wu-shu*.

Kung fu is sometimes defined as the Chinese version of the Japanese karate, which is one of those unarmed-combat disciplines that train the mind as well as the body. But it would be nearer the truth to say that karate is the Japanese version of kung fu, for the martial arts originated in China.

Kung fu – or *wu-shu* – has hundreds of classical systems of fighting, each with its own style and traditions, but they all have certain features in common. They are not intended to be used aggressively or to provoke aggression, but to promote health, well-being and a sense of moral responsibility, though victory in combat becomes the main objective in self-defence or when the fabric of society is threatened.

Victory in combat means rendering one's opponent impotent rather than doing him any deep or lasting injury. In an emergency, an exponent of kung fu will use his skill as a police officer might – in an honorable endeavor to protect fellow citizens and maintain the status quo. Vicious violence is, of course, contrary to the teachings of Buddhism and Taoism.

The various systems of kung fu appear to be combinations of boxing and wrestling, together with the occasional use of weapons. They are classified as styles: northern or southern, hard or soft, and internal or external.

The people in the north of China are taller and have longer legs than the people of the south, so they use their feet as much as their hands in fighting. They "box with their feet," we might say. The people of the south are accustomed to using their hands in planting rice, so they use their hands more than their feet.

Exponents of the hard styles use their own strength directly, and as this is clearly seen in their fighting techniques, their styles are said to be external, that is, not hidden. By contrast, the exponents of the soft styles, using will-power and skill, yield to their opponents' strength but turn it to their own advantage, which is not clearly seen, so their styles are said to be internal, or hidden.

The traditions and meditative aspects of the hard styles of kung fu are firmly rooted in the tenets of Buddhism. Buddhists believe that their souls proceed from one animal body to another in a long series of reincarnations, so it is hardly surprising that the movements of the hard styles are based on those of five animals, which include the dragon.

The soft styles are based on the teachings of the Taoist philosophy. But there are other influences. Pa Kua kung fu emulates by physical movements the qualities represented by the Pa Kua: strength, joy, illumination, forceful movement, penetration, danger, rest and submission.

Three popular hard styles are *wing-chun*, Shaolin and *tang-lang*. Three soft styles are Tai Chi, Pa Kua and *hsing-i*.

Wing-chun is a hard, or external, southern style based on punching in a straight line. It is believed to have been founded by Yim Wing-chun, who had learned some of its principles from Ng Mui, a nun from the Shaolin temple in the north of China.

Shaolin kung fu, a hard, or external, northern style, originated in the Buddhist temple at Shaolin in the Sung mountains of Honan province. As with all the hard styles, its movements are imitative of those of five animals – the dragon, snake, tiger, leopard and crane. The present system has 170 skills!

Tang-lang is a hard, or external, northern style, but it is very much an exception in so far as its movements are not based on those of five animals, as are the other external styles, but on those of the praying mantis and the footwork of the monkey.

Tai Chi is a soft, or internal, style with slow and graceful movements which are indicative of self-control and have philosophical overtones.

Pa Kua is a soft, or internal, style. It is based on eight trigrams, called Pa Kua, which are fully interpreted in the *I Ching*. Pa Kua is a very popular style.

Hsing-I is a soft, or internal, northern style with five forms of attack, which are characteristic of the five elements: metal, water, wood, fire and earth. Its series of twelve movements are characteristic of those of twelve animals, and firmly based on Taoist principles.

CHINESE WEAPONS

The martial arts have not always been gentle sports. They evolved in an age when warfare was common, and it was the exponent's purpose to put his enemy out of action without too much effort on his own part, with no injury to himself, and even with little or no injury to his enemy. But there were times when desperate measures were called for, and then weapons were used. A wide range of these were available. Those shown opposite give a clear indication of the ferocity with which men fought in those times.

That people as peace-loving as the Chinese should once have possessed this wide array of fearsome weaponry may come as a bit of a surprise. But it is probable that, like the martial arts, these weapons originated in the Buddhist monasteries and one can be sure that the monks would have claimed that they were essential to self-defence. But defence against whom? Surely not other peace-loving Chinese.

Perhaps the weapons were intended more as a deterrent than for actual use. Certainly, a would-be wrongdoer would think twice about committing an offence if he were faced with the prospect of being attacked by someone wielding a trident or a halberd. On the other hand, the chances are that some of these criminals would have armed themselves with similar weapons, so the claim that they were merely intended for self-defence is questionable.

But to say that the Chinese are peace-loving does not mean that they believe in peace at any price; while they see no virtue in aggression, they also see no virtue in abject cowardice. They would have been only too ready to use these weapons to resist invaders – and throughout history China has been invaded many times.

However, although no one could doubt the intentions of the makers and users of these weapons, they could perhaps question their effectiveness. For example, the many-sectioned staff would allow extra leverage, but along with this would come the disadvantage of being easily broken. The pronged truncheon is clearly a clumsy instrument.

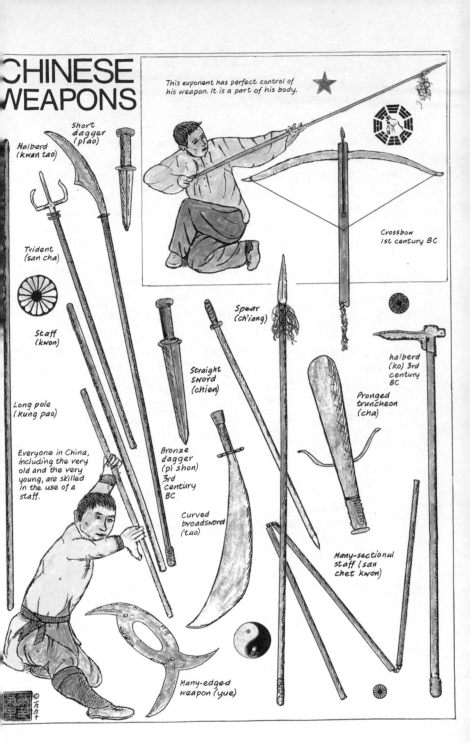

CHINESE WEAPONS

This exponent has perfect control of his weapon. It is a part of his body.

Short dagger (pʻiao)

Halberd (kwan tao)

Crossbow 1st century BC

Trident (san cha)

Staff (kwon)

Spear (chʻiang)

Straight sword (chien)

halberd (ko) 3rd century BC

Pronged truncheon (cha)

Long pole (kung pao)

Everyone in China, including the very old and the very young, are skilled in the use of a staff.

Bronze dagger (pi shon) 3rd century BC

Curved broadsword (tao)

Many-sectional staff (san chet kwon)

Many-edged weapon (yue)

GARDENS

The Chinese have much respect for the natural world, and so it is not surprising that in China there is an abundance of well-kept parks with decorative gardens teeming with many exotic forms of wild life, which are a source of delight for those with an interest in natural history.

Of particular interest in this respect are the Zen gardens, where Zen Buddhists practice their daily meditation. A Zen garden is a fount of tranquility and inspiration.

ZEN BUDDHISM

The Japanese form of Buddhism was developed from the Buddhism introduced from China and India during the twelfth century. Its adherents maintain that moral attitudes and intellectual activities are of no value without *satori*, or "deep insight." They seek *satori* through deep meditation, in which they contemplate the meaning and purpose of life and those paradoxical issues which seem to give the lie to conventional logic and scientific analysis. They contend that the gaps in our knowledge are due to the inadequacies in our systems of reasoning. We have limited knowledge because we have limited minds.

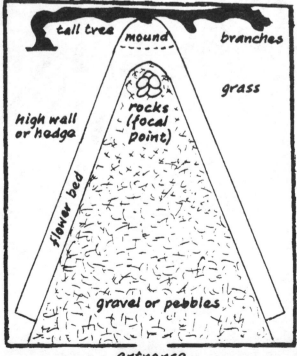

ZEN MEDITATION

In *za-zen*, which is the daily meditation practiced by Zen Buddhists, the meditators sit uncomfortably erect and cross-legged, and count from one to ten over and over again, so disciplining their thoughts.

Zen meditation could be of value to those who are victims of materialism and vanity, which are often manifested by anxiety, depression and stress.

A ZEN GARDEN

A Zen garden is intended to provide the ideal setting for meditation. It can be simple or elaborate, its essential characteristics being a rock or a small number of rocks as a focal point which, when viewed, transports the mind into a state of freedom where thought may proceed without distractions in a setting which shuts out the wider world.

FISH PONDS

Many of the parks and gardens in China have ornamental fish ponds, and most of the fish they contain are members of the carp family.

These ponds have a decorative effect, but they may also have a utilitarian purpose. Carp are a popular item of diet in China, for the Chinese insist on all their food being fresh. If they happen to live far away from the sea, their only hope of having fresh fish is to catch it in the lakes, rivers and ponds.

A HERB GARDEN

The Chinese use a large number of herbs, so many Chinese households have a small herb garden to ensure a constant supply of seasonings and medicines. In addition, many of the herbs they use grow wild in the countryside, and are there to be picked – free of charge.

There could be the same situation in the West. A small garden providing a wide range of culinary and medicinal herbs would greatly benefit health. Thyme, parsley, sage, mint and rosemary are easily grown from seeds or cuttings, and there is an abundance of herbs growing wild in the countryside. One should note that many of the plants cultivated for decorative purposes, such as the marigold and nasturtium, have medicinal properties, as do some of those grown as vegetables, such as fennel and the onion.

Mint

Wolfberry

Spring

Autumn

WEEDS

Perhaps we in the West should not be so destructive of weeds, for some of them, such as the dandelion and stinging nettle, have valuable medicinal properties. The wolfberry, which has red berries and grows in the hedgerows, is regarded as a noxious weed in the West. In China, it is highly valued as an ageing-inhibitor (see page 235).

INDOOR GARDENS

The Chinese have a liking for indoor gardens, as do the Japanese. It was the Japanese who developed bonsai, the art of cultivating ornamental dwarfed varieties of trees and shrubs.

Indoor gardens on a miniature scale are generally used for decorative purposes. On a limited scale, they are used for growing fruit and vegetables.

GROWING BEAN SPROUTS

Soya beans and mung beans are hard and difficult to digest; however, as sprouts they are easily digested, and rich in vitamin C.

Put a few beans in a clean jar, add a little water, and put aside for a few days until they have sprouted.

A MINIATURE GARDEN

Fill the bottom half of a large flat dish with small pebbles. Sterilize some garden soil by boiling it for 30 minutes, and then fill the dish with the wet soil. The pebbles will provide drainage for the excess water from the soil.

Use a glass mirror to represent a pond, gravel and small stones to make a path and a rockery, and a leafy and woody twig to represent a tree. Sprinkle small seeds on to the soil. Radish, lettuce, grass and bird seeds are suitable for this. Also plant a carrot top. This will grow to produce a "fern." Keep the soil moist and await results.

Prepare another large flat dish of soil, and plant the following: pips of apple, orange, lemon, pear and grape; cherry and date stones; sycamore fruits; peanuts; 1-inch lengths of dandelion root; small potato pieces with "eyes." Keep the soil moist and await results. You may be lucky.

When the seedlings are sturdy, they can be transferred to the garden, though those of orange, lemon, date and peanut are not likely to thrive in a cold climate. The young dandelion plants will be a source of leaves for salad dishes.

ETIQUETTE IN COMMUNICATION

The Chinese set much store by etiquette for, they would contend, it is a major component of that socially acceptable behavior – friendliness, helpfulness, patience, tact and civility – which greatly assists in creating harmonious relationships and bringing them nearer to the Confucian ideal of "making a heaven on earth for each other." Accordingly, in their conversations and social gatherings they are always meticulously careful and greet each other courteously, often using flowery language and forms of address such as "worthy gentleman" and "beneficent lady." Whatever their private thoughts, they contrive to be urbanely polite, and the most unworthy person is likely to find himself elevated to the rank of "honorable sir."

This code of etiquette extends to written communications. In personal letters, invitations and greeting cards, they will use the same flowery language and courteous expressions as they do in conversation. Moreover, as an indication of sincerity, whether it is heartfelt or mere good manners, invitations and greetings are usually written or printed on red paper because, by tradition, red is symbolic of fire, passion, power, honesty, love, benevolence and everything to do with the heart. The Chinese would not be likely to send a communication on yellow paper, for yellow is the imperial color and at one time it was forbidden, and tantamount to sacrilege, for it to be used by anyone less exalted than a member of the imperial family. As further evidence of sincerity or affection, and on the principle that actions speak louder than words, an invitation or greeting is generally accompanied by a small gift, though there are those in the West, where standards of etiquette are less sophisticated, who would be inclined to misinterpret this practice as a form of bribery.

The recipient of an invitation of greetings card accompanied by a gift generally responds by sending a gift in return. A typical reply to an invitation might be as follows:

Much esteemed friend,

You do me a great honor by your invitation and I am delighted by your gift of two gongin of rice and ten quails' eggs. Your benevolence has no bounds.

Please honor me by accepting my small token of appreciation – three chi of silk and a pair of hand-carved chopsticks.

May you live in less troublous times.

Li Mo Feng

Years ago, when most people were illiterate, it was customary to obtain the services of a professional scribe who, for a small fee, would write or read letters as required. This practice has persisted and so, even today, there are still many Chinese who rely on the services of a scribe. This applies even to the highly educated who are perfectly capable of writing their own letters, for employing a good scribe ensures that the written material is not only linguistically sound but also of ornate quality, as would be expected in a land where calligraphy is a well-established art form and a calligrapher has the status of an artist. It is also a common practice for a person to have his name engraved on the end of a stick of marble which can then be used, as we might use a rubber stamp, to make impressions on paper. Some of these engravings are of exquisite design and, when they are used with red ink, which the Chinese prefer, the effect is forceful and arresting.

It is interesting to note that it is quite a common practice for a Chinese person to engage a caligrapher to write his name in ornate characters on a large piece of paper or canvas, which is then proudly displayed on a wall where it can be admired by all. Such is the power of the written word! The characters are sometimes supplemented by small but attractive pictures.

Those readers who have absorbed the contents of this book should now be very knowledgeable about the Chinese way of life, particularly with regard to the ancient traditions and rich folklore on which have been erected a complex but extremely healthy social structure. It should be apparent that the Chinese have spared no effort in introducing the sound systems of health, divination and philosophy that are likely to yield the Confucian ideal of a "heaven on earth." This explains why the Chinese are always courteous and rarely aggressive, for nothing must stand in the way of harmonious relationships. In fact, as has been said elsewhere, if one were charged with the task of selecting a single word which would aptly sum up Chinese society, then that word would be "harmony," for it is one that not only describes Chinese society as it is perceived overtly, but that also has profound philosophical overtones.

It is this striving for harmony and the Confucian ideal which has largely determined the Chinese social order and system of government. The family is the basic unit of society, with discipline being enforced – though not unkindly – by the head of the household, on the principle that there can be no real happiness where there is disorder. The Chinese prefer a system of government which is authoritarian but benevolent, regarding Western democracy as an attempt to find a moral justification

for disharmony and dishonor. This is an aspect of the Chinese way of life which most Westerners fail to understand.

Discerning readers will also have noticed the great profundity of Chinese philosophy. Indeed, it could be said that the depth of Chinese philosophy can only be fully appreciated by those who have depth of mind. One is reminded of the English Christian missionary who, after living in China for over 30 years, made a thoroughly reliable translation of the *I Ching*; but in the introduction he declared it to be no more than a book of magic spells. In fact, the 64 hexagrams of the *I Ching* are based on the binary system which is the principle of the electronic computer. This gentleman may have been an ace with religion and the Chinese language, but he was a bit short on philosophy and mathematics.

But, more than anything else, what the contents of this book demonstrate is that the Chinese have a great capacity for survival. For them, this is as much a matter of race as it is for the individual. A sound diet and adequate exercise produce healthy people who will have healthy offspring; moderate habits ensure that illness and accidents are kept to a minimum; and respect for one's ancestors – sometimes erroneously described as ancestor worship – promotes a kind of lineal continuity and togetherness. Additionally, the Chinese are immensely patriotic, but this feeling is characterized by pride of race, not by flag-waving and other forms of jingoism.

China is now expanding rapidly in education, technology and other fields, and the signs are that she is destined to become the most powerful of all nations.

INDEX